Skiing into Modernity

SPORT IN WORLD HISTORY

Edited by Susan Brownell, Robert Edelman,
Wayne Wilson, and Christopher Young

This University of California Press series explores the story of
modern sport from its recognized beginnings in the nineteenth
century to the current day. The books present to a wide readership
the best new scholarship connecting sport with broad trends in
global history. The series delves into sport's intriguing relationship
with political and social power, while also capturing the
enthusiasm for the subject that makes it so powerful.

Skiing into Modernity

A CULTURAL AND ENVIRONMENTAL HISTORY

Andrew Denning

UNIVERSITY OF CALIFORNIA PRESS

Parts of this book were previously published in different form and appear here by permission of their original publishers: parts of chapters 3, 6, and 7, chapter 8, and the epilogue originally appeared as "From Sublime Landscapes to 'White Gold': How Skiing Transformed the Alps after 1930," *Environmental History* 19 (January 2014): 78–108. Parts of the introduction and chapters 4 and 5 appeared as "Alpine Modern: Central European Skiing and the Vernacularization of Cultural Modernism, 1900–1939," *Central European History* 46 (December 2013): 850–90.

University of California Press, one of the most distinguished university presses in the United States, enriches lives around the world by advancing scholarship in the humanities, social sciences, and natural sciences. Its activities are supported by the UC Press Foundation and by philanthropic contributions from individuals and institutions. For more information, visit www.ucpress.edu.

University of California Press
Oakland, California

Library of Congress Cataloging-in-Publication Data

Denning, Andrew, author.
    Skiing into modernity : a cultural and environmental history / Andrew Denning.
        p.   cm. — (Sport in world history ; 3)
    Includes bibliographical references and index.
    ISBN 978-0-520-28427-2 (cloth, alk. paper) — ISBN 978-0-520-28428-9 (pbk., alk. paper) — ISBN 978-0-520-95989-7 (electronic)
    1. Skis and skiing—Alps—History.   2. Skis and skiing—Social aspects—Alps.   3. Tourism—Alps—History.   I. Title.
GV854.8.A43D46   2015
796.93—dc23   2014018808

Manufactured in the United States of America

24   23   22   21   20   19   18   17   16   15
10   9   8   7   6   5   4   3   2   1

In keeping with a commitment to support environmentally responsible and sustainable printing practices, UC Press has printed this book on Natures Natural, a fiber that contains 30% post-consumer waste and meets the minimum requirements of ANSI/NISO Z39.48–1992 (R 1997) (*Permanence of Paper*).

For Whitney

CONTENTS

FIGURES AND TABLES

FIGURES

TABLES

ACKNOWLEDGMENTS

As I researched and wrote this book, I came to realize that it was not only about mountains, but it created its own topography. Books accumulated on my desk, pointing skyward like the spires of the Dolomites, while precariously arranged stacks of notes threatened to cascade to the floor in an avalanche with the slightest jostling. As I scaled this mountain, I learned what skiers and mountain climbers have known for generations—that while our efforts are often solitary, our greatest joy comes from sharing our struggles and triumphs. Here I thank those who helped me scale this mountain.

I am indebted to a number of individuals and institutions who supported this project in one way or another. The German Academic Exchange Service (DAAD), the International Olympic Committee, and the Department of History at the University of California, Davis, provided financial support to undertake research at various repositories in Europe and the United States. The Rachel Carson Center for Environment and Society in Munich generously supplied a grant that allowed me to obtain publication permissions for the wide variety of stunning images found in this book.

As all historians know, our work depends on the efforts of countless librarians and archivists behind the scenes. I am grateful to the library staff at UC Davis, Western Washington University, and the University of British Columbia for their immense skill and constant support in helping me procure a wide range of rare and fragile sources from across the globe. While I was based in Munich, the staff at the Bayerische Staatsbibliothek proved equally adept. Peter Collins and Fran Oscadal at Dartmouth College went out of their way to make my short research trips in New Hampshire as productive as possible, and each worked tirelessly to help me track down articles and images from Dartmouth's collections. Scott Taylor at Georgetown

University provided speedy access to the Sir Arnold Lunn Papers. Gerd Falkner at the Deutscher Skiverband in Planegg graciously allowed me access to the association's marvelous collection of rare publications from the early decades of skiing, and he was always willing to share his encyclopedic knowledge of European skiing history at a moment's notice. Klara Esters and Stefan Ritter of the Archive of the Deutscher Alpenverein in Munich provided access to their rich resources, and Stefan provided vital help in tracking down many of the images. Nuria Puig and Regula Cardinaux, along with their staff at the Olympic Studies Centre in Lausanne, enabled access to the wide-ranging collections held by the International Olympic Committee. The Beekley Family Foundation allowed the use of its world-class collection of skiing artifacts and ephemera, and I am particularly grateful to Natale Messina and Marianne Curling for facilitating the inclusion of these images in this book.

This project began as a doctoral dissertation at UC Davis, where it benefited from the enthusiasm and critical perspective of numerous individuals. Ted Margadant and Michael Saler offered insightful critiques at various stages of research and writing, while Bill Hagen sharpened my analytical eye and clarity of expression. Ari Kelman provided crucial support in navigating the funding landscape. Edward Ross Dickinson, my doctoral adviser, encouraged me to ask big questions and to seek out answers in unexpected places, and his close readings of my work required me to refine my approach and clarify my analyses. In the intervening years he has continued to offer personal and intellectual support, for which I am eternally grateful.

My colleagues at Western Washington University helped me hone my ideas in formal and informal settings, and I am particularly indebted to Amanda Eurich, Steven Garfinkle, Kevin Leonard, Ricardo Lopez, Johann Neem, Jennifer Seltz, and Sarah Zimmerman. A postdoctoral fellowship in the History Department at the University of British Columbia allowed me focused time to complete the manuscript. This benefit, however, was secondary to the welcoming, collegial atmosphere in the department, and I am lucky to be surrounded by such supportive colleagues. My postdoctoral adviser, Eagle Glassheim, provided wonderful advice from my earliest arrival in Vancouver, while conversations with Anne Gorsuch, Bradley Miller, Carla Nappi, and Leslie Paris helped me polish the manuscript. Chris Friedrichs deserves special gratitude for dropping a priceless resource—his late mother's diary—into my lap. His generosity and interest in this project improved it immeasurably.

Thoughtful comments and critiques offered in various forums allowed me to fine-tune the ideas in this book. Scott Casper first taught me to think and write like a historian as an undergraduate at the University of Nevada, and I continue to benefit from his support and advice more than a decade later. Jessie Hewitt heard me speak about this project at its inception, and her enthusiasm gave me continuing confidence. I am particularly thankful for her comments on a draft of the introduction. Annie Gilbert Coleman, Steve Harp, and Tait Keller offered constructive criticism and unflinching support, and the benefit of their intellectual interventions is evident. Colleagues at conferences, lectures, and seminars challenged me to approach this project in new ways. I am particularly grateful to my colleagues at the T2M Summer School in Berlin, the Environment and Society Group and the Leisure and Consumption Cluster in Vancouver, the Thinking Mountains conference in Edmonton, and the Case Western Reserve University German Studies Program in Cleveland for their thoughts and recommendations.

The administrators and staff and my colleagues at the Rachel Carson Center deserve particular praise. I was lucky to be affiliated with the center in its inaugural year while I completed my research in Munich and to benefit from the vibrant colloquia and the opportunity to discuss my work with colleagues in the environmental humanities. The center's director, Christof Mauch, is legendary for his intellectual generosity, wide-ranging interests, and tireless efforts to facilitate the work of other scholars. I am happy to count him as a mentor, friend, and colleague.

Since a chance meeting at a conference many years ago, my editor at the University of California Press, Niels Hooper, has been an unflinching supporter of this project. He served as an able guide through the publication process, and his recommendations improved the final product immensely. His assistant, Kim Hogeland, responded to an infinitude of requests and clarifications regarding the publication process with expeditious good cheer. Christopher Young, the editor of the Sport in World History series, expressed his enthusiasm for the project from the beginning, and his trenchant comments on a draft of the manuscript inspired a round of revisions that strengthened the argument and improved readability. I am thankful for such a supportive and hard-working editorial team.

Finally, this book would not have been possible without the support and sacrifice of friends and loved ones. Friends—academic and nonacademic— took an abiding interest in my book and peppered me with questions and recommendations, and the resulting book is more readable and dynamic for it. I extend particular thanks to Scott Warren, who prepared two images for this book. My parents have always encouraged my curiosity and were resolute in their support throughout the writing process, even as my work took me farther and farther away from my hometown. My deepest thanks go to my wife, Whitney. She became an unwitting mountain dweller herself, living among my piles of documentation and traversing the peaks and valleys of research and writing by my side. She accompanied me on this expedition across multiple countries, and words cannot express how much her support means to me. While my Alpine journey at times kept my head in the clouds, she always helped me plant my feet on solid ground. The view from the top of this mountain would be meaningless without her as my companion.

Vancouver, BC
April 2014

Introduction

To reach the idyllic Swiss Alpine village of Zermatt, the train departs the town of Visp at the base of the Mattertal and traces the path of the Matter Vispa river valley upward. As the train climbs three thousand feet to Zermatt, the Alpine foothills give way to taller and more dramatic summits. At the station in Zermatt, the viewer is greeted with a panorama of some of Switzerland's tallest and most celebrated *Viertausender* (mountains over four thousand meters, or 13,123 feet, in elevation). The pyramid form of the Weisshorn (14,783 feet) guards the northern entrance to the valley; Switzerland's tallest peak, Monte Rosa (15,203 feet), straddles the border with Italy southeast of Zermatt; and the iconic, crooked visage of the Matterhorn (14,692 feet) dominates the view to the southwest. An Icarian longing draws the visitor upward. Those with calves of steel climb the trails at the edge of the village, exchanging the Swiss-German greeting of *"Grüezi!"* with fellow hikers; an array of cable lifts ferries less masochistic visitors from Zermatt to the glaciers and snow-covered slopes at the village's southern rim. The view of Zermatt below recalls nineteenth-century Romantic canvases. Miniature Swiss chalets dot the landscape, and evergreen forests and verdant meadows populated by grazing cows surround the village. The tourist snaps photographs, hoping to capture this commanding view of the Alps for a lifetime. What a contrast to the hoteliers, restaurateurs, and shopkeepers of the village! For the tourist, this scene is priceless; for the denizens of Zermatt, it is all too costly. It is December. There should be snow on the ground and skiers on the slopes.

Economic life in the Alps is attuned to the seasons. This is particularly the case for those communities, like Zermatt, that depend on tourism, which

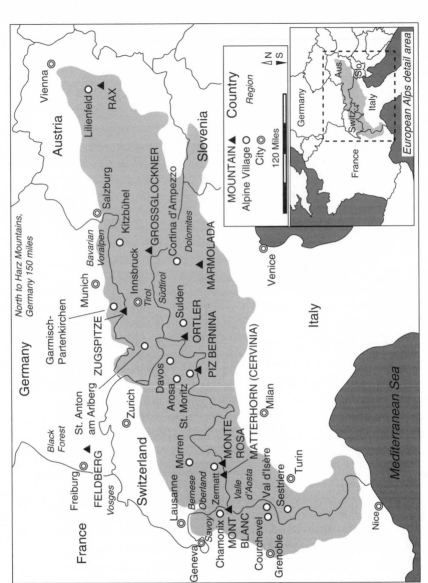

MAP 1. The Alps. Prepared by Scott Warren, Arizona State University.

came to dominate the economy of many Alpine villages in the twentieth century. Today, more than 120 million individuals visit the Alps annually, accruing 500 million rides on mountain lifts and 545 million overnight stays.[1] The Alpine year is divided into summer and winter: the former brings hikers, mountain bikers, and sightseers, and the latter is dominated by skiers. Winter tourism, originally developed in the late nineteenth century to supplement the dominant summer tourist season, has become increasingly important in the Alpine economy, particularly as summer visits have declined in recent decades.[2] Alpine skiing anchors a multibillion-dollar industry in the Alps, an economic boon that dramatically raised the local standard of living and bolstered national finances in the twentieth century. However, its dominance is both a blessing and a curse. Whereas the winter season once lasted nearly six months on average, beginning in November and stretching into April or May, since the 1980s rising temperatures have caused the beginning and end of the season to fluctuate from year to year, leading Zermatt's business owners to look out their windows onto lush, green pastures and rocky, snowless mountains far more often than they once did or would choose to. For an Alpine economy that depends on distinct, predictable seasons, climate change bears the potential for economic catastrophe.[3]

The fraught contemporary relationship between skiing and the Alps can be seen from another angle at the base of the Harakiri piste (ski slope) in Mayrhofen, Austria (figure 1). The owners of the Ski Zillertal 3000 resort advertise the Harakiri as the steepest groomed ski slope in Austria and one of the steepest in the world, with a grade of 78 percent. The name *Harakiri,* Japanese slang for the ritual suicide practiced by samurai, is pure marketing, meant to appeal to daredevil skiers. The resort operators have cleared the slope of trees, rocks, and divots to protect skiers and allow for the greatest possible speed. To maintain snow consistency, resort employees groom the piste with a ten-ton, five-hundred-horsepower vehicle with tracks like a tank. The slope is so steep, however, that the vehicle must be attached to a winch and drawn up the mountain by thick steel cables.[4] Avalanche fences have been constructed at the top of the slope, and protective fencing along the piste prevents out-of-control skiers from hurtling into trees. To satisfy the desire of most modern skiers to tempt fate without undue exertion, a chairlift has been constructed to transport them to the top of the slope.

The effects of climate change on Alpine skiing and the increasing technological manipulation of the environment have led many to speak of the alienation of humans from nature. In these interpretations, the Alps offer a

FIGURE 1. The Harakiri slope, Mayrhofen, Austria.

cautionary tale: a sport that offers the lure of getting away from it all and reconnecting with nature has scarred the landscape and placed unsustainable stress on the Alpine environment, and the intemperate use of natural resources threatens the future of skiing. Implicit in these critiques is an idealization of the Alps as a pristine natural landscape in which individuals can escape from the stresses of modern, urban existence. In this view, which has its roots in concepts of nature elaborated by the Romantic movement over two hundred years ago, the mountains, by virtue of their age and grandeur, hold the potential for soothing overtaxed minds, bodies, and souls. However, the lust for hedonistic pleasure has rendered the Harakiri piste a Frankenstein's monster—an abominable hybrid of nature and technology—while the seasonal struggles of Zermatt and countless other Alpine villages caused by rising temperatures represent divine retribution for our hubristic exploitation of nature's gifts.

As William Cronon has observed, many conflicting understandings of nature condition our perceptions of skiing and the Alps: the dream of a nature unsullied by humans; the idealization of nature as an Edenic paradise in a corrupted modern world; the view of nature as a marketable commodity to be managed and exploited; and the power of nature to frustrate the best-laid plans—as in Zermatt—as a punishment for human arrogance and rapaciousness. The narrative we construct about skiing and the Alps, indicates that, above all, nature is an ongoing debate about the relationship between human beings and the nonhuman environment.[5] Although these critiques seem particularly timely given recent concerns about global warming and the effects of technology on the mountain environment, they have driven disputes about Alpine skiing since the sport's beginnings in Central Europe (used here to describe the states comprising the Alps: France, Germany, Italy, Switzerland, and the Austro-Hungarian Empire) in the 1880s.

In 1959, the Polish sociologist Andrzej Ziemilski took the stage in Zakopane, Poland, to address a multinational congress about a movement of world-historical import: skiing. He began his speech to the Fifth International Congress for Ski Instruction by asking rhetorically whether skiing was merely one of the passing "mass hysterias" of the twentieth century, such as the hula hoop and rock-and-roll music, as some of its detractors claimed, or something more profound and enduring. Given his audience, it is unsurprising that Ziemilski came down in the latter camp. But he did so by describing skiing not as a pleasant leisure activity or a challenging form of physical exercise, but rather as a vector of civilization and modernity.[6]

Ziemilski began by noting that the history of the ski extended back millennia; indeed, other commentators have described the ski as older than both Methuselah and the wheel.[7] Spreading slowly from its Central Asian origins, the ski remained a utilitarian means of locomotion in subarctic regions for most of its history. The second phase of skiing, and the first step toward its modernization, argued Ziemilski, occurred in Scandinavia in the mid-nineteenth century, when members of the Norwegian middle class combined its practical functions with a bourgeois conception of sport adopted from Great Britain. In the second half of the nineteenth century, the connection between skiing and Norwegian nationalism expanded the appeal of the sport, attracting practitioners of both sexes and all ages and social ranks.

In Ziemilski's telling, however, the modern, world-historical character of skiing depended on a third evolutionary step: the introduction of skiing to the mountains of Central Europe in the late nineteenth century. Ziemilski recalled the fin-de-siècle Alpine winter landscape detailed in Thomas Mann's *The Magic Mountain,* in which the sanatoria and cure resorts of the Alps are nearly empty, save for a handful of diseased souls. The introduction of skiing revolutionized the region, claimed Ziemilski, by inventing the winter vacation. Alpine skiing made the local economy more stable by enabling year-round economic activity in mountainous terrain otherwise regarded as "empty economic space" and encouraging the development of a service economy.[8]

Ziemilski asserted that the import of Alpine skiing spread far beyond the economy, creating a new form of sociability especially valued in light of the anxiety and social atomization that typified the modern age. Alpine skiers behaved less formally and more democratically than their peers, thereby breaking down the social hierarchies that characterized modern metropolises.[9] The active, participatory ethos of the sport differentiated it from other popular pastimes. Skiing, opined Ziemilski, "does not displace its enthusiasts into the role of passive spectator."[10] Alpine skiing also revolutionized European culture by altering perception. For millennia, European cultures had construed the winter as "only frost and death. It is thanks to skiing that today winter is joy, beauty, and health."[11]

Ziemilski concluded his speech by arguing that the ski was a great civilizing force. The beneficial effects of skiing and the shared experience of the sport would allow individuals to transcend the artificial dichotomies of modernity, in particular the opposition between nature and culture: skiing created "a synthesis of these two eternal elements of life."[12] This bond allowed skiers to transcend modern conditions in the healing mountain landscape and thus to fashion the world anew, creating in the Alps a paradise of economic productivity, social harmony, and natural beauty.

Whereas contemporary critics of the sport view it as an actively destructive force, Ziemilski interpreted skiing as a panacea: a tool of socioeconomic modernization that, through its unification of sublime nature and modern cultural values, liberated individuals and allowed them to conquer the alienation inherent in economic development. Yet the very developments Ziemilski praised as civilizing had come under attack by critics of the sport since the late nineteenth century.

Nearly two decades before Ziemilski's laudatory speech, the British skiing pioneer Arnold Lunn had condemned the development of the sport and its effects on the Alps. Lunn's own career testifies to the transformation of skiing from a curious diversion at the dawn of the twentieth century into a mass sport that counted millions of practitioners and billions in profits by century's end; and Lunn, as the sport's greatest booster, played a vital role in this process. Born in Madras, India, in 1888 to a Methodist missionary, Sir Henry Lunn, Arnold led a remarkable life. On the family's return to England, Henry reoriented his professional activities toward a lucrative business that coordinated winter vacations in the Swiss Alps for elite Britons, and Arnold spent much of his youth shuttling between England and tourist centers in Switzerland. He attended Harrow, one of England's foremost public schools, before matriculating at Balliol College, Oxford University. Lunn ran in elite circles throughout his life, counting among his friends and confidants a diverse group of political and cultural luminaries including Evelyn Waugh, William F. Buckley Jr., and a members of royal families around the world. He left Oxford without a degree, but not before founding the Oxford University Mountaineering Club. Indeed, Lunn claimed that his true education occurred in the Swiss Alps. He first skied in 1898 at age ten and became an avid mountaineer. In 1909, he survived a frightful rock-climbing fall at Cader Idris in Wales, but the accident crushed his leg, requiring surgery that left him with an open wound for at least a decade and one leg two inches shorter than the other. Thereafter Lunn devoted himself to skiing, which his mangled leg could bear more easily. He published dozens of books on the subject, distinctive for their florid prose and constant literary allusions. He helped to form national and international ski organizations and to establish Alpine skiing as a competitive sport in the 1920s and 1930s, and he was perhaps the sport's greatest publicist until his death in 1974. Such were Lunn's accomplishments that Queen Elizabeth II knighted him in 1952 for "services to skiing and Anglo-Swiss relations."[13]

As Lunn aged, however, he became pessimistic about the relationship between skiers and the mountains. In 1941, recalling an acquaintance who spoke enthusiastically about the construction of three new cable lifts to serve skiers at Schmitzenheim, Switzerland, Lunn remarked that "the great heresy of our age is this habit of equating spiritual and mechanical progress." Far from liberating humans from the constraints of modernity and bringing them into contact with one another, "every mechanical invention for speeding up communications, from motor-cars to mountain *téléphériques* [cable lifts] breaks down barriers which are still some protection against the horrors of a standardized civilization." Whereas Ziemilski would later laud the social and hygienic benefits of skiing, Lunn highlighted its harmful effects: "Mountain railways and funiculars are not exempt from the law that mechanical progress is always balanced by spiritual regress: Skiing, which was once a culture, is degenerating into a civilization."[14] For Lunn and others like him, the popularization of skiing represented not its ascent to the realm of a social good, but instead its degeneration into the homogeneous and the banal. The development of Alpine skiing symbolized the experience of modernity in microcosm, with all of its attendant benefits and tradeoffs. If modernization resulted in greater comfort and the human mastery of once-oppressive natural forces, it also diffused the standardized tastes of a philistine mass culture. Lunn's pessimistic interpretation was a counternarrative of modernity with a long legacy in Western culture, the lament of elites about the deleterious effects of socioeconomic modernization on the mind, body, and soul.

Most important, however, Lunn, unlike Ziemilski, rejected the assertion that modern skiing successfully synthesized nature and culture. Lunn presented a scathing critique of the state of Alpine skiing:

> Skiing has passed through the Spenglerian cycle. It began as a culture in contact with Nature. In the Gothic phase of our sport we skied on snow moulded only by the natural agencies of sun and wind, frost and thaw. Ten men are too few for a skiing community, ten thousand are too many for skiing funiculars. In those days we skiers were as scattered as the primitive communities in which culture is born. Today we struggle in *téléphériques* and funiculars as crowded as the slums of our megalopolitan civilization, and the surface on which we ski is nearly as hard and quite as artificial as the city pavements which mask the kindly earth.[15]

For Lunn, skiing did not ameliorate the alienation of modern life but was instead infected with the same decadence and destructive tendencies. Indeed, it came to serve as a vector of contagion, spreading the disease of modernity to the pristine mountain landscape.

Both boosters and critics of the growing influence of Alpine skiing described the effects of the sport in terms of social relations, physical and spiritual health, and the relationship between humans and nature. For both sides, Alpine skiing had the potential to mitigate the stresses of modernity while at the same time epitomizing those very conditions. Contrary to the polarized interpretations of Ziemilski and Lunn, the effects of skiing in the Alps were not *either* civilizing *or* barbarizing, *either* triumphant *or* destructive: they were all of these things at once. Skiing both reflected and constructed modernity in the Alps. It was simultaneously transcendent and alienating, productive of an appreciation of nature and destructive of that very nature.

Since the 1880s, Alpine skiing and the meanings associated with it have expressed a complex, ongoing negotiation of Europeans' relationship with nature. Today, even though the Alps bear the evidence of direct and indirect human influence more visibly than ever before, skiers continue to depend on the unique climate and terrain of the Alps to practice their sport. The cultural meanings of skiing—whether communing with or conquering the mountains (or both)—are similarly reliant on the landscape, and skiing also sustains Alpine communities economically. These forms of dependence have inspired skiers and their representatives both to alter their perceptions of the Alps and to make material changes in the landscape itself.

DEFINING ALPINE MODERNISM

In the Alps, modernity arrived on skis. From the moment of first contact in the late nineteenth century, the Alps modernized skiing by aligning its practice with spectators' lust for mass cultural spectacles and with the rationalist dictates of modern sports, which have universal rules administered by sporting bureaucracies to allow for the comparison of quantifiable results. The sport simultaneously modernized the Alps by stimulating economic development and transforming perceptions of the landscape. When skiers arrived in the Alps in the 1880s, the sport was a strictly Scandinavian pursuit. Intellectuals in Europe's cultural centers understood northern Europe as a developing region: Scandinavians were not as deplorable and unenlightened as Eastern Europeans, but they were certainly not as advanced as the peoples of Western Europe.[16] The Scandinavian practice of skiing appeared to Europeans as bizarre, quaint, and somewhat primitive.

At the same time, nineteenth-century and early twentieth-century commentators described the Alps as a periphery—a frontier—located, ironically, at Europe's very heart (see map 1). The mountains were an economic wasteland located at the geographic edge of modern metropoles such as Germany, France, Italy, and the Austro-Hungarian Empire. Similarly, the Alps were seen as a cultural periphery, a retrograde space suited only for simple mountain dwellers and for urbanites in need of relaxation and contact with nature in its most elemental form. Before coming into contact, both skiing and the Alps were peripheral to the concerns of metropolitan Europe; when they were considered at all, each suggested backwardness and a decided lack of modernity.

The appearance of the ski transformed the subordinate status of the Alps in modern Europe: both the sport and the landscape became modern and central to European concerns, and the Alpine wasteland became a winter wonderland. Like a number of other contemporary leisure practices, skiing cultivated a particularly modern relationship with space and the landscape through active movement. As John Urry has observed, mobility affects "how people appear to experience the modern world, changing both their forms of subjectivity and sociability and their aesthetic appreciation of nature, landscapes, townscapes, and other societies."[17] Hiking and mountain climbing (Alpinism), the bicycle, the automobile, and the airplane cultivated important new relationships with the landscape. However, Alpine skiing was characterized by a distinct and notable bond to space and place that drew on disparate elements from various leisure cultures.

Skiing practices and motivations had much in common with Alpinism, and indeed many of the first skiers were mountaineers who used skis to traverse snowfields and glaciers. Both climbers and skiers took to the Alps to test their courage and build camaraderie while escaping lowland civilization. Like skiers, Alpinists cultivated an intense relationship with the mountains, but their methods and outlook appear quite traditional when compared to the practices and beliefs of Alpine skiers. Alpinism largely remained a contemplative realm of leisure, an aesthetic, spiritual pursuit that was at least theoretically exempt from competitive endeavors and certainly lacked the rationalist practices of modern sporting competitions. By contrast, Alpine skiing increasingly exemplified the new era of modern sport.[18] The cultures surrounding the bicycle, automobile, and airplane, on the other hand, were tightly linked to modern culture; each in turn appeared as the very embodiment of all of the thrills and nuisances of modernity. Those who embraced these forms of transport deemed them particularly modern for their dramatic ability to collapse time and space. In these pursuits, the act of riding, driving, or flying itself provided the thrill, rather than any relationship with or appreciation for the landscape. To apply terms drawn from art, these adventurers celebrated the *form* and experience of technology. The environmental *context* that so enraptured Alpinists was largely incidental to the enjoyment of the mobile act itself, and landscapes were thus perceived as interchangeable space to be consumed, rather than a distinctive place to be appreciated.

Alpine skiing is unique because it synthesized the Alpinists' appreciation of nature with the formalist celebration of speed and movement in modern transport media. Although the ski was thousands of years old, it was new to the inhabitants of Central Europe. Much of the sport's appeal came from its delicate balance of modernity and tradition, providing the modern ecstasy of speed without demanding mechanical accoutrements. In the words of the midcentury French journalist Michel Clare, skiing was at once a vector and an embodiment of modernity: "The reasons for its success are simple. . . . Downhill skiing is one of the physical activities that best fulfills the desires of modern man. . . . In the century of the airplane and the automobile, one experiences in the downhill that fascination that is the myth of the contemporary world: speed."[19] Skiing placed its practitioners into intimate contact with nature. Indeed, for many skiers, the opportunity to experience the aesthetic beauty of nature with only two planks of wood strapped to one's feet was the main appeal of the sport.

When describing the significance of sport in modern societies, historians and sociologists have generally emphasized the relationship between sport and the definition of social categories such as class, gender, race, and nation.[20] In many of these excellent studies, sport is seen as an echo of changes in the political, social, and economic realms. Alpine skiers certainly enjoyed the sociable aspects of their sport and, consciously or otherwise, used skiing as a way to define social difference, as the expense and danger of the sport proved formidable barriers to the less affluent and daring. Like other leisure pursuits, Alpine skiing gained in popularity as cultural, economic, and political trends in the first half of the twentieth century combined to democratize leisure time and to lower the costs of equipment and transportation.

Nevertheless, Alpine skiers argued for the cultural distinctiveness of skiing, elaborating a dynamic and volatile cultural ideology that I term *Alpine modernism.*[21] Alpine skiing was at once reflective of the dynamics and velocity of modern times and uniquely suited to counteract the stresses of these very same modern conditions. Individuals seeking meaning and transcendence in a disenchanted world were stifled by the institutions, practices, and mores of modern civilization, which conspired to force individuals into unnatural and unfulfilling modes of existence.[22] The rapid growth in the ranks of skiers and the cultural influence of the sport in the early twentieth century stemmed from the distinctive ideology that motivated skiers and the aesthetic principles that they developed and then disseminated. Alpine skiers believed that their sport allowed them to master time and space by neutralizing the dangers of winter and covering great distances, thus reenchanting an increasingly banal and instrumental world by enabling acts of heroic self-assertion. Simultaneously, skiers claimed to escape the crowds and materialistic concerns of the lowlands by reconnecting with nature in its most arresting form. The motivations and cultural beliefs that inspired Alpine skiing (and, by extension, other leisure pursuits in the age of mass culture) were as much cultural as social, and they demand more serious scholarly attention.

By taking to their skis in the Alps, moderns endeavored to reclaim their roles as agents of modernity, rather than its passive objects.[23] Drawing a distinction between the Romantic aesthetic that inspired nineteenth-century tourists and their own motivations, Alpine skiers argued that their sport and the cultural landscape they fashioned were not antimodern, but were instead exceptionally modern.[24] Both Alpine skiers and modernist artists celebrated the cult of speed and formalistic and functional movements and representations. More important, both groups critiqued modernity in order to save it and make it more responsive to human needs. Similarly, both skiers and artists forged transnational connections based on their common aesthetic principles and a shared worldview. The development of Alpine modernism thus demonstrates how leisure practices are reflective and interpretive, and how their combination of sociability, introspection, and physical activity served as a conduit through which individuals defined, challenged, and disseminated cultural practices and ideologies in the modern era.[25]

Examining the relationship between Alpine skiing and modernism also increases our understanding of how this amorphous cultural movement affected everyday life. Historians usually characterize modernism—whether understood narrowly as the (high) cultural modernism of artists and philosophers or more broadly as "social modernism," which includes professional groups such as engineers, bureaucrats, and scientists—as an urban, socially elite movement.[26] Although economic barriers and ingrained social practices discouraged the working classes from practicing the sport, skiers of varied nationality, social standing, and gender popularized cultural modernism before World War II, spreading awareness of the sport among skiers and nonskiers alike, thanks to the symbiotic relationship between skiing and the international mass media (particularly the sporting press and the film industry). As a mass phenomenon, Alpine skiing extended modernist ideas and practices beyond the socially circumscribed milieu of high culture into the realm of popular action and experience.[27] Simultaneously, Alpine skiers transported modernism from the cafés and salons of Berlin, Vienna, Paris, and Zurich to the undeveloped landscapes at the continent's geographical heart.[28] Unlike the pure formalism of most urban modernists, Alpine modernism was inherently linked to the distinctive landscape of the Alps. In the early decades of the twentieth century, the practices and writings of Alpine skiers transformed the common perception of the Alps from a benighted landscape into a modern, progressive realm.

Alpine skiers were not doctrinaire modernists: thus Alpine modernism was a hybrid ideology, one that illustrates how individuals seized ideologies from aesthetes and philosophers and combined them with a wide array of seemingly unrelated practices and ideas in the age of mass culture.[29] Alpine modernism had vernacular appeal because it synthesized the pastoralism and nature worship of Romanticism with the cultural iconoclasm and celebration of technology seen in modernist submovements such as futurism. Both Romantics and modernists criticized the cultural, political, and socioeconomic structures of the modern world as alienating and inhumane, but whereas Romantics celebrated sublime, pristine natural landscapes as the antithesis of industrial society, various modernist movements embraced modern technologies and ideas to emancipate themselves from an increasingly banal existence. Alpine skiers synthesized and reconciled these viewpoints, combining the modern medium of sport and the timeless milieu of the Alps to translate aesthetic abstractions into practices that stimulated both body and mind.

The study of Alpine skiing in this period also challenges the usual understanding of the relationship between modernist movements and modernity. Even when construed as an active and creative response to modern conditions, cultural modernism remains epiphenomenal. By these readings, modern conditions inspired modernism, and the latter constituted a defensive response to the changes wrought by modernization. Alpine skiing certainly depended on modernization processes such as industrialization and democratization and derived much of its power from the way it addressed the perceived deficiencies of modern life, but Alpine modernism was more than a descriptive intellectual abstraction. Once Alpine modernism infiltrated the Alpine winter landscape, it became a propulsive rather than reactive force, spurring socioeconomic modernization through the development of the winter tourism industry. Skiers gave shape to Alpine modernism, and their modernism affected both European societies and the Alpine landscape.

As a result, Alpine modernism was never a static ideology. The delicate tension between modern culture and timeless nature made the sport appealing to a wide constituency, but it also produced divergent understandings of the sport, such as those espoused by Arnold Lunn and Andrzej Ziemilski. Early Alpine modernism, as a form of vernacular modernism, appealed to individuals by allowing them to experience the modern cult of speed and the timeless beauty of nature simultaneously. A variety of interest groups marshaled Alpine modernism to their own causes. The visceral allure of skiing extended beyond practitioners to spectators, making competitive Alpine skiing increasingly popular in the interwar period. As a result, the sport came under the influence of sporting bureaucracies like the International Olympic Committee and the Fédération Internationale de Ski, equipment manufacturers and tourism officials who sought to monetize athletic accomplishments, and, after World War II, event planners and television producers who strived to make the sport more marketable and profitable. Sport, which Matthew McDowell has characterized as "one of the rare nexuses between community, capitalism and politics, at the regional, national and global levels," extended the reach of Alpine modernism by making skiing widely appealing and lucrative, but the ethos of modern competitive sport changed Alpine modernism and the Alps in important ways.[30]

Similarly, the appeal of Alpine modernism helped stimulate the massive expansion of the winter tourism industry. As the quasi-spiritual implications of Alpine modernism came into contact with the amalgamation of goods and services that constitutes modern tourism, hoteliers, transportation companies, advertisers, and even national governments pushed to democratize access to the sport and increase profit margins, exerting increasing influence over the practice of the sport. Projects to build lift infrastructure, expand hotel offerings, and create ski resorts attempted to engineer the Alps to better accord with the popular appeal of Alpine modernism. In the process, they brought the perceived problems of urban modernity—environmental degradation, overcrowding, and the industrial mindset—into the Alps, often to an extent unseen even in Europe's largest lowland metropolises. Alpine modernism thus came to absorb the allure of modern tourism as well as that industry's more materialist concerns.

Clearly, Alpine modernism was replete with ambivalence and contradiction. Practitioners of the sport balanced expressions of euphoria and angst.

Europeans understood both the Alps and Alpine skiing to be at once a remedy for and the troubling apotheosis of modernity. Skiers shaped debates that lie at the heart of twentieth-century European culture: nature versus culture, urbanity versus ruralism, cosmopolitanism versus nationalism, and values and aesthetics versus economic materialism. Alpine modernism often bridged these divisions, illustrating the constructed nature of these dichotomies, as well as the dialectic and dependent relationship between their constituent concepts.

In short, Alpine skiing was not merely a mindless pastime: it was an attempt by individuals and groups to make sense of the relationship between modern ideas and practices (i.e., culture) and the Alps (i.e., nature). Viewed through the lens of Alpine modernism, modern leisure, sport, and tourism emerge as active, critical pursuits, not unthinking acts of capitalist consumption or faint facsimiles of political, social, and economic changes. Further, modern leisure played a vital role in bringing individuals into contact with nature in the twentieth century, and the Alpine landscape affected the practice of the sport just as skiers transformed the landscape. Alpine skiers created, elaborated, challenged, debated, and altered their ideology continually, but its fundamental attempt to synthesize nature and culture through skiing remained constant.

THE CONTEXTS OF ALPINE SKIING

The historical significance of Alpine skiing is apparent only when viewed on the proper spatial and temporal scales. Historians are highly attuned to such questions, as the geographical and chronological limits of a study and the process of plotting a narrative shape historical arguments in important ways.[31] A study of skiing from its ancient origins suggests humankind's millennia-long struggle to tame and order nature, with the shift of skiing to the realm of leisure in the nineteenth century highlighting humanity's successful mastery of the elements. On the other hand, studies of Alpine skiing that focus solely on the era before World War II present heroic and dramatic narratives of pioneers and adventurers exploring uncharted territory and conquering nature.[32] After the war, real estate developers and government bureaucrats crowded out heroic trailblazers as the primary actors in the development of Alpine skiing, but it was after World War II that the sport became more democratized, profitable, and significant in the development of European culture, society, and the Alps themselves.

In modern European history, the two world wars and the Cold War tend to structure historical understanding, with 1914 and 1945 functioning as definitive breaking points in historical developments. Studying the historical relationship between skiers and the Alps from the first modern contacts in the 1880s through the late 1970s demonstrates, however, that World War II was no historical zero hour; rather, the war capped off changes that had been in motion for decades. The historical significance of Alpine skiing lay at the intersection of multiple social and political currents: the economic development of the Alps, the changing European consumption practices that created a leisure society, the creation of a modern mass culture, and shifting attitudes toward nature. Examining Europe's twentieth century through the parallel, mutually dependent processes that constituted Alpine skiing disrupts the accepted political chronology of twentieth-century Europe, tracing continuities that spanned dramatic political shifts on the continent. The physical and discursive modernization of the Alps was largely complete by the 1970s, and more recent developments and debates in Alpine skiing have occurred within the framework set by the sport's democratization and its symbiotic relationship with mass culture, which began in the interwar era and solidified in the decades after World War II.

Examining the changing relationship between skiers and the Alps also presents an opportunity to study the relationship between the natural environment and modern culture on a transnational scale. Much of the historical study of modern Europe has become ossified in a statist mode of interpretation, in which historical development is seen as emanating outward from European political centers such as Berlin, Paris, Rome, and Moscow. Historians have increasingly recommended supplementing traditional histories of the nation-state with transnational and polycentric understandings of the past, in which local, regional, transnational, and global processes conspire to produce historical change.[33] The tools of environmental and cultural history are particularly well suited to writing such histories.[34] Indeed, as J. R. McNeill observes, "For many sorts of history, including environmental history, the nation-state is the wrong scale on which to operate. Ecological processes unfold with no regard for borders, and cultural/intellectual trends do so nearly as blithely."[35] Thus the study of the subject demands not an international or comparative history, in which the experiences of skiers in separate countries are treated in turn, but instead a truly transnational, entangled history that examines how mobile groups of people intersected and interacted, and how these movements and connections produced the cosmopolitan culture of Alpine skiing.[36]

An entangled history of Alpine skiing must, then, be a regional history. Regions are best understood not as a specific geographical areas but rather, in the words of Celia Applegate, as "a set of practices" and "a cognitive structure" given shape by economic, cultural, and geographical characteristics.[37] The relationship between skiers and the Alps illustrates the coexistence and interdependence of physical and cultural definitions of the Alpine region, and skiers helped shape the socioeconomic, cultural, and geographical characteristics that defined the Alps in the modern era. As a geographically and culturally distinct region, the Alps are well suited to a transnational, regional approach.[38] They are defined in part by their liminal status between civilization and nature, and between core and periphery.[39] Tracing the cultural and environmental effects of Alpine skiing across national borders shows how the Alps, once deemed a periphery paradoxically located at the geographic heart of the continent, became increasingly central to historical change in Europe during the twentieth century.

Alpine skiing presents an intriguing test case for the study of transnational European cultures in the modern era because it was created virtually ex nihilo, and from its earliest beginnings, Alpine modernism was highly reflexive. Skiers and nonskiers vied to define, adapt, and contest the material practices and the sport's cultural ideologies. These debates occurred not only on the ski slopes and in bars and meeting halls across Europe, but also, and most strikingly, in the mass media. Alpine skiers created a culture that flourished in newspapers and magazines, in guidebooks and vacation prospectuses, and in film, radio, and television. As skiing grew in tandem with the mass media, a number of savvy skiers developed into celebrities. Sir Arnold Lunn was not only an innovator in the sport and an active member of its first regulatory bodies but also a prolific author on subjects ranging from Alpine skiing to scientific materialism and the rise of communism. Hannes Schneider was an Austrian ski champion, movie star, tour operator, and transatlantic ski instructor who rose to fame in the early twentieth century. The Frenchman Jean-Claude Killy won multiple gold medals at the Grenoble Winter Olympics in 1968 before becoming an actor, racecar driver, and global pitchman for products ranging from Head Skis to Chevrolet cars and Schwinn bicycles.

Alpine skiing produced a cosmopolitan culture stretching from the foothills of Nice to the gates of Vienna, with enthusiasts based in skiing centers such as Chamonix (France), Davos (Switzerland), Cortina d'Ampezzo (Italy), Garmisch-Partenkirchen (Germany), and St. Anton am Arlberg (Austria).

These cosmopolitan networks spread beyond skiing villages into the urban centers of metropolitan Europe. Even so, skiers were not a monolithic group, and they often disagreed on their vision for the mountains. Like the white-outs that pummel Alpine peaks in winter, the sport stripped the mountains of previous reference points and in the process inspired new ways of seeing, experiencing, and manipulating the Alps in the form of Alpine modernism.

PART ONE

Taking Root

ONE

___

An Uphill Climb

THE AGE OF DISCOVERY

In late 1894, a Scottish doctor and novelist took to the pages of the famed British literary digest *The Strand* to relate his experiences in the Alps with an obscure means of locomotion: the ski. The author balanced expressions of fascination and bemusement at an activity that proved both bizarre and captivating. The doctor's account of his adventures on "ski" (the word appeared in quotation marks throughout the article because the Norwegian term had not yet been naturalized into English) recalls the thick description of contemporary ethnographers who studied isolated peoples in the age of imperialism. Indeed, the doctor's use of the primitive ski in the barren Alpine landscape alongside Swiss villagers proved just as foreign and fascinating as the religious practices and social mores of peoples encountered in Africa and Asia. In breathless tones, the author meticulously described the practice of skiing while also attempting to convey the visceral thrill of the sport in writing. His days in the Swiss Alps with skis on his feet afforded him an incomparable experience of speed, the exotic, and the conquest of nature's elementary forces. His narrative aligned this bizarre practice with the values of modern mass culture. And indeed, this was an author who was deeply familiar with fin-de-siècle mass culture. His most enduring literary creation, Sherlock Holmes, similarly tapped into that era's lust for adventure, excitement, and novelty.

In the sport of skiing, Arthur Conan Doyle detected a new sensation. His narrative of his skiing adventures acquainted the *Strand's* nearly half a million subscribers with a sport that quickly became fashionable among Europe's middle classes. At the turn of the century, skiing offered the allure of a primitive practice in an unforgiving landscape of austere beauty, combining the inclination of imperialists to discover new lands with a Romantic appreciation of the landscape. As skiers like Conan Doyle began to take to the Alps in significant numbers, they exhibited the daredevil courage usually reserved for fictional detectives and imperial heroes.

Conan Doyle described skis as deceptively simple tools that suggested "nothing particularly malignant. . . . No one to look at them would guess at the possibilities which lurk in them." In short time, however, the author found himself crashing head-first into snowbanks, slipping in cartoonish fashion, and generally entertaining his friends with his clumsiness. It did not take him long to determine that "the 'ski' are the most capricious things upon earth." He found himself veering from master to novice with little warning, a humbling experience destined to produce "a fine moral effect" for anybody "who suffers from too much dignity." He recognized the absurdity of the whole scene to an outsider, especially in the context of Victorian conventions of propriety, and resorted to contemporary imperialist idiom to describe the activity as "an exaggerated nigger dance." To protect the new skier's ego, Conan Doyle recommended that "one can do very well without a gallery when one is trying a new experiment on 'ski'" (figure 2).[1]

Thanks to his wife's prolonged winter stay at the tuberculosis cure center in Davos, however, Conan Doyle became quite adept at skiing. He even claimed that summiting a peak or traversing a mountain pass in winter was in fact easier than the same trip during the summer. With skis, "your trouble is halved" through the effortless glide downhill, and the "crisp, pure air" of the wintry mountains was far better suited to physical exertion than the summer climate. Conan Doyle described a day trip from his hotel in Davos to the village of Arosa over the intermediate peaks of the Plessur Alps, a distance he estimated at twelve to fourteen miles. To undertake such a trip in winter would have struck all but the hardiest contemporary readers as a death wish. Along with his local guides, the Branger brothers, Conan Doyle departed Davos at 4:30 A.M. The party easily slid across "virgin snow" of indeterminate depth that would have stopped walkers in their tracks. He effortlessly traversed "that great untrodden waste," averring that "it was glorious to whizz along in this easy fashion." By 9:30 A.M., the men had Arosa in their sights. Fashioning a toboggan out of their skis to negotiate a particularly steep final slope, they reached their destination at 11:30, astonishing the residents of Arosa, who had calculated that it would be impossible for Conan Doyle to arrive before 1 P.M.[2]

FIGURE 2. Arthur Conan Doyle in the Swiss Alps, 1894. Arthur Conan Doyle, "An Alpine Pass on 'Ski,'" *Strand,* July–December 1894, 659.

Conan Doyle's description of his early exploits on skis highlights three major themes that defined Alpine skiing in its early years. First, it reflects the rapid shift from derision to appreciation of skiing. Whereas Conan Doyle sheepishly described his early efforts as reminiscent of "primitive" colonial peoples, after practicing the sport and completing Alpine ski tours, he became a proselyte for the sport. By World War I, skiing had become a popular leisure activity, an economic stimulant in the previously barren Alpine winter, and a vital means of defense along the Alpine battlefronts of the Great War. In a short time, Central Europe had naturalized this Nordic activity and came to view it as uniquely Alpine. Skiers also understood their equipment to be particularly modern, despite both its ancient provenance and its associations with Scandinavian (and particularly Norwegian) culture in the nineteenth century.

Second, Conan Doyle highlights the exotic and heroic nature of the sport. Skiing in the austere, uncharted winter Alpine landscape conveyed a sense of adventure and discovery that other modern leisure activities, whether organized sports like soccer or rugby or less rigorous recreations in the summer Alpine resorts, did not evoke. He wrote, "I believe that I may claim to be the first save only two Switzers to do any mountain work (though on a modest enough scale) on [skis], but I am certain that I will not by many a thousand be the last."[3] Although Conan Doyle exaggerated his own role as a trailblazer (numerous locals and tourists skied in the Alps in the 1880s), his attitude illustrates the perception of the sport's novelty and the feeling of conquest and exploration it afforded its practitioners.

Third, Conan Doyle recognized the potential of skiing for both visitors and the residents of the Alps. Alpine skiing made the seemingly impossible— a winter traverse of high mountains—not only possible but immensely enjoyable. For many residents of the Alps, this newfound mobility drastically affected everyday life. Even today, traveling by road from Davos to Arosa requires a circuitous journey of some fifty miles. As a result, for mountain residents who did not live near the rather sparse Alpine rail network, skiing afforded much greater mobility in the harsh Alpine winter. And because of the appeal of skiing to tourists and holidaymakers, Conan Doyle predicted "that the time will come when hundreds of Englishmen will come to Switzerland for the 'ski'-ing season."[4] The hundreds of thousands of Britons who read his rapturous account of skiing in the Alps in the *Strand* would prove invaluable to the further development of the sport in the following decades.

Conan Doyle's description of the joy of speed and movement in wintry landscapes could just as easily have been written in 1920, 1970, or 2010. But his account is particularly striking because it posits the ski as a catalyst for historical change. It aligned with the contemporary fascination for the exploration and conquest of extreme, barren landscapes, and it would revolutionize social and economic life in the Alps for year-round residents and foreign tourists alike. To better understand the nuances of Alpine modernism and to place these revolutionary changes in context, we must first examine the Alps before skiing and skiing before the Alps.

THE ALPS BEFORE SKIING

The society, economy, and culture of the Alps developed in response to the geographic and climatic challenges the region posed to human settlement.

One of the first historians to look carefully at the role of mountains in history, Fernand Braudel, lamented that "the historian is not unlike the traveller. He tends to linger over the plain, which is the setting for the leading actors of the day, and does not seem eager to approach the high mountains nearby. More than one historian who has never left the towns and their archives would be surprised to discover their existence. And yet how can one ignore these conspicuous actors, the half-wild mountains, where man has taken root like a hardy plant?"[5] Indeed, in describing the varied mountains ringing the Mediterranean Sea, Braudel conceded that the cultural and physical composition of the Alps were so exceptional that he could differentiate them only tautologically, writing, "the Alps are after all the Alps."[6]

In spite of the exceptional mass and elevation of the Alps, they are generally easier to traverse and more habitable than other European mountain chains, such as the Pyrenees, because the unique geomorphology of Alpine peaks and valleys connects the mountain heights to the European lowlands, rather than sequestering Alpine communities.[7] As a result, the Alps have a long history of human settlement, and Alpine communities have at times influenced mainstream European culture, as during the Protestant Reformation and Catholic Counter-Reformation of the sixteenth and seventeenth centuries.[8] Like all mountains, the Alps can be described as a sort of circuit breaker. At times they allow for the circulation of goods, ideas, and people.[9] At other times, they serve as an obstacle, impeding mobility and cultural and economic exchange.

For centuries, the Alps evoked fear because of the hazardous nature of the terrain and climate. Even in relatively modern times, this combination of land and weather could prove deadly; in the winter of 1888, a series of avalanches killed fifty-three residents and 510 head of cattle and destroyed 103 homes in the Austrian state of Tirol.[10] As late as the fin de siècle, the Alps were considered be impassable in winter to all but the healthiest and bravest individuals.

The rugged landscape was difficult to reconcile with the increasingly influential capitalist imperatives of rationality and productivity. In general, nineteenth-century industrial practices did not transfer well to the Alps because production in traditional Alpine economic spheres, such as agriculture or handicrafts, could be executed more cheaply and efficiently in the lowland metropolises, which combined a larger labor pool with better connections to rail lines and navigable rivers. As a result, established Alpine trades such as metallurgy and glass making had to compete with lowland manufacturing. Although the Long Depression that began in 1873 inspired economic protectionism by European states to shield domestic producers from international competition, the main beneficiaries were not Alpine producers but rather established industries in lowland Europe.[11]

Alpine industrialization was further arrested by the growth of centralized states, which developed well-defined, highly regulated borders to expand control over their realms and thus disrupted inter-Alpine commerce.[12] Following decisions emanating from the lowland capitals of Paris, Vienna, and Rome, Alpine communities such as Innsbruck that had served as economic and cultural hubs before the nineteenth century (the Holy Roman Emperor Maximilian I ruled from Innsbruck in the late fifteenth century, making the city a center of considerable political and religious power) were downgraded to secondary, provincial status. As a result of these policies and attitudes, the Alps came to be seen as geographically, economically, and culturally marginal.

In an industrialized Europe, Alpine communities remained isolated, with the majority of mountain dwellers living near the subsistence level. Many commentators considered the Alps to be wasted space populated by a cultureless, backward people.[13] The mountains possessed few of the natural resources that fueled industrial development, such as coal, and production of goods in the Alps was uneconomical in comparison to urban production. One Swiss historian estimated in 1945 that nearly a quarter of the land in mountainous Switzerland was "unproductive" and would remain so, placing the Swiss at a severe economic disadvantage.[14]

The common attitude toward the residents of the Alps during the nineteenth and early twentieth century mixed pity and derision. Some commentators, such as Luis Trenker, a South Tirolean author and director of German-language *Bergfilme* (mountain films), observed a quiet dignity in the Alpine denizen who engaged in an "eternal struggle" against "the sum of nature's elements." This struggle was multiplied in the winter, when snow "fences him in and closes him off from the world."[15] Other commentators were less empathetic. The German philosopher Ernst Bloch viewed the Alps as a vibrant landscape inhabited by a moribund people who could not overcome the obstructive essence of the mountains: "The mountain world . . . is always an encircled one in comparison with the heath and the ocean; its stoniness is rigid, and liable to promote an especially stagnant, undialectical, settled-in state of mind, inimical to exodus."[16] Despite his love of the Swiss Alps, Arnold Lunn spoke even more derisively of the mountain folk, writing of Switzerland's Gems Valley in the wake of World War I: "The chalets are all extremely black and old and dirty. So are most of the natives. Nothing in this valley seems much less than three hundred years old, except the children who only look about seventy—queer little wizened trolls, carrying vast baskets of manure on their backs."[17]

At the same time, European attitudes toward the Alps were influenced by Romanticism. As Luis Trenker contended, mountains play a dual role: they "bind and split," serving as both "cultural field and cultural vault."[18] The initial impetus for connecting lowland society to the Alps in the modern era came not from formal economic initiatives but from broad cultural shifts. One of the primary consequences of the rise of capitalism was the marginalization of land in the public imaginary. Whereas land had provided the most reliable basis for status and power in precapitalist Europe, the shift to capitalism displaced the foundations of economic and social capital from the land to the control of the means of production.[19] In response, capitalist European societies generally valued land less as an economic or social commodity and more as a cultural one, serving a moral and aesthetic purpose.[20] The landscape nurtured values such as simplicity and fortitude in individuals, implicitly returning them to a natural state of existence from which they had become alienated by capitalist, industrial modernity.

Disciples of the Romantic movement cultivated a worldview that celebrated the moral potential of the landscape, and perhaps no landscape underwent a more dramatic reappraisal than the Alps. The classicist aesthetic construed the Alps as unappealing. Their asymmetry offended artistic sensibility, while the Alpine climate and landscape thwarted endeavors to manipulate nature to serve human needs. In response, Europeans composed myths and legends for millennia to explain the mountains' otherworldly power.[21] Starting in the late eighteenth century, Romantic authors and artists reversed this longstanding fear and disdain when they began to praise the sublime power of nature as a remedy for the corrupting power of industrialization and the hubris of Enlightenment rationality. The Alps appealed directly to human emotions with their timeless beauty and grandeur, making them the consummate Romantic landscape. When early Romantics like Jean-Jacques Rousseau critiqued modern civilization (implicitly urban and lowland), the Alps appeared pristine and uncorrupted in comparison. According to the German author and critic Arnold Zweig, who in the dark years of World War II saw in the multicultural Alps a metaphor for human cooperation and progress, the popularization of Romanticism meant that these mountains "no longer stood as a barrier, but rather as a bond between the North and South of the continent."[22] The Alps became a meeting ground for individuals disaffected by modern civilization, including acclaimed Romantic authors such as Johann Wolfgang von Goethe, who climbed Switzerland's Rigi-Kulm in 1775, and the parade of English Romantics who vacationed in Switzerland in the early nineteenth century, the Shelleys and Lord Byron among them.

Although Romanticism began to wane as an artistic movement by the mid-nineteenth century, the Romantic veneration of the Alpine landscape continued to inform the public imaginary.[23] A late nineteenth-century German Alpinist averred that mountaineers and hikers found in the Alps "the source of purest joy, spring of rejuvenation and the renewer of strength, where spirit and body dive into nature's fountain of youth."[24] But despite the Romantic opposition to industrial modernity, the naturalization of its landscape aesthetic in European culture paradoxically encouraged the economic development and modernization of the Alps. The mountain landscape, a disadvantage to primary or secondary industrial activity, proved to be a tremendous asset in the development of the tertiary economic sector, and specifically tourism. As Romanticism moved from the fringes of European culture to the mainstream by the mid-nineteenth century, public interest in touring the Alps, and especially Switzerland, skyrocketed. The famed German guidebook publisher Karl Baedeker published his first guide to Switzerland in 1844, and the British Thomas Cook Company conducted its first organized trip to Switzerland in 1863, in response to growing demand among the British population. As more Europeans developed the cultural desire and the economic means to explore the Alps in the fin de siècle, membership in European Alpine clubs grew dramatically (see table 1). The local population was at first confused by outsiders' fascination with the barren Alpine landscape but quickly moved to exploit this interest.[25]

Although Alpine tourism was not unheard-of before the mid-nineteenth century, the primary and secondary effects of industrialization, including a growing focus on work, made it both more popular and more lucrative. Middle-class Europeans began to imagine the Alpine landscape as a "modern space of experience" in which identities—adventurous mountain climber, contemplative hiker, cosmopolitan socialite—could be defined and performed.[26] The concept of leisure gained steam among those members of the middle class who could afford it. The appreciation of free time, combined with a regard for the aristocratic tradition of travel (such as the European Grand Tours that flourished in the seventeenth and eighteenth centuries) and rising discretionary spending, created great demand for tourism.

TABLE 1 Membership in the German and Austrian
Alpine Association, 1874–1914

Year	Number of Members	Number of Local Sections
1874	4,074	46
1884	13,878	108
1894	32,163	214
1904	63,041	307
1914	102,092	407

SOURCE: Dagmar Günther, *Alpine Quergänge: Kulturgeschichte des bürgerlichen Alpinismus (1870–1930)* (Frankfurt, 1998), 79.

Romanticism thus provided advance publicity for the Alps. As socioeconomic and cultural forces converged to stimulate tourism in the second half of the nineteenth century, Europe's burgeoning middle classes increasingly flocked to Alpine summer resorts and cabins (*Sommerfrische*), where they socialized, hiked, and swam.[27] By the turn of the century, the Alps were celebrated by the "back to nature" movements that gained popularity as responses to modern life, connecting Alpine leisure to contemporary movements such as nudism, vegetarianism, and landscape conservation.[28] Businessmen and state officials saw great economic potential in tourism and quickly invested in the development of Alpine hotels and rail lines to transport urban tourists to Alpine destinations.

Beginning with the completion of the first standard-gauge Alpine railway in 1854 (Austria's Semmeringbahn), Alpine train travel developed rapidly in the second half of the nineteenth century.[29] The completion of the Gotthardbahn in 1882 reduced travel time between the Swiss town of Chiasso, on the Italian border, across the Alps to Basel from three and a half days to ten and a half hours.[30] The railway redrew the map of tourism, opening up spaces that had once been too remote for all but the most affluent and leisured travelers.[31] Now a day of travel sufficed to transport most Europeans from their homes to Alpine tourist centers. This ease of transport also internationalized Alpine tourism. By the end of the nineteenth century, only 20 percent of tourists in Switzerland were Swiss citizens: the remaining 80 percent were mostly Germans and Britons.[32]

As tourist numbers ballooned, some lamented their effect on the Alps, arguing that the mountain landscape had begun to reflect the industrialization and commercialization of Europe's urban metropolises. In 1904 a British tourist and author, Alexander Innes Shand, described the dramatic changes in the Alpine landscape that he had witnessed during his lifetime: "Railways traverse the length and breadth of the land; tunnels are being driven through the bowels of the Alps, lifts have been fitted to the hills wherever a solitary eminence offers commanding points of view; magnificent hotels have been springing up everywhere; rude shelter huts have been turned into commodious inns. . . . The Playground of Europe has been swamped with sightseers, and the sanctuaries where Chaos and Old Night once reigned supreme have been desecrated and vulgarized."[33] Other commentators spoke more positively, including Arnold Lunn, who contended that "the Alps have been humanized rather than vulgarized by human contacts. Their austere majesty has, perhaps, been diminished, but there has been gain as well as loss, for even trippers and picture postcards contribute something to the personality which the Alps have acquired by long association with Man. Man is at home in the Alps."[34] It must be noted, however, that this favorable assessment was written in 1943, two years *after* Lunn's polemic against the democratization of Alpine skiing and the spread of tourism infrastructure (see introduction). Regardless of the tenor of the responses, however, the Alpine landscape, which had grown in popularity as an imagined escape from the challenges of modern life, progressively came to reflect modern conditions and debates.

The use of hypermodern Alpine railways to get back to nature highlights the uneasy tension between the modern and the natural in Alpine tourism. Express trains from distant locations such as Berlin, Paris, and Calais (to serve the British market) delivered tourists to barren landscapes inhabited by mountain dwellers who struggled to survive in primitive conditions. While the railways brought the trappings of metropolitan culture to towns like Davos and St. Moritz, nearby villages remained profoundly isolated. At the same time, the growth of the tourism sector held out the promise of self-sufficiency and even prosperity for mountain communities. Yet almost all tourist activity occurred in the summer. For the vast majority of tourists and mountain residents, the Alps in winter remained a forbidding wasteland.

SKIING BEFORE THE ALPS

Archaeological digs from Norway to the Bering Sea have produced evidence of ancient forms of the ski as a tool used by Eurasian peoples to aid in hunting and transport for the last eight millennia. Where skis played an important role in everyday life, they began to appear in cultural productions, including art and mythology. Rock carvings and cave paintings depicting skiing are scattered across the Eurasian landmass and date back three to five thousand years. In the thirteenth century, skis began to appear in Norse sagas. The god Ullr and the goddess Skadi, also known as Öndergud, or "ski god," carry bows and arrows and move effortlessly about the winter landscape on skis.[35] The infiltration of skiing into myth demonstrates the importance of skiing to everyday life in the subarctic regions and implies the godlike power it afforded mere mortals.

In 1555, Olaus Magnus, the exiled Catholic archbishop of Uppsala, Sweden, composed a work of history and descriptive geography in which he chronicled the use of skis in Scandinavia for transport and hunting.[36] The German Johann Christoph Friedrich GutsMuths devoted a short section to "snow-running, or running on snowshoes" in an 1804 update to his revolutionary 1793 treatise on physical education, *Gymnastik für die Jugend.* GutsMuths described the popularity of skis in Scandinavia and, notably, their use in the Danish army (Norway was politically united with the kingdom of Denmark in one form or another from 1396 to 1814). He argued that although Germans did not inhabit cold climates and snowy landscapes on a par with those in Scandinavia, snow accumulations in parts of the German lands often limited or entirely thwarted movement and communication in the winter. GutsMuths saw in skis a multifaceted civilizing force: they would allow for normal communication and transportation in extreme climates and would bolster the skiers' strength and flexibility, thus improving physical and mental health.[37]

Recreational skiing developed slowly in the mid-nineteenth century, with Norwegian skiers leading the way. The 1814 Treaty of Kiel ended the union of Norway and Denmark and forced a Norwegian union with Sweden after a brief war between the two Scandinavian nations. In an attempt to define an identity distinct from that of their new overlords, nationalistic Norwegians celebrated their ancient, spiritual connection to skiing, idealizing the sport as distinctly Norwegian in the early to mid-nineteenth century.[38] Intellectuals dredged up references to skiing in Norwegian-language publications and Norse myths, describing a bond between the Norwegian people and the stark landscape to spark a recognizably Romantic form of nationalism. In the context of what many considered a Swedish conquest and colonization of their homeland, nationalistic Norwegians elaborated the concept of *Skiidrett,* a term that connected the physical act of skiing with broader principles of national identity, in much the same sense as the contemporaneous Romantic-nationalist German *Turnen* gymnastic movement.[39] In both cases, the importance of physical activity went beyond utility and individual health: it had the potential to produce deep spiritual meaning and to cultivate group identity.

As Romantic nationalist intellectuals deliberately fostered connections between skiing and national identity, skiing grew steadily as a leisure activity in Norway. The first organized ski race was held in 1843 in the Arctic port of Tromsø, some one thousand miles north of Christiania (today's Oslo). The ancient Viking capital of Trondheim, located three hundred miles north of the capital and surrounded by rolling hills, became a hub of ski touring during the 1840s and 1850s. Although the sport developed first in the geographic periphery of Norway, intellectuals expounded the animating nationalistic and athletic ideologies from Christiania by associating the sport with an organic folk culture.[40] The capital lagged in terms of the actual practice of skiing, holding its first organized ski tour only in 1860. In the 1860s, organized ski tours and races proliferated throughout Norway, raising the sport's public profile. The growing popularity of the sport necessitated the establishment of bureaucratic organizations to guide skiers' activities, making skiing both a reflection of the modern practice of state centralization and a conduit of socioeconomic and cultural modernization.[41] The more popular the sport became, the more uniquely Norwegian it seemed, and the more widely it appealed to nonpractitioners as a manifestation of national identity, whether they skied or not. In 1875 skiers founded the first ski club in the world, the Christiania Ski Club.

Despite the efforts of Christiania's intelligentsia to cast skiing as a distinctive national practice, the practice of the sport varied widely with the local terrain. Rolling hills, steep slopes, and forested flatlands inspired variations of equipment and the celebration of nearby geographic features.[42] These variations in fact aided in the creation of Norwegian nationalism. The historian of Germany Alon Confino has interpreted nationalism as a "local metaphor" through which individuals developed overlapping group identities that fed into the imagination of an overarching nationalism.[43] Skiing allowed Norwegians to cultivate local bonds by forming ski associations and fostering attachments to specific landscapes. Simultaneously, the sport mediated the relationship between the local and the national. From its earliest modern developments in Norway, skiing has served as a political and cultural tool, contributing to Norwegian identity formation and cultural perceptions of place. The transformative power of skiing reached new heights as it came into contact with the forbidding peaks of the Alps, and the sport would in its turn be transformed.

FROM SCANDINAVIA TO CENTRAL EUROPE

In the modern era, certain mobile classes of individuals, including teachers, students, government bureaucrats, and businesspeople, have played a formative role in the global diffusion of sport.[44] A modern map of cricket-mad nations bears a striking resemblance to that of the nineteenth-century British Empire, while the spread of soccer and rugby from England to Europe can be mapped to continental ports such as Hamburg and Le Havre that did significant business with British firms. Similarly, Norwegian students in Germany were instrumental in the transmission of skiing from Norway to Central Europe in the 1880s.[45]

Germany emerged in the late nineteenth century as a premier industrial power, with particular strengths in sciences with industrial applications, such as chemistry, mining, and engineering. Germany's technical institutes attracted budding engineers and scientists from across Europe, including a sizable number of Norwegians.[46] Many of these Norwegian students had been young boys precisely when skiing became popular in the 1860s and thus could not imagine winters without skiing. Carl Luther, an arbiter of German skiing culture and practice at the turn of the century, noted that skiing grew markedly in Germany from 1883 forward, notably in the Harz Mountains of central Germany and the Black Forest near Freiburg im Breisgau.[47] Not coincidentally, the technical universities in Hannover, Clausthal, Braunschweig, and Chemnitz, as well as the traditional universities in Göttingen and Leipzig, all lay within a hundred-mile radius of the Harz, making this upland region accessible for weekend getaways. Similarly, Freiburg was home to an esteemed university with strengths in mining and the metallurgical sciences.

Norwegian students near the Black Forest and in the areas surrounding the Harz found these landscapes reminiscent of the their native ski terrain, with rolling hills rather than soaring peaks or steep inclines. Summarizing his experiences in the Harz, a Norwegian student wrote in 1885, "A normal winter [in Germany] . . . offers a Norwegian great opportunities to limber up with that sport which is dearest to him."[48] By contrast, the steep descents of the Alps and the flat expanses of northern Germany held little appeal for Norwegian skiers. Thus the Norwegian model of skiing first took hold not in the high Alpine communities that are today synonymous with the sport, but rather in what Germans would call *Mittelgebirge*—relatively low mountain ranges, including not only the Harz and the mountains of the Black Forest but also the Vosges of France and Germany, the Jura of Switzerland and France, and the Riesengebirge of the Austro-Hungarian Empire (today's Poland and Czech Republic).

The early importation of the Norwegian sport of skiing to Central Europe was a matter not of formal initiatives but rather of hundreds and thousands of informal, individual contacts, as attested by the experiences of Wilhelm Paulcke, the German skiing pioneer and proponent of skiing in the Black Forest. As the sickly child of a Leipzig pharmacist, the seven-year-old Paulcke was taken to Switzerland to enjoy the curative air of the Alps in late 1879.[49] By coincidence, Agnes Duborgh, the nurse who cared for young Wilhelm while the Paulckes resided in Davos, was a Norwegian. She dazzled him with her tales of the men of Telemark, who used skis to hunt, whizz downhill, and fly off jumps. Duborgh's stories, Paulcke recalled, "awakened such longing in me." In 1883, Paulcke received a pair of skis for Christmas and began practicing the sport in the area around Davos. He continued to ski while studying geology in Freiburg in the early 1890s, and he began to undertake trailblazing and dangerous skiing tours in the Alps: his 1896 climb of the 10,919-foot Oberalpstock in the Swiss canton of Glarus was the first ascent of a *Dreitausender* (a 3,000-meter peak) on skis.[50] Early skiers in Central Europe, whether Norwegian or native, had to overcome the initial incredulity of the local populations, who in the 1880s and early 1890s viewed skiers "as a blend of madman and clown." Many skiing pioneers resorted to making clandestine tours and practicing their sport at night to avoid the stares and mockery of the local population.[51]

In a parallel development, the growth of winter Alpine tourism laid the foundation for the expansion of skiing. Hotel operators took advantage of the vogue for Alpine cure centers. Doctors believed that the hygienic qualities of cold, dry mountain air could ameliorate or even cure a range of diseases that afflicted modern urbanites, including neurasthenia and tuberculosis. The Alps also symbolized recreation and leisure for the healthy, and many of the English, German, and French pleasure seekers who visited the Alps for months in summer expressed their desire to stay into the winter. This was the basis for Sir Henry Lunn's successful tourism company in Britain. By 1888, four of the major Swiss Alpine-tourism centers, aided by technological developments such as improved rail service and central heating, had opened their doors for winter business: Davos in 1865–66, St. Moritz in 1883–84, and Arosa and Grindelwald in 1888.[52]

These four locales remain prominent centers of Alpine skiing to this day. This continuity suggests the enduring influence of summer tourism. Other summer destinations that became popular in winter included the *Sommerfrische* of the Alpine state of Tirol (Austria), the village of Megève (France), the established thermal spas of Kitzbühel (Austria) and Bagnères (France), Alpinist centers such as Zermatt (Switzerland) and Chamonix (France), and medical cure centers such as Davos (Switzerland). Existing accommodations, transport infrastructure, service cultures, and established patterns of tourist activity made these Alpine communities well prepared to welcome winter-sport enthusiasts.

Skiing in the Alps did not emerge in a vacuum, nor did skiers necessarily search out and develop virgin terrain. Instead, they took advantage of existing infrastructure and leisure cultures, while tourist businesses wooed skiers by supplementing their offerings. This relationship between skiers and the tourism industry proved symbiotic and mutually beneficial from their earliest contact.

Although staying through the winter sounded charming, many were surprised by the isolation and boredom of snowed-in Alpine villages. To cope, guests looked to amuse themselves, and many turned to winter sports. In the nineteenth century, the use of obsolete forms of transport such as horses, sleds, and skis for leisure not only made old technologies newly viable but was also freighted with deep cultural meaning.[53] As Arthur Conan Doyle's description illustrates, the use of skis for leisure evoked a return to the primitive, the simple, and the natural among Europe's cosmopolitan middle classes, aligning skiing with the Romantic critique of civilization and the movement's primitivist celebration of the Alps and its peoples.

Skiing did not take off immediately at Alpine resorts: other winter entertainments preceded it. The first ice skaters took to Davos Lake in the late 1860s, and tobogganing and bobsledding gained in popularity in the 1880s. Similarly, at St. Moritz, ice skating and tobogganing became popular leisure pursuits soon after the first winter opening in 1883.[54] Retrospectively, Arnold Lunn described skating in the late nineteenth century as "the Queen of Winter sports." In comparison, skiing was "an uncouth intruder," and at St. Moritz, haughty skaters referred to skiers derisively as "plank-hoppers."[55]

Lunn recalled that when he first tried skiing in 1898, "the few visitors who bothered to ski in Chamonix were regarded as reckless faddists."[56] The first Alpine skiers largely confined themselves to forests and foothills that resembled Scandinavian landscapes. Theirs was a curious and disadvantaged sport, one that required more practice and exertion to enjoy than skating and tobogganing. For elite tourists and frail cure seekers, this was no minor difference, though many were nevertheless drawn by the novelty and exoticism of skiing.

The development of European skiing outside Norway in the last two decades of the nineteenth century was informal and isolated. The belief that skiing was only suited to Nordic landscapes plotted the early geographic diffusion of the sport. The growth of skiing benefited from conjunctural socioeconomic and cultural shifts in Europe such as secondary industrialization, the rise of the middle class, and the growth of leisure culture. A growing public interest in leisure and sport fortuitously converged with the economic processes that lured Norwegian university students to German universities. Although early skiers outside Scandinavia followed Nordic models closely, they left much of its nationalistic and ideological baggage behind and gradually altered the practice and meaning of the sport to suit the dramatic socioeconomic and cultural changes of the fin de siècle. As we shall see in the next chapter, the diffuse skiing movement in Central Europe coalesced markedly in the wake of what was essentially an informal, unplanned advertisement for skiing in Europe, consonant with the values of a nascent mass culture.

TWO

A Civilizing Force

IGNITING SKI FEVER

Fridtjof Nansen's upbringing was largely unremarkable. Born near Christiania in 1861, Nansen took up skiing at age four, and his childhood was infused with the same sporting-nationalist *Skiidrett* that animated the Norwegian engineering students responsible for introducing skiing to Central Europe in the last decades of the nineteenth century. But Nansen promoted skiing in a way that hundreds of Norwegian students could not. While studying zoology at the University of Christiania in 1882, Nansen's professor invited him to observe and catalogue animal life on a five-month voyage of discovery in the Arctic, during which Nansen shot some five hundred seals and fourteen polar bears in the name of science.[1] Upon his return, Nansen began to devise a plan that combined his love of skiing with the spirit of discovery and adventure cultivated on his Arctic journey. He settled on traversing one of the globe's last remaining frontiers: the massive and forbidding Danish territory of Greenland. Nansen plotted a 420-mile journey across the island from east to west that he estimated would take one month, adopting the motto "Death or the west coast of Greenland."[2] Little did Nansen realize that his 1888 traverse of Greenland would help transform skiing from merely one option among many for winter pleasure seekers in the Alps into the winter recreation activity par excellence at the turn of the century.

The attempt to cross Greenland was a test of human endurance and ingenuity in one of the world's most extreme landscapes. The barren terrain and lack of significant settlements required that Nansen's party of six be entirely self-sufficient. Yet Nansen and his traveling companions were confident that their journey would be successful thanks to their mastery of the ski, which would allow them to glide easily through the menacing glacial landscape. As Nansen wrote in his account of the Greenland expedition, "All our prospects of success were based upon the superiority of 'ski' in comparison with all other means of locomotion when large tracts of snow have to be traversed."[3]

Nansen's journey was successful, although delays on the boat journey to Greenland and during the ski traverse required him to alter his route, shortening the traverse by nearly one hundred miles, and forced him to wait out the winter in the western settlement of Godthaab (today's Nuuk) before a boat arrived to deliver him back to Norway in April 1889. Meanwhile, word of his success circulated throughout Europe. In the summer of 1889, Nansen frequented the drawing rooms of London, gave well-attended talks to the Royal Geographical Society and the British Association for the Advancement of Science, and received further honors from scientific and geographical societies across Europe. Nansen published an account of his journey in 1890 that was soon translated into English (1890), German (1891), and French (1893).

Although Nansen's expedition certainly had scientific significance, and it also set the stage for his trailblazing journey in the polar ice from 1893 to 1896, the most enduring legacy of Nansen's Greenland traverse was its effect on skiing in Central Europe. At the time of his journey, most Europeans south of Scandinavia still regarded skiing as exotic and obscure. As readers followed daily newspaper reports of Nansen's expedition and later devoured his published account of the traverse, they came to see skiing not as a curious, faddish pastime but as a tool of adventure and a vector of civilization. Nansen used skis to explore blank spots on the map and to overcome obstacles once thought to be impassable, putting his voyage on a par with contemporary imperial exploits such as the Briton Henry Morton Stanley's Central Africa expedition, the Frenchman Pierre Savorgnan de Brazza's exploration of the Congo, and the German Carl Peters' colonial endeavors in East Africa. Appearing in the context of adventure novels such as Henry Rider Haggard's *She* (1887) and Jules Verne's *Around the World in Eighty Days* (1873), Nansen's exciting—and true—narrative of his struggles in a faraway and primitive land captivated the European public. His was a feat perfectly suited to the growing mass media of the fin de siècle and the attendant public appetite for spectacle and novelty.[4]

Nearly all of the early proponents of skiing, including Arnold Lunn, Austria's Mathias Zdarsky, and Germany's Carl Luther, praised Nansen for his role in popularizing skiing. Wilhelm Paulcke commented that Nansen's heroism in Greenland stood "in contrast to the everyday throngs of 'modern man;' it nourishes in us the heroic spirit of the olden days. Nansen shows that human willpower and vigor lead us to victory over the horrors of natural forces."[5]

Nansen's traverse inspired thousands of curious Europeans to try skiing, and "Nansen fever" transformed the sport from a curiosity to be practiced surreptitiously, out of sight of mocking spectators, into a cultural sensation. Even so, its practice and meanings remained aligned with the Norwegian style of skiing. In Central Europe, the most obvious, direct effects of Nansen's traverse were to increase the number of skiers and to serve as a modernizing force in the Alps. Mountain dwellers began to use skis for winter travel and to exploit skiing as an attraction for winter tourism. Equally important, however, was the modernization of Alpine skiing culture. The influx of new practitioners led skiers to organize themselves into clubs and associations to represent their interests, to direct the development of the sport, and to organize and adjudicate competitions. These organizations not only increased the influence of skiers but also contributed to the self-definition of a cosmopolitan middle class in the fin de siècle.

Nansen's traverse thus marks an inflection point in the history of Alpine skiing. Not only did it associate skiing with heroism, conquest, and the new mass culture of spectacle, but it also presented new opportunities to Alpine residents and made the organization and cultural meanings of the sport conform with the values and aptitudes of its primary practitioners, the middle classes. A small group of particularly evangelistic skiers interpreted Nansen's expedition as proof that they could consciously and deliberately spread civilization to the Alps and nourish body and soul.

The growth of Alpine skiing had unexpected effects. It altered the daily life of mountain dwellers, but not as champions of the sport assumed it would; and the growing popularity of skiing initiated a civilizing process within the sport itself, which required skiers to critically assess their goals and ideals. Skiing engendered contradictory impulses. It was an ancient tool that engaged symbiotically with modern mass culture; its practitioners rhapsodized its power to modernize everyday life in the Alps while celebrating the simplicity of the landscape and its peoples; and skiers sought to expand their ranks while simultaneously policing the social boundaries of the sport. Skiing could thus be all things to all people, and it is in the last decades of the nineteenth century that we can see the beginnings of the synthetic, amalgamating ideology of Alpine modernism. However, such tensions also had the potential to divide skiers. Modernizing trends within the sport laid bare these contradictions, culminating in the definitive separation of Alpine and Nordic practices of skiing in the years before World War I.

CIVILIZING THE ALPS

Central European skiers before World War I may be broken down into two groups: those who skied for utility and those who skied for pleasure. This divide reflected social and geographical differences. Early celebrations of skiing repeatedly described it as a liberating force that would release hapless and dull mountain peoples from the shackles of winter, laying to rest, in the words of Arnold Lunn, "the old legends of the impracticability of Alpine passes, of the inhospitability of the high regions in winter, of the perpetual danger of avalanches, and of the intense cold."[6] The French pedagogue and early skiing proselyte Jules Payot epitomized the combination of triumphalism and rank condescension inherent in this early attitude: "In the past, the snow was an imprisonment for weeks. It represented a reduction of liberty. . . . Thus, people shut themselves away. Immobilized, in airless rooms, the villagers became sensitive to the cold. They endeavored to fill the cracks through which pure air from outside could enter. Sedentary, breathing contaminated air, [they] led a life that smelled musty, analogous, in certain remote villages, to [hibernation]. A weakened life, which made the blood anemic [and] aggravated nervous conditions. The boredom of an unhealthy and reclusive life incited alcoholism." Skis, however, "transformed local life[,] . . . exorcis[ing] the evil spirits of the snow. The ski is liberating. It afforded an enormous extension of liberty to the mountain dwellers . . . and has more importance for the future of the [Chamonix] valley than thirty ministerial changes."[7]

Across Central Europe, middle-class observers described skis as the perfect tool for integrating backward mountain people into the modern world by giving them greater freedom of movement. In 1901, Wilhelm Paulcke wrote, "Transport brings progress." Alpine peoples suffered from the disease of immobility, and it was their lack of connection with the outside world that made mountain life a constant struggle. They experienced "a *vita minima* in both bodily and spiritual terms" for which the only remedy was mobility and activity. In response, Paulcke recommended that the German and Austrian Alpine Association (Deutscher und Österreichischer Alpenverein—DÖAV)

TABLE 2   Membership in the German Ski Association (DSV) and the
Swiss Ski Association (SSV), 1905–14

	1905	1906	1907	1908	1909	1910	1911	1912	1913	1914
DSV	2,459	—	3,718	9,116	11,100	17,619	21,161	27,913	32,843	32,292
SSV	620	1,169	1,893	2,403	2,854	3,210	3,676	4,131	4,561	5,192

NOTE: DSV membership for these years includes Austrian members.

SOURCES: Dr. Tenner, "Der Weg des Deutschen Skiverbandes," in *Deutscher Skilauf: Ein Querschnitt*, ed. Carl Luther (Munich, 1930), 27. Annual Swiss figures drawn from *SSV Jahrbuch*, 1905–14.

organize courses to teach mountain residents to use skis.[8] He pointed to the great success of skiers in the Black Forest area of Germany and the Austrian state of Styria in persuading the local population to adopt skiing, largely by example. The local populations, Paulcke believed, embraced skiing because they could see its usefulness with their own eyes. By exposing residents of the high Alps to skiing, leisure skiers would fulfill what Paulcke believed was the primary mission of the DÖAV: "the opening of the Eastern Alps, the improvement of transportation, and with it the improvement of the entire *Alpenland*."[9]

Many middle-class leisure skiers thus considered themselves to be agents of civilization, doing for Europe's internal frontier what valorous contemporary imperialists did for their "little brown brothers" overseas. As leisure skiers enjoyed the visceral and intellectual pleasures of the sport and the sociability of club culture, they believed their example would inspire Alpine residents to emancipate themselves and enter the modern age by becoming active and productive year-round. Many mountain dwellers did use skis to aid in a variety of occupations and activities, including forestry and hunting. A number of them became quite proficient, and within a generation, most of the preeminent racers and instructors at Alpine resorts were locals of modest means whose parents worked in the tourism industry and who had grown up skiing.

The greatest impact of skiing, however, was more indirect and accidental than advocates like Payot and Paulcke had predicted. Many Alpine residents saw in skiing the potential for a new vocation and adapted their activities to benefit economically from the growth of winter tourism. The presence of summer crowds in Alpine leisure centers such as Chamonix and Davos had already given rise to a service economy and boosted tourism-related activities, including agriculture and handicrafts. As skiers began to reach a critical mass in the early twentieth century (see table 2), mountain dwellers could adjust their economic activities to serve a year-round clientele.

By the late nineteenth century, some Swiss communities had already developed services to attract winter tourists. With the growing popularity of winter sports, and skiing in particular, other regions followed suit. In 1908, the owners of two major Chamonix hotels journeyed to St. Moritz and Davos, along with two representatives from the Paris-Lyon-Méditerranée rail company, to assess what Chamonix, a prominent French summer tourism center, needed to do in order to compete with Swiss resorts for winter guests. They found that the greatest difference lay in the volume of trains serving the Swiss resorts. Whereas Chamonix was served by only three trains per week in the winter of 1908, Davos and St. Moritz each welcomed seven trains per day carrying visitors from distant metropolises such as Zurich, Paris, and London.[10] The railway officials quickly addressed this deficit, allowing Chamonix to gain in prominence as a winter tourism station in the 1910s and 1920s.

Early winter-tourism figures illustrate the effects of skiing on Alpine socioeconomic development. In winter 1899–1900 in St. Moritz, only 1,851 guests arrived, staying a total of 37,014 nights. By winter 1913–14, those numbers had increased to 14,710 guests who stayed a total of 237,399 nights, at which point the number of overnight stays in St. Moritz was nearly evenly split between the height of the winter season (December–March) and the height of the summer season (June–September). After the war, the balance tilted heavily in favor of winter stays.[11]

Similarly, rail companies expanded train services to serve winter tourists, with economic effects that extended far beyond mountain villages. In Bavaria, special weekend winter-sport trains between Munich and the Bavarian highlands south of the city proved increasingly popular. In winter 1905–6, 9,166 passengers traveled on 81 trains; only two years later, those numbers had more than doubled to 19,207 passengers on 188 trains.[12] Thus skiing changed the lives of mountain dwellers not primarily by extending traditional Alpine occupations into the punishing winter season, as early enthusiasts had anticipated, but by creating balance and stability in an Alpine economy that had long been marked by seasonal ebbs and flows.

The growth of winter tourism had marked effects not only on producers but also on patterns of consumption. In the first decade of the twentieth century, skiing and sport periodicals were filled with advertisements for Alpine hotels, ski equipment, and announcements of new skiing guides. Products and services targeted at skiers helped shape a transnational, cosmopolitan Alpine culture. German and Austrian skiers encountered advertisements for French and Swiss resorts in their newspapers, while English and

Italian skiers absorbed sales pitches from German ski manufacturers. In 1914, the national railroad authority in Austria circulated a pamphlet that described Austria's abundant winter-tourism options, directing potential customers to tourism offices in every major European metropolis, as well as Beijing, Cape Town, Jerusalem, San Francisco, and Sydney.[13] Thanks to the tight bonds between Alpine skiing and capitalist enterprise, the allure of the sport extended across the globe.

SKIING, CLASS, AND GENDER

In Central Europe, the rising popularity of skiing, a conspicuously modern sport, coincided with the rapid expansion of the middle classes tied to the expansion of white-collar professions in the second half of the nineteenth century. Despite its utilitarian applications among poorer mountain dwellers, skiing in the fin de siècle was primarily middle-class in both imaginary and material terms, while its associations with elite British tourists in towns like Davos, St. Moritz, and Chamonix gave it an aristocratic cachet. Thus much of the sport's appeal issued from the aspirational strivings of the middle classes. In societies of increasing class divisions, the working classes had little interest in participating in a transparently bourgeois sport and instead turned to sports like soccer, bicycling, and boxing. The poor mountain dwellers who took to skiing did not threaten the cultural cachet of the sport but in fact added to it by supplying a touch of the exotic, primitive, and authentic.

The high cost of skiing excluded the less affluent, reinforcing its middle-class composition. A 1913 skiing guidebook recommended the following items for a safe and successful ski tour: a snow suit, hat, gaiters, gloves, undergarments, and either a sweater or a leather vest; outerwear, such as a wind jacket; boots, with crampons if the soles were not nailed; skis with good bindings and a set of reserve bindings; a carrying harness for the skis; climbing skins made of seal fur to attach to the ski bottoms for ascending slopes; ski crampons; a ski-repair kit; ski poles; a backpack; sunglasses; and a portable stove with fuel.[14] A ski tour in this era was a survival test in the harsh mountain landscape, requiring a wide range of expensive equipment.

Skiing quickly came to reflect contemporary debates about gender relations among the middle classes. Male skiers interpreted women's participation in the sport according to Victorian moral codes. Women accompanied their husbands and fathers on winter vacations to Alpine resorts, but women

FIGURE 3. Lithograph by Candido Aragonese de Faria advertising Cachat's-Majestic Hotel, Chamonix, France, ca. 1910. Courtesy of the Beekley Family Foundation, Hartford, CT.

and men were generally expected to remain in separate spheres. A prewar advertisement for the Cachat's-Majestic Hotel in Chamonix shows the snow-covered hotel at the center, framed by Alpine foothills (figure 3). In the foreground, two women clothed in knee-length dresses and stylish coats speak animatedly with a man on skis. One holds a leash or rope attached to an unseen object, and two young children cavort nearby, under the apparent care of the other woman. This advertisement implies that winter resorts were an arena for earnest social exchanges between men and women as well as ideal settings for family vacations. Yet skiing implicitly remained an activity for men.

The barriers to women's participation in skiing were significant. Doctors worried that women's bodies were inherently unsuited to physical exertion and to the steep terrain and extreme climate of the Alps. Max Nassauer, a Munich gynecologist, argued that modern medicine had proved that repeated, intensive movements could cause harm to women: it had been shown that excessive exertion on a bicycle could lead to "sickness of the ovaries." Similarly, concerns about the circulation of blood precluded women from undertaking physical activities while menstruating.[15] These perceived biological impediments reinforced male objections to women's participation

FIGURE 4. Men and women on a ski tour near St. Moritz, Switzerland, 1903. Archive of the Deutscher Alpenverein, Munich.

in the sport. A Viennese engineer and devoted Alpinist encapsulated the feelings of many men when he wrote in 1912 that mountains have an intimate relationship to man's "urge for struggle and bodily activity," whereas those with "more passive natures are given to an appreciation of nature outside the mountains." Because the Alps possessed such "overwhelming gravity" and represented an "expression of struggle, strength, [and] stored-up energy," many conceived of the mountains as an exclusively male realm.[16]

Despite these arguments and complaints from some quarters, middle-class women came along on winter vacations and took part in short tours (figure 4). Their participation was governed by social norms: women skiers were almost entirely from the middle class, and, as the British skier Olive Hockin wrote of her experience before World War I, their enjoyment of skiing was conditional on male approval: "While a man may ski to please himself, she is expected to pursue no sport or occupation for the sake of her own joy in it—but only incidentally to please her men-folk."[17] But the physical mechanics of skiing enabled women to make inroads into the male preserves of sport and the Alpine landscape. Despite his worries about women's overexertion, Max Nassauer noted that in order to avoid a variety of physical and spiritual ailments ranging from nervousness to hemorrhoids, women required some form of moderate physical activity. Further, he argued that for women as well as men, experiencing the mountain landscape produced psychological and spiritual benefits that compounded the virtues of activity.[18] The pioneering French skier Marie Marvingt argued that skiing was well suited to women's participation because it was not "violent" or "brutal" like other contemporary sports, and its flowing, graceful movement made it socially acceptable for women.[19] The mountain air proved liberating, and skiing rapidly became both a vector and a symbol of women's increasing independence during the fin de siècle.

Winter conditions in the mountains and the necessity of free, flowing movement to ski safely allowed women to challenge conventions about suitable attire. Traditional dresses and corsets were wholly unsatisfactory. While trousers remained too provocative, many women experimented with bloomers and other skirt-pant hybrids to allow ease of movement while conforming to accepted standards of feminine modesty.[20] Hockin wrote that women's clothing on the slopes became a flashpoint because it fulfilled such contradictory purposes: women's clothing was to be "practical, beautiful, fashionable, workman-like, becoming, and feminine all at once." Increasingly, however, men and women came to judge women's attire on utilitarian grounds, with the "chief consideration," in Hockin's words, being "complete freedom of movement."[21] The authors Henry Hoek and E. C. Richardson agreed, fulminating in their 1907 guidebook against the contemporary practice of wearing a skirt over long pants because snow would get lodged between the two garments and restrict movement. They concluded that the utilitarian ethic of sport trumped decorum.[22] Hockin concurred: "Even the glory of a sunlit mountain peak or the exhilaration of a glacier-run can be dimmed, or even annihilated, by the fret and worry of clothes that all the time are furtively attempting to propitiate drawing-room conventions."[23]

Skiing altered the social relations between men and women. Marvingt argued that men and women could meet as equals on skis and that mountain excursions composed of men and women proved especially gratifying because "a charming camaraderie is established among them, much more sincere than that of the vapid conversations that take place in the salons." The mountains in winter were desolate and dangerous, requiring women to be self-sufficient. As Marvingt averred, "there are neither taxis nor carriages" on the mountain, and a woman who became exhausted on a ski outing would be a dangerous burden to her party.[24] While women were still expected to know their place—the Austrian Mathias Zdarsky acidly proclaimed in 1915 that "women must learn to hold four things: the pole, the trail, spacing, and their tongues"—men generally viewed women as partners and comrades on ski outings.[25] In consequence, most ski clubs allowed women full rights of membership, although organizational control remained a male preserve.[26] Women even took part in races organized by their clubs, so long as they obeyed "certain hygienic rules," and race organizers protected women's health by canceling races if snow conditions were dangerous.[27] For this reason, women's races before World War I were generally simple and short, and women were excluded from competitions that covered longer distances or steep terrain.[28]

Women on skis slalomed between Victorian cultural conservatives, who considered all physical exertion for women physically and morally damaging, and progressive feminists, who argued for women's equality in the voting booth and in society generally. Women flocked to skiing for the same reasons men did: it was fun; it fortified mind, body, and soul; and it provided a new, exciting forum for middle-class sociability. Even if most women skiers did not regard skiing primarily as a tool of emancipation, they put equality into practice on skis, demonstrating their skill and hardiness so that men came to consider them comrades rather than burdens. Later, in the interwar era, women came to symbolize the mass cultural allure and the seductive charm of Alpine skiing, often against their own wishes.

SOCIALIZING THE MIDDLE CLASSES

A German aphorism proclaims, "Two Germans, a discussion; three Germans, a club," and the Germanic enthusiasm for associational life quickly became visible among skiers.[29] In a process that first developed in the late eighteenth century but accelerated in the second half of the nineteenth century as the number of participants expanded, sport played a modernizing role (analogous to that of eighteenth-century coffee shops and salons) by creating middle-class social networks.[30] The earliest non-Scandinavian ski clubs and associations in Europe were formed in German-speaking Central Europe: eastern Switzerland, the German Empire, and Austria and Bohemia. The popularity of skiing, spurred by "Nansen fever," drew on informal connections with Norwegians in German and Austrian cities and towns as well as the cultivation of winter leisure cultures at German-speaking Swiss resorts. Often, a short demonstration of the sport by a Norwegian was sufficient to pique the curiosity of the local populace and inspire some to sample the sport. For example, in 1892 a Norwegian baker's apprentice living in Vienna, W. B. Samson, wowed a small crowd of Austrians by using a snow-covered manure heap as a ramp to jump nearly thirty feet in distance.[31] The ability of wooden planks to expand human capabilities proved captivating, and the sport gained many converts in the 1890s, whether through such personal experiences or through the breathless mass-media coverage of skiing exploits such as Nansen's.

The primary goal of early ski clubs was to expand the popularity of the sport. Because of its steeper learning curve, skiing had to compete with other entertainments for the attention of winter tourists and holidaymakers. Arnold Lunn noted that "the man who is new to winter sports is particularly amenable to the temptations of the skating rink and the toboggan run."[32] Wilhelm Paulcke, who in 1895 helped found the Ski Club Schwarzwald (Black Forest), one of the most influential German regional ski clubs of the fin de siècle, argued that the primary function of a ski club was to advertise the benefits of the sport through action, particularly by staging races, which served as "the best means of propaganda for the masses."[33] Paulcke and other proponents of skiing were shrewd enough to recognize that spectacles of competition and daring, whether in the form of skiers racing downhill or flying off jumps, would attract more proponents than the announcement of other, loftier goals.

The promotion of skiing as a competitive sport required the drafting of regulations and teams of bureaucrats and judges to administer and monitor competitions. The ethos of modern sport, which includes professionalization, the quantitative assessment of individual performance, and competition, proved especially appealing to Europe's middle classes. Because modern sport depended on a well-integrated network of middle-class professionals—doctors and trainers; social reformers and pedagogues; politicians, bureaucrats, and military strategists; and advertisers and journalists— ski clubs proved modernizing in multiple senses.[34] Not only did they foster middle-class associativity and the expansion of the private sphere, but they also developed a more Weberian form of modernity in skiing that focused on rationalizing and bureaucratizing in the name of fairness and efficiency in the sport.[35]

Beyond staging races, Paulcke envisioned that ski clubs would engage in a wide range of promotional activities, including publishing a journal featuring articles on equipment and skiing technique, race reports, skiers' personal narratives of their adventures, and information about snow and weather conditions. Clubs would offer instruction to neophytes, teach winter survival techniques, stage races, adjudicate racing rules, mark winter routes, distribute skis to Alpine residents, and host lectures and slide shows.[36] These recommendations were based on the practices of extant Alpine clubs, which sought to publicize Alpinism, regulate mountain climbing, and advocate stewardship of the mountain landscape.[37]

Central European sporting associations, so often assumed to be a faint echo of nineteenth-century British models, began to alter sport and leisure practices at the turn of the century to make them more attuned to the needs of a growing middle class. When the British founded the Ski Club of Great Britain (SCGB) in 1903, a debate immediately broke out as to whether the club should imitate the social exclusivity of the British Alpine Club (safeguarded by requiring new members to possess an indeterminate level of mountaineering experience and to be sponsored by an existing club member), which Arnold Lunn noted would cultivate more class-based esprit de corps, or instead emulate the more democratic approach of continental Alpine and ski clubs in the interest of expanding the sport and strengthening its civilizing mission. When the SCGB chose the more democratic route (as Lunn advocated), competing organizations sprang up to serve the British elites, including the Public Schools Alpine Sports Club, founded in 1905, which booked up entire hotels to allow its members to commingle without interference from their social inferiors. Splinter associations proliferated, including the British Ski Association and the National Ski Union, before the various British clubs finally agreed in 1914 to convene the Federal Council of British Ski Clubs to organize national championships and represent Britain at international congresses.[38]

Central European skiers organized their clubs on a more democratic but also a more hierarchical basis. They started at the local level, with clubs such as the Erste Wiener Ski-Club of Vienna (founded October 31, 1891). These local clubs banded into regional associations with greater bargaining power and the ability to stage larger races, tours, and instructional courses, such as the Verband Steirischer Skiläufer (Association of Styrian Skiers), centered in the early Austrian skiing mecca of Mürzzuschlag, in February 1893, and the Ski Club des Alpes, founded in France in 1896.

The varied activities undertaken by skiing clubs are exemplified by the efforts of the Munich Snowshoe Association (Schneeschuh-Verein München, or SVM), a small club founded on November 16, 1893. In December 1892, the two founding members of the SVM, Theodor Neumayer and Karl Hölzl,

FIGURE 5. Skiers await transport in Munich, Germany, 1890. Archive of the Deutscher Alpenverein, Munich.

tried skiing for the first time after purchasing their skis from Max Schneider of Berlin, the editor of the popular German journal *Der Tourist* and an important early supplier of Norwegian skis for the German market.[39] The two men investigated their local ski club—the Ski Club München, founded in 1890 and the first ski club in Central Europe—but refused to join when the club leadership told Neumayer that he had to promise not to ski in the Alps "because, as experience shows, skis are not suited for the mountains." This stance demonstrated the tensions between those who rigidly adhered to Norwegian practices and those who believed that the sport could (and must) evolve in accordance with the unique Alpine landscape. In response, Neumayer founded his own club the following winter with nineteen members (five of whom were from Norway).[40]

The SVM hosted its first races in February 1894 but fell into the doldrums for the remainder of the 1890s, hampered by a series of snow-poor Bavarian winters beginning in late 1895 (demonstrating that skiers' recent concern over the effects of climate on snowpack is not a new phenomenon). In late 1901, the club organized a series of races, hosting them in the Munich suburb of Starnberg as opposed to sites further afield with the expressed goal of attracting more spectators. Like Paulcke, the organizers recognized the power of modern competitive spectacles to woo new skiers. In spite of these concerted efforts, by 1903 the membership of the club had fallen to sixteen members, a decline that the directors of the club attributed to the years of poor snow conditions and the inability of the SVM to raise interest in skiing among members of the local Alpine, gymnastic, and bicycling clubs.[41] The relative lack of success was also due to the multiplicity of small skiing clubs in Munich, which endorsed different skiing styles (see chapter 3).

Small, local ski clubs like the SVM were in a precarious position that could be easily undermined by circumstances such as unfavorable weather, poor access to skiable terrain, and dissension among competing clubs. When the directors of the SVM attempted to negotiate with local railroad authorities in 1905–6 to establish more reliable train connections to Schliersee, a ski area located some thirty miles south of the city center, they were told that their numbers were insufficient to guarantee the profitability of such service.[42] For ski clubs to exert a greater influence, they would have to expand their associations beyond the local level.

ESTABLISHING AN INSTITUTIONAL PRESENCE

Skiing clubs made concerted efforts to publicize the sport in the 1890s and the first decade of the 1900s. Advocates of skiing became participants in modern print culture, publishing articles in local community publications as well as the specialist sporting press. In the 1890s, articles on skiing appeared most often in the Alpinist periodicals such as the *Annuaire du Club Alpin Français* and the *Mitteilungen des Deutschen und Österreichischen Alpenvereins*. Skiing information also circulated via ephemeral media such as pamphlets and mailed circulars.

By the first decade of the twentieth century, specialist periodicals had developed to promote skiing and other winter sports. Unsurprisingly, given the popularity of the sport in German Europe, German-language publications led the way, including *Deutscher Wintersport* (which first appeared in 1891 but increased its skiing coverage markedly around 1900) and *Der Winter* (first published in 1906). These were followed by the appearance of the French journal *Sports d'hiver* in 1908. In the first issue of *Der Winter*, the editors laid out the mission of the publication, noting that "winter sport has in the course of recent years undergone such an enormous expansion in all of Central Europe that it has become a highly significant factor for our entire culture, for our entire economic life, especially as the most effective remedy for the damage done to our health by nerve-shattering, exhausting professional occupations."[43] The magazine quickly became a clearinghouse for all information related to winter sports in German-speaking Europe. Its circulation numbered eight thousand in its second year of publication, and by the end of the decade, the journal abandoned coverage of other winter sports to cater to the rabid public interest in skiing.[44] Simultaneously, the market for instructional books, especially in German and English, grew massively between 1895 and 1910 (with one of the most popular ski manuals being a collaboration between a German and an Englishman, Hoek and Richardson).[45]

From 1905 forward, specialist journals multiplied and became the main organs for publishing information about skiing. By World War I, British ski clubs (the National Ski Union and the Ski Club of Great Britain) published a common yearbook, as did the Swiss Ski Association (Schweizerischer Skiverband, or SSV). *Der Winter* served as the official periodical of the German Ski Association (Deutscher Skiverband, or DSV) and the Austrian Ski Association (Österreichischer Skiverband, or ÖSV), while the SSV published *Ski* beginning in 1904. The dynamic German skiing scene produced the heterodox journal *Der Schnee* (1905–14), edited by the Austrian skier Mathias Zdarsky to serve as the official organ of his Alpen-Skiverein, as well as *Ski-Chronik* (1908–13), the official journal of the Central European Ski Association (Mitteleuropäischer Skiverband, or MESV). The intellectual ferment surrounding skiing made ski culture highly self-reflexive from its earliest development. The sport proved to be a media sensation, with photographs and accounts of races and tours proliferating in both the skiing and nonspecialist media.

As the membership of local and regional skiing associations swelled, skiers attempted to scale up their organizations to the national and then to the transnational level to better represent their interests. The most vociferous proponent of this expansion was Wilhelm Paulcke, who on September 12, 1905, under the auspices of the Ski Club Schwarzwald, circulated an invitation to ski clubs and associations across Germany, Switzerland, and Austria to establish separate German and Austrian national skiing associations (the national Swiss Ski Association had been established in 1904 with seven hundred members drawn from sixteen clubs) and, more important, to unify the three national associations into an international association of German skiers, the MESV. In the invitation, the representatives of SC Schwarzwald echoed Paulcke's recital of the advantages of forming a Central European association: the publication of a common journal, universal racing rules, an authoritative racing calendar (so as to avoid scheduling conflicts among the rapidly multiplying races in Central Europe), and the study of "technical questions" such as the proper construction of bindings, marking of race courses, and construction of jumping hills.[46] Thus Paulcke and others hoped to create a unified organizational network for the sport, coordinating the fragmented efforts and practices of the diverse local and regional clubs.

When the representatives of the assorted Austrian, German, and Swiss ski clubs met in Munich on November 4, 1905, they agreed to found both the DSV (comprising 2,450 members in eleven associations) and the ÖSV (with 700 members in eleven associations). On the following day, the German and Austrian Associations joined their Swiss counterpart to found the MESV, a joyous unification that in hindsight appeared doomed to fail. The Swiss were apathetic about the MESV, whereas the Germans and Austrians were fervent supporters. In its first three years, the association achieved none of Paulcke's goals, save for the publication of a common journal. Even this achievement was unimpressive and insignificant, as the MESV merely gave its imprimatur to *Ski,* the existing journal of the SSV, whose format and content remained largely unchanged. In 1908 the Swiss withdrew, with the SSV's president writing, "We feel that we need all of our energies in order to first establish orderly and stable affairs within our own small association, before we can reach out a hand in fruitful activity to associations beyond the borders of our country."[47] The MESV lasted another five years as a joint undertaking of the German and Austrian national associations and produced its own journal, *Ski-Chronik.* In 1913, however, the MESV was dissolved because of its "faulty organizational structure."[48]

The rise and fall of the MESV suggest a significant shift in the nature of the skiing movement. With the founding of national and then multinational bureaucratic organizations and the annual assembly of the International Ski Congress (first convened in 1910) to bring skiing officials from across Europe together to discuss the rules and regulations of the sport, skiing organizations began to shift their focus away from the informal sociability and associativity of the local and regional ski clubs and toward centralization and rationalization. What they lacked in local flavor and personal touch they made up for in influence. No longer were skiing clubs content to organize races and offer instruction; they now began to lobby transport companies and operate financial schemes, like insurance to protect skiers against catastrophic injury.[49] Similarly, as skiing associations began to operate at the national level (though still as private associations), they adjusted their mission, undermining the local associativity of the early organizations. The founding statutes of the DSV listed three goals for the national association: the advancement of skiing for sport and transport; the opening of the mountains in winter; and the improvement of the physical capabilities of the youth and the training of skiers for the army.[50] This final goal, seen in the context of heightened military tension in Europe and the trans-European anxiety about decadence and degeneration in the fin de siècle, suggests that although the DSV was not directly manipulated by the government, it deliberately aligned itself with the goals of the German state.[51]

Whereas the establishment of national ski clubs suggests a shift toward standardization and bureaucratization in skiing organizations, their structure reflects a countervailing trend. Despite increasingly larger scales of organization, skiing remained, paradoxically, a profoundly local sport. Skiers identified not with the national organization but with their local club and, more important, with the landscape in which they skied. Despite improvements in transportation, the vast majority of skiers (excepting the British) practiced the sport in their immediate environs. In German-speaking Europe, this meant that each community of skiers cultivated strong relationships with their local *Hausberg,* a mountain with particular resonance for local identity and connected to the German idea of *Heimat.* Thus, Freiburgers celebrated the Feldberg, Müncheners explored the Bayerischen Voralpen south of the city, and the Viennese skied the Schneeberg and the Rax. The cultural and physical landscapes of winter sport in these areas were circumscribed, making Alpine skiing quite local in nature.

National and international organizations established broad-based training and instructional initiatives and worked to set the rules and regulations that governed races, although these affected only a very small minority of skiers. These initiatives were implemented at the local level through training courses and races. At the local and regional levels, the sociable and associative nature of the early clubs persisted and grew. The average skier had little connection with the national club, and the Swiss, German, and Austrian national associations adopted a federal structure—they were founded as associations composed of associations—that fostered local and regional identity. Thus, while the intellectual lights and racing enthusiasts who drove the public discourse pushed for greater national and international coordination of efforts to both universalize and popularize the practice of the sport, the average weekend skier was more likely to be interested in a tour of a nearby *Hausberg* with fellow club members. These countervailing orientations continue to characterize the sport: skiers have long been attracted by the commonality of experience at the local level, fostered by an intense connection to the landscape, whereas regulatory organizations at the international level have relevance for only a tiny minority of elite skiers.

Despite the snow-capped peaks within their own borders, the French and the Italians lagged behind German-speaking skiers and English tourists in their adoption and organization of skiing. Skis first appeared in Italy in 1897, when Adolf Kind, a Swiss engineer living in Turin, introduced some acquaintances to skiing. The first Italian skiing competition occurred in 1901, and skiers in Turin formed the Ski Club Torino in the same year. Skiing grew relatively slowly in Italy, however; by 1911 Italian ski clubs counted only 530 members, compared with over 20,000 German skiers in the DSV in the same year.[52] The military drove much of the early skiing development in Italy, as officers in the army deemed skis a useful tool to defend Italy's Alpine frontiers. In 1908, the Italian military published a ski manual for its celebrated Alpini troops, and military officials in the other Alpine nations also trained skiing troops on the Italian model.[53] In this same year, the national L'Unione Ski Clubs Italiani was established at the suggestion of the Turin club, but it disbanded in 1910. After another abortive attempt in the 1910s, Italian skiers founded the Federazione Italiano della Ski in 1920.

A few French skiers embraced the sport in the 1880s and 1890s, inspired either by Nansen (although his narrative of crossing Greenland proved much less popular in France than in either Britain or German-speaking Europe) or by informal contacts with other skiers. The father of French skiing, Henri Duhamel, discovered the sport by chance when he became fascinated with a pair of skis in the Scandinavian pavilion at the 1878 Universal Exposition in Paris. Duhamel convinced the Swedish representative to give him the skis and set about learning to ski in the mountains around his hometown of Grenoble. Unfortunately, he could not ascertain how to bind the skis to his feet, and he gave up until a chance meeting with a Finnish diplomat in 1889 allowed him to fashion bindings. By the mid-1890s, he and approximately a dozen friends skied in the area around Grenoble, eventually founding the first French ski club, the Ski Club des Alpes, in 1896.[54] In France, however, skiing was not the immediate sensation that it was in German Europe, because of the lack of informal contacts with dedicated skiers such as

Germany's ubiquitous Norwegian students as well as the greater distance of major French cities from skiable landscapes in the Alps or Pyrenees.

As in Italy, skiing in France was boosted by the military. From 1901 to 1903, the French army imported Norwegian military advisers to train ski troops in France. In 1904, the French established a military skiing school, the École Normale de Ski, in the Alpine village of Briançon. Here, the French state introduced military recruits to the sport, and the officers at the school also provided training and equipment to local residents in an attempt to naturalize the sport in the French Alps.[55] By the end of the decade, skiing had gained a foothold in France, although private skiing activities remained subsumed under the Club Alpin Français until the creation of the Fédération Française de Ski in 1924.

FROM UNITY TO DIVISION

The development and increasing influence of skiing institutions and the impressive growth of the sport in the fin de siècle masked inherent contradictions. As skiers grew in number, the scale of their organizations expanded from the local to the regional, national, and eventually, international levels. Yet while national and international ski bureaucrats worked together to centralize control over the sport and to standardize its practice at annual meetings in hotel ballrooms, the common experience of the sport remained decidedly local. Most skiers emulated Henri Duhamel, exploring their local environment while socializing with fellow club members on weekend outings. Even so, skiing localism and internationalism did not threaten one another: both supported the growth of the sport. The larger organizations confirmed the popularity, international import, and modern allure of the sport, while their federal structure allowed skiing to foster local identities that connected leisure, landscape, and sociability.

Not all contradictions in the sport of skiing proved so beneficial, however. Because most skiers experienced the sport not in the rarefied cosmopolitan air of Swiss resorts but instead in their local mountains, their practices and motivations quickly diverged. As the withdrawal of the SSV from the MESV in 1908 shows, the local worldview of most skiers made international organizations seem superfluous and even harmful to the ethos of the sport.

The social composition and cultural meanings of skiing were also marked by contradiction. The ski was an ancient and primitive tool that skiers paradoxically understood as a vector of modernity. While skiing remained a modestly sized movement, these contradictory meanings coexisted, but as its popularity expanded and skiers exerted more influence over European culture and socioeconomic development in the Alps, debates erupted between those who treasured the simplicity of the sport and those who celebrated its cosmopolitan, modern implications. Similarly, skiers described their sport as a means of uniting socially disparate groups, and yet the vast majority of early skiers were leisured, middle-class, urban males. The middle-class desire for associative leisure found an ideal outlet in Alpine skiing, but the rational and bureaucratic nature of modern sport had the power to recast skiing in its own image, leading to the profusion of sporting bureaucracy and ever larger and more complex skiing organizations.

The most significant division among fin-de-siècle skiers was based in many of these unresolved contradictions. Should Central European skiers emulate Norwegian skiers, accepting their techniques and practices as sacrosanct? Or should they break from their Norwegian forebears and develop their own form of skiing, one better suited to the steeper terrain of the Alps? As the debate developed, differing relationships to the mountain landscape proved decisive. By 1910, Central European skiers had split off into two rival camps: the Nordic skiers, who practiced the sport in the undulating terrain of Scandinavia and Europe's *Mittelgebirge,* and the Alpine skiers, who responded to the steeper Alpine environment with a modern, uniquely Alpine skiing practice and ethos.

THREE

A Family Feud

MONTAGUES AND CAPULETS

At the turn of the century, two extended families, the Salzöhrl clan and the Kratzbürschtl family, dominated the social and political life of a small Bavarian village. Although the Salzöhrls were Catholic and the Kratzbürschtls were devout Protestants, their friendship had not been affected by centuries of often brutal sectarianism in the German lands. Their spirit of camaraderie appeared unbreakable until a minor disagreement sparked a bitter feud. At the end of the nineteenth century, both took to the novel sport of skiing with alacrity, and one year they planned a friendly race. When the family heads proved unable to agree on a racing route, the spirit of amity rapidly devolved into an enmity of Shakespearean proportions. At its base, this was a doctrinal dispute: the Kratzbürschtls practiced the Norwegian tradition of skiing that had been imported into Central Europe in the late nineteenth century, whereas the Salzöhrls had become disciples of the heterodox Lilienfelder, or "Alpine," school.

When it became clear that the young Mizzi Kratzbürschtl and Franz Salzöhrl were in love, the elder Kratzbürschtl forbade his daughter to consort with the heretical Alpine skier, preferring instead to introduce Mizzi to a good Norwegian boy. The prohibition of Mizzi's father only caused the young couple's love to grow deeper, and they decided to skip their families' respective weekend ski excursions to spend time together. The young sweethearts lost track of time, a fierce storm pummeled the mountains, and the two families conducted a harrowing search before finally finding their children safe and sound. After this experience, both sides agreed that skiing technique was a poor excuse for a feud: they reconciled and resolved that in the future, they would teach their children in a hybrid Nordic-Alpine style, a synthesis that resolved tensions and created well-rounded skiers.[1]

This piece of short fiction, "Montecchi und Capuletti," appeared in 1921 as part of a collection of poetry and short stories meant to entertain skiers after a long day on the slopes. While it might appear frivolous, it dramatizes a vital episode in the history of skiing in Central Europe. From approximately 1895 to 1910, Central European skiers were engaged in an internecine conflict between the "Alpine" and "Nordic" schools of skiing. By associating the dispute with familiar fictional and historical narratives of conflict and division—Shakespeare's Montagues and Capulets, Catholic and Protestant—the author demonstrates that the choice of a skiing style was not merely a dispassionate choice or a casual recreation; rather, it entailed deep moral meaning and shaped personal and group identities. A minor plot point in the allegory reveals the essence of the debate. In the abstract, the families were able to overlook their differences, but when they were forced to agree on a racecourse and thus map their practices onto the landscape, the divisions became irreconcilable. The debate over technique revolved around the physical landscape and reflected skiers' sense of place.

As the appellations *Alpine* and *Nordic* indicate, the landscape dictated the practice of skiing. Whereas Nordic-leaning skiers like the Kratzbürschtls sought out forests and rolling hills, Alpine-oriented skiers found that higher mountains offered both better snow cover and longer, steeper descents, allowing them to enjoy the most appealing aspect of skiing for many of its Central European practitioners: speed. The adaptation of the sport to suit the Alps demonstrates that Alpine skiing was not a superficial or unreflective leisure pursuit; instead, skiers actively interpreted the mountain environment in the context of modern conditions. Before this dispute, *Alpine skiing* merely described the physical act of skiing in the Alps, practiced in compliance with the sport's Nordic heritage, whereas *Nordic skiing* was redundant and meaningless. By 1910, the two terms delineated separate schools of thought defined by their own practices, aesthetics, and landscapes.

The Alpine/Nordic dispute also illustrates the role of the Alps in the practice and perception of skiing. These acrimonious debates occurred among compatriots in local clubs and associations as well as in national and international associations and the cosmopolitan print culture that served skiers. Skiing opened fissures within national groups while at the same time forging alliances across national boundaries. Yet, despite its vehemence, the dispute ultimately expanded the popularity of skiing by stimulating the development of a cosmopolitan Alpine modernism.

THE "SKI POPES"

The leading representatives of the two warring styles were Wilhelm Paulcke and Mathias Zdarsky. The two men came to be known as the "ski popes" because their acolytes treated their word as gospel and because each claimed to speak the truth, contrary to the heresies of his rival. Their version of the Great Schism developed on the slopes of Central Europe and in the European ski press and ended with the definitive separation of Alpine and Nordic skiing. Yet Paulcke and Zdarsky were merely the point men for a long evolution of ski styles in accordance with local landscapes.

The two ski popes were a study in contrasts. After taking up skiing during his childhood convalescence in Davos, Paulcke became a major force behind the foundation and administration of the Ski Club Schwarzwald. He served as a professor of geology at the Technische Hochschule in Karlsruhe, where he published on a wide range of topics, including avalanche science.[2] Although he is usually associated with skiing in the Black Forest, Paulcke was also a pioneer of skiing in the Alps and undertook many dangerous tours over great Alpine peaks in the 1890s and 1900s, thus illustrating the somewhat artificial nature of the distinction between Alpine and Nordic skiing before the construction of ski lifts. All early skiing in Central Europe, even in Alpine landscapes, was fundamentally Nordic in character: skiers used Nordic techniques and equipment to roam the terrain, not merely ski down it. Most early skiers in Davos and St. Moritz did not scale great peaks or schuss (make a straight, fast downhill run) exclusively, preferring instead to traverse rolling hills and flat expanses.

The first concerted challenge to Nordic teachings came from Mathias Zdarsky. Zdarksy was born in 1856 in Iglau, Moravia (now Jihlava, Czech Republic), as a subject of the Austro-Hungarian Empire. Zdarsky cultivated a rather bohemian persona. He trained as a painter and sculptor at the Academy of Fine Arts in Munich and traveled throughout the Austro-Hungarian Empire as a teacher and artist. Zdarsky fancied himself a Renaissance man with eclectic intellectual tastes, and he believed that a healthy, virile body was a necessary complement to an active mind. He found

60 · TAKING ROOT

an ideal outlet for this philosophy in the German *Turnen* movement, through which he became internationally known. In 1889, at the age of thirty-three, Zdarsky moved to the small village of Lilienfeld in the Alpine foothills of Austria (elevation 1,257 feet) in search of artistic, scientific, and pedagogical inspiration. Once there, he discovered that the snowy winters and steep terrain made even basic outdoor activity difficult. After reading of Fridtjof Nansen's 1888 exploits in Greenland, he procured a pair of skis.[3]

Like many early skiers, Zdarsky found Nordic skis difficult to use on steep, rocky slopes like those that surrounded his Lilienfeld home. The skis were too long (often approaching ten feet in length) and too narrow to control on descents of slopes steeper than thirty-five degrees.[4] Securing the skis to one's boots posed a major difficulty for skiers in this era.[5] Steep terrain, which required quick changes in speed and direction, aggravated these problems. In response, Zdarsky—ever the polymath—experimented with a variety of homemade bindings. He produced over two hundred prototypes and eventually received a patent for his binding from the Vienna Patent Office in March 1896.[6] His innovations later led his friend, the German skier and Alpinist Willi Rickmer Rickmers, to refer to him as "the Newton of the ski laws."[7]

Some historians have speculated that the Zdarsky-Paulcke quarrel extended beyond technical questions to matters of business. Zdarsky allied with a Lilienfeld businessman by the name of Engel to market and sell skis outfitted with his patented bindings, while a close associate of Paulcke's in the Black Forest marketed a competing ski through the Austrian ski manufacturer Fischer.[8] In fact, the business competition between the two ski popes was a manifestation of their larger conflict over skiing practice: the markedly different skis and bindings sold by their associates reflected their preferred skiing styles.

With his new bindings, Zdarsky found that he was able to tackle steep Alpine slopes that students of the Nordic school had deemed unsafe. The pioneering German Alpinist and early skier Theodor Wundt summarized the initial disappointment of Alpinists who attempted to use skis for mountain traverses: "Climbing a mountain with skis is exceedingly boring and difficult; descending the mountain is exceedingly dangerous."[9] Josef Müller, a factory owner from Guntramsdorf, Austria, toured the Rax, southwest of Vienna, in 1893 and also described his disappointment: he climbed the mountain on skis but had to descend on foot, carrying his skis, because the steep slopes offered no "egress." Only after reaching the valley could he continue on skis.[10] Similarly, a German medical doctor argued in 1907 that

FIGURE 6. Mathias Zdarsky demonstrates his "Alpine" skiing technique near Lilienfeld, Austria. Archive of the Deutscher Alpenverein, Munich.

skiing in unsuitable landscapes posed a great danger to knee and foot joints. He believed that only "a section of the Black Forest" and "a small section of the Vosges, the Ore Mountains [along the current German-Czech border], and the Bavarian Alpine foothills" were suited to skiing. In the steeper landscapes of the Alps, he argued, Nordic-style skis were too long to allow the skier to navigate around obstacles such as rocks and trees.[11]

Using shorter skis and sturdier bindings, Zdarsky developed a new system of skiing that relied less on long, sweeping turns than on short, rapid changes in direction, aided by the use of a long staff, to negotiate steep slopes (figure 6). Zdarsky's technique became known as the Lilienfelder technique and later the Alpine technique, following the custom of associating skiing styles with the landscapes in which they arose; similarly, the Nordic style incorporated styles of turns associated with different places, such Telemark and Christiania. In 1896, Zdarsky published an instructional book on the Lilienfelder technique. It went through eighteen editions between 1896 and 1925, giving Zdarsky a vital role in defining Alpine skiing. Even subtle semantic shifts are telling. The first edition taught the Lilienfelder *Skilauf-Technik* (ski-running technique), whereas by the fourth edition of 1908, it referred to the *Skifahr-Technik* (ski-riding technique).[12] This change indicated a sport that focused not on arduous traverses of horizontal space but on the harnessing of gravity that allowed Alpine skiers to "ride" effortlessly downhill and thus conquer seemingly intractable vertical space.

In December 1900, Zdarsky founded the Internationaler Alpen-Skiverein to represent the interests of Alpine skiers. It was designated an "international" club because it welcomed not only Austrian ski enthusiasts but all Alpine skiers, regardless of nationality.[13] Zdarsky's club provided a number of services to skiers, including negotiating with rail authorities to organize trains to Alpine destinations and the publication of a journal, *Der Schnee,* beginning in 1905. Implicitly, then, Zdarsky and his followers believed that skiers should be organized not according to political or cultural boundaries, but instead according to the landscapes that informed their conception of the sport.[14] Although Zdarsky's club did not attract a huge number of members, it was large enough to have a prominent voice in skiing debates and to achieve near parity of membership with the competing Austrian Skiing Association (Österreichische Skiverband, or ÖSV) in the fin de siècle (table 3).

As it evolved farther from its Nordic roots, the Alpine style of skiing attracted criticism from traditionalists. Nordic skiers often accused Alpine skiers of laziness, arguing that the downhill pull of gravity allowed them to avoid exertion. A Norwegian, Thor Tangvald, argued that the only "natural" form of competition for a sport that involved gliding on top of the snow was "to traverse in the quickest way a certain distance with the natural obstacles that the chosen route gives." To Tangvald, long-distance Nordic races were true sporting competitions that demanded strength and willpower, whereas Alpine races suited only women and untrained men.[15] Similarly, Paulcke and others mocked Zdarsky's methods, which depended heavily on the use of the staff for braking and turning: Arnold Lunn, an early antagonist of Zdarsky, called the resulting style "a clumsy, slow, timid type of skiing."[16]

For their part, Alpine skiers believed that their sport presented far greater tests of courage and masculinity than Nordic skiing. Zdarsky himself wrote that "for the Alpine skier," archetypal Nordic activities such as "jumping,

TABLE 3 Membership in Mathias Zdarsky's
Internationaler Alpen-Skiverein, 1900–1914

Year	Number of Members
1900–1901	39
1901–02	83
1902–03	106
1903–04	197
1904–05	320
1905–06	539
1906–07	832
1907–08	1,005
1908–09	1,092
1909–10	1,209
1910–11	1,361
1911–12	1,576
1912–13	1,847
1913–14	1,889

SOURCE: Hugo Vondörfer, "Der Alpen-Skiverein," in *Zdarsky: Festschrift zum 80. Geburtstage des Begründers der alpinen Skifahrweise,* ed. Erwin Mehl (Vienna, 1936), 115.

Telemark turns, [and] the Christiania turn, in spite of their magnificence, are only useful as a diversion on the training ground." These Norwegian methods, claimed Zdarsky, were useless in the Alps, which demanded utilitarian, often violent changes in direction aided by the staff. Whereas "there are gentle enough areas in the Alps" to apply the Nordic style, "these do not give the mountains their reputation."[17] When Wilhelm Paulcke mocked Zdarsky's admonition to carry a repair kit while skiing, Willi Fleischmann of Munich, a Zdarsky supporter, retorted: "In the *Mittelgebirge,* where one can always come to an inhabited area after a short time, it is perhaps not necessary to carry repair materials." By contrast, the high Alps, "with their giant dimensions, where one potentially will not encounter an occupied house or a human being for days," were exceedingly dangerous and required hardier men, making such preparations vital.[18] Proponents on each sides of this debate thus condemned the other style as a lazy, decadent, and effeminate form of skiing. Nordic enthusiasts championed the skier's battle to overcome fatigue over long (horizontal) distances, whereas Alpine skiers focused on the conflict between the skier and the technical challenges posed by the steep slopes of the Alps.

The Nordic/Alpine dispute often proved petty. Paulcke and his disciples maneuvered to keep Zdarsky's Alpen-Skiverein out of both the ÖSV and the MESV when they were founded in November 1905, in spite of the fact that Zdarsky's club represented nearly as many Austrian skiers as the ÖSV did. Paulcke argued that "the stress of dissenting viewpoints in the debate could possibly jeopardize the successful foundation of the association."[19] In fact, both sides agreed on a fundamental issue: they believed skiing could serve as a modern *Volkssport* (sport of the people) that could remedy contemporary physical, spiritual, and moral deficits. They disagreed, however, as to how to pursue this remedy. Paulcke adopted the Romantic, quasi-spiritual meanings associated with skiing in Norway. In 1905, he wrote: "Scandinavia is and remains our model for skiing; in the north skiing came to its as-yet highest blossoming, to its highest technical achievement."[20] He thus endorsed the philosophical and aesthetic implications of *Skiidrett* for Central Europeans. Through skiing, Paulcke argued, individuals would learn self-discipline, cultivate physical and mental health, and experience the grandeur of nature.

Zdarsky's approach differed greatly. Ever the pedagogue, he focused on developing a method of teaching skiing quickly, thus permitting unpracticed skiers to enjoy the physical and spiritual benefits of the sport in the shortest possible time. Zdarsky argued that Norwegians were virtually born with skis on their feet, allowing them to develop muscle memory as children that made them expert skiers in adulthood. In addition, the long winters and relatively backward economic conditions afforded Norwegian skiers more time on the snow. In Central Europe, by contrast, snow conditions as well as "economic concerns" prevented individuals from "whiling away every free hour on the snow," and the Norwegian technique, with its steep learning curve, discouraged prospective skiers. Zdarsky crafted a technique and teaching method with which he promised that "in two to six days anybody can master the ski to the point that he can overcome any terrain."[21] In the Central European milieu, marked by the industrial logic and time discipline of the cities, skiing instruction needed to be efficient and versatile.[22]

Zdarsky began teaching ski courses at his home in Lilienfeld, instructing 719 students in the winter of 1901–2 and 1,051 the following winter.[23] In the winter of 1910–11, the Austrian emperor Franz Joseph I attended Zdarsky's course.[24] Over the course of his career, Zdarsky personally taught about twenty thousand individuals to ski, in addition to those who were instructed by his acolytes throughout the Alps and beyond. (One of his students, General Major Theodor von Lerch of the Austrian Army, served as a military attaché to Japan and introduced skiing there in 1911.)[25] Zdarsky taught many of these early courses for free to democratize and popularize the sport.[26] Carl Luther, an early opponent of Zdarsky (who later came to appreciate the Austrian's contributions to the development of skiing), nevertheless observed one of Zdarsky's instructional courses and came away impressed, deeming his teaching methods more "systematic" and advanced than Nordic ski instruction.[27] Zdarsky thus achieved his goal of enabling novice skiers to undertake Alpine tours after only a brief course of instruction. New skiers' philosophical commitment to the sport and the aesthetic appreciation of the landscape, he believed, would follow organically.

The "German Norwegians," as Paulcke and his followers were sometimes called, did not dispute Zdarsky's claims that the Alps were well suited to skiing, as some Norwegians did. Instead, they criticized the novelty of Zdarsky's methods and questioned their soundness. Often the personal aspects of the feud seeped into the technical dispute, as when Paulcke reproached Zdarsky for claiming to have opened the door to the Alpine landscape: "We, and not the Lilienfelders, had undertaken the first groundbreaking ski tours in the Alps—with many slopes over 30 degrees—on Norwegian skis."[28] Paulcke criticized Zdarsky's technique for depending too heavily on the ski staff to regulate speed and direction, which resulted in a "patchwork" style that emphasized "the extreme cultivation of speed-inhibiting turns" over the development of general proficiency on skis. Although Zdarsky could teach skiers to negotiate steep slopes more quickly than Nordic-style instructors could, his Alpine technique produced skiers who would never be able to experience the ultimate joy of the sport, "the practice of pole-less, rapid downhill."[29]

British skiers who practiced the sport in Switzerland cultivated close ties with Norwegian skiers and considered themselves at the forefront of the endeavor to adapt Norwegian practices to the Alpine landscape. Unsurprisingly, a vocal contingent of Britons criticized Zdarsky. In 1913, Arnold Lunn argued that Zdarsky had allowed his distaste for the Norwegians' summary dismissal of the Alps to blind him to the substantial value of Nordic methods. Zdarsky, wrote Lunn, was correct in his view that Nordic techniques and equipment were unsuited to steep Alpine terrain, but he failed to recognize that he had "discovered nothing new in the way of ski technique, and failed to rediscover at least nine-tenths of the common heritage of all expert Norwegians." Lunn regretted that Zdarsky's inferior technique was "such poor fun." Zdarsky failed to understand that "skiing is not merely a means of locomotion. It is an art, and a beautiful art."[30] Similarly, in a 1913 skiing guide in 1913 titled *How to Ski and How Not To,* Lunn's friend and compatriot Vivian Caulfeild averred that Zdarsky had developed a flawed technique to suit his faulty bindings and short skis, and as a result, his teachings "encourage timidity as well as clumsiness." Although Zdarsky's ambition to teach initiates to ski quickly was admirable, his school managed to produce "ski-runners quickly by allowing them to run badly." The resulting methods were "a waste of energy . . . for it is doing clumsily by brute force what can be done more comfortably, gracefully, and effectively by skill."[31]

Most important, Paulcke and Zdarsky understood the concept of *Volkssport* differently. Paulcke and his allies emphasized the Romantic, spiritual nature of skiing, whereas Zdarsky focused on spreading the sport to the masses. Paulcke and the status-conscious Britons envisioned skiers as a committed elite and, like Lunn, considered skiing more meaningful than a mere pastime or means of locomotion. These critics of Zdarsky implicitly presented an argument about the nature of their sport consistent with the nineteenth-century political and cultural beliefs of middle-class liberals, whose focus on individual liberty often enabled and excused social divisions. Skiing, they argued, should indeed be open and made available to all, but it had to be undertaken with a keen understanding of tradition and practiced with the proper philosophical motivations. In their view, Zdarsky had debased the sport by dumbing it down and making it an object of mass consumption, too readily accessible to casual practitioners.

Zdarsky, for his part, believed that all could benefit physically and socially from skiing, whether they were deeply committed skiers or only dabblers. For Zdarsky, skiing was to be understood in populist democratic, not liberal terms: his primary aspiration was spreading the sport as widely as possible. If fin-de-siècle Europeans needed skiing to cope with the stresses of modern life, as both Paulcke and Zdarsky agreed, then Zdarsky believed that it should not be made artificially difficult in the interest of preserving outdated foreign traditions.

By 1905, the personal feud between Paulcke and Zdarsky and the broader debate among skiers about the relative merits of the Alpine and Nordic schools began to dissipate in favor of a hybrid approach that could be applied in a wide variety of terrain and snow conditions, from the hills of the Harz to the slopes of Mont Blanc. Although the tone of the Alpine/Nordic debate was often dogmatic and unyielding, skiers in Central Europe in the era before ski lifts were likely to encounter a great variety of terrain on any given day. A day of skiing from an Alpine village would require uphill climbs, hill traverses, and steep descents. Skiers thus required a wide array of skills, and the hybridization of the sport occurred in response to the conditions.

Most skiers could not identify with the doctrinaire public faces of the debate; indeed, by 1905 even staunch allies of Paulcke and Zdarsky began to tire of the hostilities. Zdarsky's ally Willi Rickmer Rickmers complained that the technical struggle between the two schools obscured a fundamental unity: skiers should consider themselves as a "brotherhood" who all recognized the transformative power of skiing, not enemies wrangling over arcane technical matters.[32] A more unified international ski culture developed in the first decade of the twentieth century, as skiers devoured early guidebooks written primarily in German and English, such as the volume by Richardson and Hoek.[33] The acknowledgments in Arnold Lunn's 1913 history of skiing read like a Who's Who of skiing pioneers, including Wilhelm Paulcke, Henry Hoek, Carl Luther, E. C. Richardson, and Vivian Caulfeild.[34] The culture of skiing quickly became so internationalized, in fact, that in the interwar period Carl Luther compiled a skiing dictionary in five languages: English, French, German, Italian, and Norwegian.[35]

The most prominent role in the technical hybridization of the sport was played by an Austrian army officer, Georg Bilgeri, who drew on both schools of thought to develop a more versatile set of skills. Like Zdarsky, Bilgeri sought "to make possible for everyone an effortless, quick, and safe training in skiing" and also "to allow the full exploitation of this sport in the most difficult of conditions."[36] Bilgeri's hybrid technique, which he called Alpine skiing, blended Zdarsky's innovation of connecting a series of sharp, short "stem" turns to control speed with a solid grounding in the elegant, swinging turns developed by Norwegians. He cemented his influence by organizing and training the Alpine divisions of the Austro-Hungarian army on Zdarsky's model, which in turn shaped the ski troops of the other Alpine nations during the Great War. After the war, many of these highly trained skiers became ski teachers in Alpine villages, further disseminating the new technique.[37]

Although this hybrid technique discarded many of Zdarsky's technical innovations, his revolutionary reimagination of the skiing landscape persisted. Trailblazing skiers such as Wilhelm Paulcke took to the Alps to climb peaks in winter on ski tours, but it was Zdarsky who envisioned the Alps as a suitable landscape for skiers of all capacities. If skiing in the last decade of the nineteenth century had consisted largely of practices and ideals imported wholesale from Norway, by 1910 skiers in the Alps had established a competing tradition. As tempers cooled in the wake of the Alpine-Nordic debate, former critics of Zdarsky (such as Arnold Lunn and Carl Luther) helped to promote this approach as distinctly Central European and quintessentially modern.

ALPINE SKIING BEFORE WORLD WAR I

By World War I, Europeans had come to associate the Alpine form of skiing with modernity, adventure, and luxury. In a short time, Nordic skiing receded into the background and came to be viewed as a regional, Scandinavian sport. Hassa Horn, a famed Norwegian skier who met Mathias Zdarsky on the slopes of Lilienfeld in 1905 as part of a staged competition between the Alpine and Nordic schools of skiing, noted that he was originally skeptical of Zdarsky but quickly recognized that the Alps had become a center of innovation in the sport. Horn cautioned his countrymen that if they turned a blind eye to the developments in the Alps, the day would come when the Norwegians would be outstripped by the newcomers.[38] Although the Norwegians deserve credit for developing the modern form of the sport, it was in the Alps that the practice of the sport began to shift to accord with the modern lust for speed and the consumerist desires of modern mass culture.[39] The foundations for Alpine modernism, and thus for the global popularity of the sport, were laid in the Alps in the years before World War I.

As the Alps moved to the forefront of the Central European skiing imaginary, the *Mittelgebirge* receded. In comparison to the speedy, flowing movements inspired by the Alps, skiing in the flatlands was, in the words of the filmmaker Luis Trenker, "a walk on all fours."[40] The use of ski poles to propel the skier forward made Nordic skiing appear to be a more animalistic and unrefined activity. In contrast, the upright stance and effortless glide of the Alpine skier projected an image of progress and elegance that was both sport and art. Carl Luther, writing in the 1930s, noted that the Alps had inspired the development of "an astonishingly versatile" technique during the fin de siècle. The equipment and practices developed in response to the challenges of the Alpine landscape had left the "still-simple Norwegian school" behind. Even Norwegians came to use the techniques developed in the Alps. As a result, Luther wrote, "the academy of skiing is to be found in the Alps. . . . It has become the craving of every skier of the *Mittelgebirge* to experience this ski area at least once and in it to perfect himself."[41]

Skiers in the fin de siècle established that different landscapes and different styles of skiing produced different types of skier. In 1913, the famed Austrian skier Sepp Bildstein wrote that "a skier in the mountains is something entirely different from a skier from the flatlands; both again are something different from a skier from the hilly Alpine foothills." Downhill skiing upset the tranquil culture of skiing, argued Bildstein, because "it is a child unlike other children." By bringing skiing to the Alps, skiers assimilated with this most powerful of landscapes: "The mountains wish to enrich us, to delight us. Free men, artists shall emerge from us! We will be considered not as your slaves, but as your darlings!" The Alps produced a method of skiing more "individual" and "artistic" in nature than those practiced in Norway and the *Mittelgebirge;* Alpine skiing was "proud, uncompromising," and would not allow itself to be "constrained." In response, skiers offered their "entire devotion to the mountains" and experienced "total aesthetic pleasure."[42]

In short, Alpine skiers considered their relationship with the Alps uniquely profound and transformative. If Norwegians celebrated the Scandinavian landscape through Romantic-nationalist *Skiidrett,* Alpine skiers, regardless of nationality, engaged with the landscape to create an unparalleled affinity between their sport and the Alps. Ultimately, the Alpine/Nordic debate had a unifying effect on the sport, connecting skiers' local practice in familiar landscapes to broader, transnational conceptions of the sport. In 1904 Rickmers wrote, "Eternal thanks be to Norway for the original fruitful notion of gliding on wood, but we, and above all Zdarsky, have developed everything else under our own power and thus we will not abandon it, as it is our true property."[43]

Although the popularity of the sport increased massively in the wake of World War I, with a particular explosion of activity in the Alps, not all skiers viewed the democratization of the sport as universally positive. From its very beginnings, there existed ethical tensions between the transcendent potential of Alpine skiing and the materialist, international-capitalist exploitation of the sport. Advertisers constructed, manipulated, and exploited the modern, cosmopolitan, luxurious cachet of Alpine skiing. As a result, the sport quickly came to mirror the modern society that many skiers hoped to escape in the Alps. Isolated voices began to question the direction of the sport. They echoed the Paulcke-Zdarsky debate about the nature of *Volkssport* and questioned the

FIGURE 7. "Once . . . and Now" offers an early warning about the growing popularity of Alpine skiing. Source: Olaf Gulbransson, "Einst . . .
und jetzt," *Simplicissimus* 18, no. 36 (1913), 591. © Artists Rights Society
(ARS), New York/BONO, Oslo.

mass popularization of the sport. Many commentators invoked the specter of
fin-de-siècle cultural degeneration. As early as 1907, Henry Hoek lamented,
"Already decadence is appearing in skiing. Already many a ski club has become
a winter sport and tourism association. Already the love of the festival prevails
over the love of sport in some places, already the ski has begun to become the
advertising bait of the resourceful hotel owner. The growth upwards is nearly

complete; now comes the development in breadth, with all of its positives and negatives."[44] Zdarsky, too, lamented the spread of winter-sport festivals, which pitched the sport to the masses by sensationalizing it. He described the festivals as an "epidemic," staged by organizers solely to draw crowds. The organizers, Zdarsky wrote sarcastically, would quickly replace the skiers with a dancing camel or harmonica-playing ape if it guaranteed more profits.[45]

Other voices began to question the meaning of this growth not only for the sport but also for the Alpine landscape. These concerns are nicely summarized in a 1913 cartoon from the German satirical magazine *Simplicissimus*. The cartoon, "Once . . . and now," shows a wintry mountain in its "natural" state, before the arrival of skiers (figure 7). The second panel shows the same mountain, but a monochromatic, faceless horde has driven away the birds, and the snow has been scarred by ski tracks and befouled with trash. Thus, while advocates of skiing sought to democratize the sport and trumpeted both the visceral appeal of the sport and its potential to strengthen body, mind, and soul, others feared that expanding access to the sport could diminish its distinctive charms.

Alpine skiing proved unique in the way that it bridged and synthesized the contradictions of modernity. By the First World War, Alpine skiing was a cosmopolitan sport that cultivated local affinities, in which skiers used an ancient tool to feed modern desires for speed, leisure, and relaxation. It was an important component of mass culture that nevertheless reinforced social distinctions, illustrating the tension between liberal and democratic concepts of identity in this era. Skiers celebrated Romantic aesthetics while depending on industrial advances and technological innovations. Contradictions and paradoxes in skiing persisted in the following decades. Alpine skiers created a culture that was distinctively modern not only because it spurred modernization but also because it drew its dynamism from the often-imperfect synthesis of antinomies, as skiers attempted to balance conflicting values.[46] The following chapters examine this dynamic, ongoing expression of Alpine modernism, beginning with a study of how skiers' movement through the landscape accorded with cultural change in the early twentieth century and inspired new ways of seeing nature through movement.

PART TWO

———

Modern Mobilities

FOUR

Joy in Movement

HARMONY AND MASTERY

From its first appearance in the Alps, scattered skiers described their sport of choice not merely as a means of locomotion or a pleasing leisure activity but as an art form. But how did artists interpret it? The Austrian artist Alfons Walde's 1931 painting *Aufstieg der Skifahrer* (The Climb) presents the viewer with a complicated vision of the sport's meaning in the decades before World War II (figure 8). In the foreground, skiers reach the crest of a hill, with the majestic, snow-capped peaks of Austria's Tirolean Alps in the background. Their faces obscured by shadows, they move through a sublime Alpine landscape that is seemingly devoid of other human presence or influence. Although the viewer's eye is drawn to the three skiers, they are dwarfed by the massive dimensions of the Alps. The work invokes the Romantic vision of the sublime in suggesting the role of skiing in mediating the human relationship to the landscape. Such Romantic implications proved increasingly popular in the critiques of modern urban life that abounded in the 1920s and 1930s. Viewed in this context, *Aufstieg* suggests that the attraction of Alpine skiing in the early twentieth century lay in its combination of vigorous activity and appreciation of nature as a retreat from modernity.

But Walde's painting is more nuanced. A straightforward Romantic reading obscures an underlying tension: are the three skiers communing with nature or conquering it? Whereas Alpine peaks frame the skiers, the true subject of the painting is the skiers who engage in the climb of its title. The skiers reach the crest of the hill thanks to the civilizing power of their skis, demonstrating the triumph of human ingenuity over the climate and terrain of the Alps. Their short-sleeved shirts mock the extreme conditions: they are

FIGURE 8. Alfons Walde, *Aufstieg der Skifahrer*, 1931, depicts skiers in the Austrian Alps. © Artists Rights Society (ARS), New York/Bildrecht, Vienna.

working up a sweat, but they are doing so purely for pleasure, and they will return to their warm chalets before the chill of night sets in. The sociocultural critiques of the modern world in the 1920s and 1930s inspired not only Romantic yearnings for a return to nature but also demonstrations of the human power to tame natural forces through speed and movement.

A year after Walde completed his painting, Carl Luther echoed the contradictory motivations and implications of skiing in early twentieth-century Europe:

> Because our work in the daily routine and in the cities, in factories and in offices has become prosaic, atomizing, and devoid of adventure—because we live faster and must demonstrate greater resistance—because we do not wish to age, but rather wish to remain young, fresh, and slender—because we are anxious and know that only new thrills and new visions can rejuvenate us.... Spring, summer, and fall, the former seasons of relaxation, no longer suffice for us.... We have also discovered the winter, the most alien to us of all manifestations of nature, thus for us nature in its most modern and most youthful form.... The ski entered into the world ... to allow men to flee excessive snow and cold. Today, however, skiing is also flight, but flight from the metropolis [in search of] all remote winter environments.... Fortune is with the skis, because they overcome the awkwardness of urbanites estranged from nature and have so far evaded natural [limits upon] speed that they make man and speed consubstantial.[1]

Luther, the doyen of German ski culture before World War II, idealized skis as both an ancient instrument and a modern cultural necessity. For all Alpine skiers, regardless of nationality, class, or gender, the appeal of the sport in the early twentieth century lay in its combination of sublime nature and super-human speed, of harmony with and mastery over nature. Put more generally, skiing synthesized the timeless and the modern, allowing skiers to transcend the boundaries erected by urban modernity.

Skiers of a less philosophical bent than Luther often described the sport's unique appeal more concisely as "fun." The experience of Nellie Friedrichs, a German Jew from Braunschweig, is representative. In 1934 and 1935, Friedrichs took three-week vacations to the Italian Dolomites with her fiancé, enticed by the sunnier climate of the southern Alps and the cosmopolitan milieu —no small concern for a Jewish woman in the Third Reich. In her diaries, Friedrichs recorded her daily routine, which mixed skiing lessons, short ski tours, copious sunbathing, and evening social diversions.

During her March 1935 stay in Sulden, Italy, Friedrichs undertook a three-day tour with her fiancé and other companions, demonstrating the growing acceptance of women on strenuous Alpine tours. Friedrichs and her party departed Sulden (6,253 feet) and climbed steeply for ninety minutes to reach the Düsseldorfer rest hut (8,927 feet). On arrival, they "sat for three hours in the blazing sun with an indescribably beautiful view of the Ortler" (a 12,812-foot peak).[2] After spending the night at the Düsseldorfer Hut, her party climbed a steep slope and skied alongside a glacier and its moraines before crossing the glacier itself. They continued climbing to the Hintergrat Hut (8,730 feet), where they took a break for lunch. After lunch, they climbed once more to reach the summit of the Hintergratkopf (9,203 feet). Friedrichs gushed to her diary that she had just summited her highest peak and took in an "unforgettable" panorama of the Königsspitze, Zebrù, and Ortler peaks (figure 9) before returning to the Düsseldorfer Hut, adding, "The descent was also totally marvelous. I was so overjoyed." The next morning, the party climbed to view the glacier once more before making their way back to their hotel in Sulden. For Friedrichs, "the descent was truly the most beautiful that I have ever experienced, it was so blissful [*überselig*], at times schussing in open terrain, at other times wide turns, then the valley became very narrow and difficult, and to finish, one more indescribable schuss."[3] Ski tours like this, involving both climbs and descents in varied terrain, were typical. They offered a combination of physical exertion, natural panoramas, and the excitement of speed. Although ski lifts became more popular in the 1930s, it

FIGURE 9. Ortler, Monte Zebrù, and Königsspitze as seen from the Düsseldorfer Hut outside Sulden, Italy. Laternbildsammlung, Austrian Alpine Association Museum, Innsbruck.

was not until after World War II that Alpine skiing became synonymous with downhill skiing.

Regardless of its more poetic or prosaic articulations, the combined allure of speed and natural beauty proved irresistible, and the number of skiers on Alpine slopes grew exponentially in the first decades of the twentieth century.[4] Skiing was the only activity that combined the nature appreciation of Alpinism with the ecstasy of speed celebrated by bicyclists and motorists. Skiers understood their sport of choice not as a mere pastime but as art. They saw its rhythms and motions as the basis for a healthier life and a stronger connection with the natural environment. This kinaesthetic, or aesthetic of movement, led Alpine skiers to understand the sport as reconciling modern divisions between body and mind and between nature and culture. Chapter 5 examines how skiers' precise control and visceral experience of speed became the cardinal appeal of the sport and led them to interpret their sport as an act of mastery, both of self and of the natural environment.

The tensions between the discourses of harmony and mastery were defining features of Alpine modernism: indeed, Alpine skiers celebrated rather than lamented them. Nevertheless, the combination of nature and modern culture was never a stable one. In the first two decades of the twentieth century, Alpine skiers, while celebrating speed, generally emphasized the sport's harmony with nature, a product of its roots in Romantic, nineteenth-century forms of Alpine leisure and criticisms of the tempo of modern urban life during the fin de siècle. In the 1920s and 1930s, however, skiers began to downplay their connection with nature in favor of a celebration of speed and mastery. This "heroic" form of modernism prevailed in the wake of wartime destruction and the feeling of impotence in the face of subsequent economic and political crises.[5]

COPING WITH MODERNITY

A 1909 article by a Bavarian Alpine enthusiast, Eugen Oertel, both encapsulated the contradictory cultural motivations that animated Alpine skiers in the early twentieth century and outlined the Alpine modernist aesthetic.[6] As Oertel understood them, mountain sports, and Alpine skiing in particular, were more than mere diversions: they were as significant and potentially transcendent as art. Placing the popularity of sport in the context of European modernity was a vital issue for Oertel and other committed skiers, as many traditionalist Alpine enthusiasts lamented the invasion of modern sport into the Alps, which they viewed as a place of retreat from the competitive ethos that governed modern, capitalist societies. Skiers like Oertel, who worked as university professors, medical doctors, lawyers, and businessmen and who imbibed the ideologies of cultural modernism without themselves becoming committed modernists, provide evidence of the vernacularization of avant-garde modernist ideals through Alpine skiing.

Oertel argued that despite human endeavors to advance, "civilization has not eliminated the human struggle for existence but has systematically reshaped it."[7] He shared a common perception that the "civilizing" forces of the late nineteenth century had solved a number of vexing problems but replaced them with newer, more burdensome ones. The struggle for existence had been transformed from a conflict with nature into humanity's own struggle against itself. The novel and rapidly changing practices, institutions, and processes that constituted modern civilization, intended to make individuals more prosperous and secure, instead made them acutely aware of their own insecurity and lack of agency.

The accelerating pace of change in Central Europe beginning in the second half of the nineteenth century reshaped everyday life. The second phase of the Industrial Revolution and the liberalization of European economies wreaked havoc on long-established institutions of economic production such as guilds, family businesses, local market economies, and artisanal modes of production. In the process, they transformed the social hierarchies created by traditional networks of economic activity. Simultaneously, the economic cycle slipped into a prolonged bust phase with the Long Depression of 1873–96.[8] Rapid urbanization turned cities into hotbeds of disease and incubators of social unrest. Democratization produced both mass politics and mass culture, which in turn led to ethnic, class, and gender-based conflicts, while the unification and centralization of states established potent solidarities as well as volatile new divisions in Europe. The growing power of the state and the rapid changes wrought by capitalist economic practices produced a disconcerting sense of individual helplessness.

Cultural changes compounded the sense of disorientation. Citizens and subjects of modern European states considered their lives progressively circumscribed by the disembodied world-historical forces of modernity, variously identified as the tyranny of capital (Karl Marx), the iron cage of rationality (Max Weber), the herd mentality (Gustave Le Bon), or the subconscious workings of the human mind (Sigmund Freud). In an era of relative peace and prosperity, material and intellectual innovations revolutionized nearly every aspect of everyday life.

Commentators lamented that modernization was destroying social connections. In 1903, Georg Simmel wrote in "The Metropolis and Mental Life" that "one never feels as lonely and as deserted as in this metropolitan crush of persons."[9] The objective and figurative rhythm of modern urban life was staccato (literally, "detached"). The cacophony of omnibuses, streetcars, millions of footsteps, and voices echoing through the streets and alleys made the metropolis deafening and unpredictable.[10] Many modernist artists represented the staccato rhythms of urban life in sound, image, and word, as in the harsh cuts of Sergei Eisenstein's montage films and the asymmetry of Georges Braque's cubism. A perception of increasing social dissonance exacerbated these jarring rhythms, as atomization and alienation replaced an idealized (and perhaps imagined) social harmony. Intellectuals and politicians rejected the conception of a "social," extroverted human nature and reconceived it as fundamentally "psychological" and introverted.[11] A new breed of politician described unbridgeable social divisions and appealed to the emotions and instincts of constituents, while Freud outlined the tempestuous interrelationship between the id, ego, and superego. Social and psychological experiences in the urban sphere decidedly lacked harmony.[12]

Oertel argued that, viewed in the context of these dramatic and often troubling changes, the development and popularity of modern sport were far from accidental. Modern societies adhered to an instrumental rationality to increase productivity, ignoring what Oertel described as the individual's "natural needs" for spiritual edification, mental well-being, and physical vigor. Sport, implied Oertel, brought body, mind, and spirit back into balance by satisfying the human desire for spontaneity, movement, and creative action. He therefore understood sport as more than a "hobby" or mere diversion: it was a desperately needed means of meeting innate and often unconscious desires that modern life repressed or trivialized.[13]

Sport allowed individuals to release pent-up energy and offered relief from the drudgery of everyday life. Whereas the drunk and the gambler found this release by surrendering to morally suspect and ultimately unfulfilling distractions, Oertel believed that the athlete shared more in common with the artist, because both "search for and find their satisfaction in the performance itself."[14] Artists and athletes alike responded to modern conditions in creative and spiritually edifying ways. Both sport and art possessed value independent of outside acclaim and monetary rewards. Both artists and athletes adhered to modernist aesthetic principles: both groups found beauty in and derived merit from the sporting or artistic act itself, independent of audience or convention. Modernists rejected the mid-nineteenth-century liberal belief in innate individual "character," instead arguing that individuals defined their identity through artistic expression.[15] Oertel contended that even in sporting competitions that required an adversary, such as an automobile race or a soccer match, athletes' internal struggle with their own corporeal, cognitive, and spiritual limits was the true source of joy, as opposed to the act of vanquishing opponents. In the field of sporting action, the opponent stood apart as something impersonal, an abstract "sum of resistances" to be overcome.[16]

Although all sports, to a certain degree, addressed the modern needs to restore atrophied muscles and to engage in recreation, some sports were particularly effective in reconstituting the fractured modern self.[17] Oertel believed that sports performed in nature were especially salubrious because they combined the physical benefits of exertion with spiritual refreshment. And just as some sports proved more therapeutic than others, certain landscapes were more beneficial than others. The mountains possessed the highest potential in this regard, because it was among the peaks that moderns could experience "nature's most meaningful side."[18]

Even as Romanticism was fading as an artistic movement in the second half of the nineteenth century, Oertel and hundreds of thousands of other Alpine enthusiasts in the fin de siècle continued to interpret the mountain landscape through the lens of Romantic aesthetics. The mountains were described as not merely beautiful but sublime: their beauty, their scale, and their age inspired awe and terror, revealing the hubris of human attempts to master and subjugate nature. The sublimity of the mountains revealed the transitory nature of human institutions and conventions, thus freeing individuals from the strictures of modernity.

Oertel contended that the desolation of the mountains allowed moderns "the opportunity to cast off the shackles and chains of our civilized life," while their sublime combination of danger and beauty "reveal to us the man as he is and what is inside of him, without masks and makeup."[19] Because skiing allowed them to escape the crowds of the summer and literally go off the beaten path, Oertel and other early skiers perceived the mountains as elemental and isolated, requiring them to ignore modern social customs and to reconnect with more natural modes of existence to survive. Similarly, the beauty of the Alps could not be understood from afar but had to be experienced firsthand. Like modernist artists, skiers purged their bodies and minds, discarding artifice, constraint, and regard for conventions in order to fulfill the Nietzschean dictum to "become who you are" and rediscover their "true," presocial selves.[20]

Oertel asserted that skiing offered greater benefits than the more established mountain pastimes of hiking and climbing: "Skiing calls forth in us a feeling that we perceive in no comparable way in Alpinism: the mastery over time and space.... It comes not only from the speed of movement but also is borne by the infinitude of the snowfield, which builds an uninterrupted bridge from mountain to valley and from valley to mountain, which covers colors and possesses no color itself, which blurs all borders and knows no borders itself."[21] Skiers climbed mountains by gliding on the snow that had once sequestered the mountains (and their inhabitants) from civilization. The descent conveyed a more striking sense of mastery with its speed, condensing a foot journey of hours into a matter of minutes and rendering the landscape in a new light. The Alps were no longer to be feared or passively observed but experienced and consumed by skiers who had mastered the forces of nature. Skis, despite the simplicity of their design, were the epitome of modernity, "cousins of the automobile and the airship," not only because of their swift and recent rise to popularity but also because they "correspond to the modern spirit, which cowers before no natural obstacle."[22]

Clearly, skiers were motivated by contradictory impulses. They wished to experience the sublime and primitive beauty of the mountains, but they also wanted to conquer the terrain. Whereas the Alps in summer had become overcrowded and commodified, skis allowed moderns "to discover the frontier [*Neuland*] of winter."[23] The skier was unique among moderns in conquering both time and space (made clear by Oertel's juxtaposition of the spatial and temporal terms *frontier* and *winter*) without mechanical assistance, simply by using skis to harness natural forces. Thus skiing appeared uniquely positioned to return agency and health to exhausted and defeated modern individuals. No other field of experience or form of locomotion so directly synthesized the appreciation of nature's raw power with the human ability to master that power and use it to their advantage.

This antinomy inspired early Alpine skiers but also laid bare troubling contradictions in Alpine skiing. Skiers' enjoyment of an apparently pristine landscape was highly dependent on human interventions, from roads and railroads to hotels and, later, ski lifts. Until the late 1920s, lovers of the mountains were relatively untroubled by this contradiction: as Marco Armiero has written, "Romantic appreciation and modernization of nature were two sides of the same coin."[24] Increasingly, however, the popularity of skiing disrupted this delicate balance. The mastery of nature through speed came to dictate the practice of the sport. By the dawn of World War II, the appreciation of sublime, elemental nature had largely faded from the public discourse about Alpine skiing.

THE ALPINE KINAESTHETIC

Regardless of their nationality, gender, or class, Europeans were remarkably unified in their descriptions and interpretations of Alpine skiing before World War II. They saw the sport's beneficent synthesis of nature and modern culture as beginning with the movement of the human body. Alpine skiers claimed that the instinctive, functional, and rhythmic movements of skiing accorded with both the modern spirit and fundamental human needs. These characteristics made the sport potentially transcendent. In the early part of the twentieth century, Alpine skiers developed a distinctly modernist kinaesthetic that responded to the Alpine landscape and to modern conditions in equal measure.[25]

The Alpine kinaesthetic was not merely instrumental; it was also expressive. To counter the staccato rhythms of modernity, many longed for a legato, or "connected," cadence. In the modern period, according to Sigmund Freud, Georg Simmel, and others, individuals had become alienated from themselves and from one another as the real or imagined former foundations of society—harmony with nature, social unity, and balance between mind and body—had evaporated. The kinaesthetic of Alpine skiing was distinctly modernist in that it simultaneously reflected and challenged modernity. Alpine skiers celebrated the pragmatism and rationality of their sport in an almost Taylorist manner. Yet unlike Taylorism, in which rationalization led to heightened productivity at the expense of individual freedom, the Alpine kinaesthetic connected the functional motions of Alpine skiing to a restorative celebration of balance and fluidity of movement.

The kinaesthetic of Alpine skiers was implicitly connected with formalist modern aesthetics. In 1908, the founder of the modern Olympic Games, Pierre de Coubertin, praised the graceful, balanced, and fluid movements demonstrated by skiers, which were marked by "moderated energy . . . without jerks or thrashes." These characteristics, argued Coubertin, made skiing particularly suited to calming modern anxiety and nervousness.[26]

Whereas many Europeans of the early twentieth century, and commentators since, believed that the modern kinaesthetic was a stilted reflection of mechanized modernity, others, including choreographers and physical education pedagogues, believed that changing the nature of movement could foster mental and emotional well-being. The cultural historian Hillel Schwartz shows, for example, how commentators interpreted torsional movements beginning in the upper body and "spinning out from a soulful center" as physical expressions of internal fluidity, rhythm, spontaneity, and harmony.[27]

Alpine skiers' unaffected, free-flowing movements were a direct response to the extreme danger posed by the Alps in winter. In 1917, Arnold Lunn wrote to a friend: "Break your leg on the Gabelhorn [Switzerland] in February and you will probably die before they can get you down," as unforgiving weather, isolation, and the brevity of daylight would make evacuation difficult.[28] In the era before ski lifts, the Alpine winter inspired caution and respect, an attitude shaped in part by centuries of cultural memory, which construed the winter landscape as desolate and deadly.[29]

To survive the Alps in winter, skiers had to call not only on agility but also on their intuitions and instincts. One of the greatest hazards, the avalanche, was dependent on such a complex relationship among snow composition, weather, and terrain that it was impossible to objectively define when a slope could be considered safe. Instead, skiers had to cultivate an understanding of snow conditions based on experience and instinct.[30]

Skiers shared this celebration of instinct with modernist artists, philosophers, and politicians.[31] Alpine skiing addressed a common anxiety that modern society dulled individuals' natural instincts and urges to action and instead rendered them passive theorists and philosophizers. To ski required determination and bravery; negotiating the hazards of the Alps in winter required quick, instinctive decisions and actions. Alpine skiers rejected modern decadence by eschewing artifice and baroque ornamentalism in favor of simple movements, much as modernist artists celebrated pure form and despised ostentation and extravagance: form was to follow function, emancipating the artist and athlete from superfluous conventions.[32]

The correct style glorified an economy of effort and motion, the goal being to achieve "the greatest results with the least effort."[33] Thus, the kinaesthetic of skiing paralleled the prevailing Taylorist logic of European society in the early decades of the twentieth century. Alpine skiers, rather than rejecting this logic as dehumanizing, stripped it of its nihilistic and exploitative implications and imported it into the Alpine landscape, where its rationality allowed them to traverse the wintry terrain pleasurably and safely. They thereby consummated what Marshall Berman has described as the modernist vision "to get a grip on the modern world and make themselves at home in it."[34]

The connections between Alpine skiing and the modernist project extended to a shared celebration of primitivism as a revolt against the sober, contrived conventions of contemporary European societies. Arguing that the sport must not be theorized and philosophized into meaninglessness, skiers invoked Goethe's aphorism: "All theory is gray, but the golden tree of life springs evergreen." In 1908, the editors of the *Revue Olympique* described Alpine skiing as a field of decisive, instinctive action, in which "neither explanations nor theories are worthwhile."[35] Unlike figure skating or ski jumping, Alpine skiing required no list of rules or codes to judge performance; instead it stressed functional efficiency. In skiing, form followed function: it was a simple and purposeful activity that served as a counter to the growing artificiality and labyrinthine complexity of modern life. Alpine skiers, rejecting the functional rationality of modern capitalism, paradoxically embraced a sport that demanded functional and rational responses to natural obstacles. It is because of such apparent contradictions that Alpine modernism must be described not as antimodern but as differently—and, in the minds of its practitioners—more benevolently modern.

Alpine skiers, like many modern artists, believed that true knowledge could only be gained through experience. In their 1907 instructional guide, Richardson and Hoek wrote that the overly intellectualized modern individual had to shun the role of the pedant conversant with the "dry grammar" of skiing but lacking in experience and improvisational spirit. Instead, the successful Alpine skier executed "unknown, instinctive, sudden adjustments to unforeseen situations" and, like a great conversationalist, deftly supplied "the 'clever answer to the unexpected joke.'"[36] To become an expert skier, the civilized individual had to shed any systematic, grammarian inclinations in favor of a more subtle, unconscious, and vernacular form of knowledge.

The glorification of rhythm and primitive instinct in the Alpine aesthetic closely paralleled developments in modernist art. For example, Vaslav Nijinsky's choreography and Igor Stravinsky's music for the modernist ballet *Le sacre du printemps* celebrated the primitive through rhythmic music and crude movements.[37] At a formal level, Alpine skiing was characterized by the unique "fusion of movement and equilibrium" that differentiated it from other sports. In 1913, the year that *Le sacre du printemps* premiered in Paris, the Viennese professor Oskar Ewald described skiing as a cultural necessity, writing that if modernity was defined "above all [by] its rhythm, the incomparable acceleration of its tempo," then "a true overcoming of turbulence and discontinuity is only possible if one seeks equilibrium in movement itself."[38] Through skiing, enthusiasts sought to enact the modern kinaesthetic values of fluidity, harmony, and equilibrium in their own lives. This was not a struggle against the powerful current of modern forces but the complete acceptance of rhythm, acceleration, and movement. Skiers celebrated and wielded these forces to become, in Berman's words, "subjects as well as objects of modernization," rather than lamenting their effects.[39]

BALANCE THROUGH MOVEMENT

If modernity was mechanical and artificial, Alpine skiers claimed to reestablish the organic harmony between humans and nature by reviving mimetic forms of mobility. Whereas premodern forms of transport depended on and responded to the rhythms and movements of nature, made tangible in the list of a ship under sail or the reverberations of a horse's gallop, the industrialization of mobility dissolved the mimetic relationship between nature and movement, making motion regular and predictable but also dull and alienating.[40]

The kinaesthetic of skiing responded directly to the Alpine environment, liberating skiers and allowing them to reconnect with nature. Skiers thus imagined the Alps as a heroic cultural landscape that, through its danger, inspired instinctive, fluid, and natural movements.

As shown above, many enthusiasts argued that Alpine skiing created inner harmony by nurturing the instinctive and intellectual features of the human character in equal measure. Similarly, the dependence of the skier on the Alpine environment and the feelings of awe engendered by the size and beauty of the mountains suggested a harmony between the modern individual and the natural environment. The ability of Alpine skiers to bridge the stark binaries of modern society—instinct and rationality, action and contemplation— constituted one of the cardinal appeals of the sport. Skiing helped them achieve a healthy balance between instinct, sociability, and intellect (not coincidentally, the three divisions of Freud's tripartite model of the mind).

Skiers softened the polarities of cultural modernism with a balanced Alpine modernist kinaesthetic. Skiing, they claimed, brought about a synthesis of physical and mental activity and of instinctive movement with deep intellectual and spiritual contemplation. Nineteenth-century industrialization and bureaucratization had promoted the cultivation of specialized practices and knowledge, encouraging physical feats (such as the impressive musculature of the famed German bodybuilder Eugen Sandow or the construction of the Suez Canal) and intellectual advances. Contemporaries lamented that as an unforeseen consequence, the number of well-rounded individuals with a wide array of physical and mental skills had declined. Pierre de Coubertin (among others) established the modern Olympic Games in 1896 partially as an attempt to reunite physical and intellectual achievement. Coubertin insisted that the quadrennial sporting competitions be paired with exhibitions of art and literature, conceiving of the Olympic Games as "'the spring of mankind,' a festival of supreme efforts, multiple ambitions and all forms of youthful activity."[41] By juxtaposing sport and art, Coubertin aimed to blend action with contemplation to celebrate youth and improve society.[42] Alpine skiers saw in their sport a unique opportunity not merely to juxtapose sport and art but to fuse them.

Enthusiasts argued that the kinetics of Alpine skiing, the goals of its practitioners (whether in sporting performance or nature appreciation), and skiers' spiritual relationship with the Alpine landscape elevated skiing above other modern sports such as soccer or boxing, transforming the Alpine skier into a philosopher-athlete. As Eugen Oertel argued in 1908, this celebration of apparent contradictions branded skiers as particularly modern, and corresponded "in high measure to every facet of modern cultural development, which demands spirituality through athletic activity and values body-strengthening deeds as much as the world of abstract thought."[43] Alpine skiing served to reconstitute the fractured modern subject by harmonizing the individual's mental, spiritual, and physical functions in the heroic Alpine landscape.

Skiing thus reestablished the bond between individuals and nature that many believed had been severed by modern urbanization, industrialization, and mechanization. The historian Joachim Radkau has written that it is "only in a society that has over-cultivated wide swathes of its environment" that an untamed and savage landscape can become culturally valuable: "Only a social stratum that hardly knows hunger any more has an eye for the aesthetic of the wasteland, the panorama of rocky crags."[44] In a modern world in which all seemed to have been systematized and made predictable, the Alps forced moderns to confront the overwhelming and unpredictable power of nature. To a class of elite Europeans who no longer depended on their bodies for daily survival, the winter landscape represented a return to the harmony between body and mind and between humans and nature and a liberation from the suffocating rationalism and materialism of modern Western society.

The Alps in winter were frequently equated with paradise. The concept of a *Skiparadies,* first invoked in the German-language skiing literature in 1913, became increasingly popular in the 1920s and 1930s. In 1935, Carl Luther wrote that the "white empire" of Europe's mountains was characterized by abundant snow, diverse terrain, stunning vistas, clear skies, and still air, with few "modern human ingredients" such as crowds, trains, or hotels.[45] Ancient societies imagined paradise as a verdant refuge from the dangers of nature, want, and human corruption. The "ski paradise" was no less a product of mythology, but it reflected the more modern concerns implied by Joachim Radkau: it was not an escape from want, but a privileged escape from excess. In similar terms, Wilhelm Paulcke argued in 1936 that while all people celebrated the *Heimat* (homeland) of their youth, skiers of his generation had discovered in the mountains "a wonderful second *Heimat.*" This *Heimat* served all skiers as something "infinitely beautiful and great," and given the cosmopolitan composition of skiing culture, formed a counterpoint to the social and national divisions that plagued modern societies.[46] The Alpine environment offered skiers a chance to reestablish their internal equilibrium.[47] Simultaneously, it enabled skiers to turn a blind eye to social conflicts, unequal gender relations, and environmental degradation, both in their sport and in the world at large.

As Alpine skiers conceived of it, the "ski paradise" not only offered an escape from the concerns and problems of metropolitan civilization but also reflected the idealized harmony between nature and modern culture. They imagined their relationship with the Alps as a symbiosis, an act of artistic creation as well as of aesthetic appreciation. In 1910, the German Alpinist F. Siebert described the experience of the mountain landscape as "a creative construction of the world according to the aesthetic values within us.... [T]he creator flows together with the creation as one ... [in] a purely artistic act."[48] Thus, in the minds of skiers, Alpine modernism constituted an evolutionary step beyond both Romanticism and urban cultural modernism. Alpine skiers did not merely observe or experience natural panoramas: they broke down the wall between the artist and the observer by performing both roles simultaneously.

Alpine skiers' directive to return to nature and their idealization of the "ski paradise," while purportedly universal, reflected the cultural values of elites. Whereas leisured urbanites embraced primitive simplicity by skiing in their free time, mountain peasants had little use for aesthetic rumination, and social customs and economic barriers blocked urban laborers from the sport. Further, the immense danger of early skiing reinforced its bourgeois character, as only men of leisure possessed both the knowledge necessary to navigate the Alpine winter safely and the expendable income to travel to the mountains and procure expensive equipment.

Alpine skiing appeared distinctive in the way that it created harmony between body and mind and between the skier and the landscape. Whereas other pleasure seekers, from drunks and gamblers to tourists and athletes, often appeared hedonistic and uninterested in mental or spiritual stimulation, skiers claimed to leaven their instinctive action with contemplation and spiritual engagement, while at the same time fostering an intense connection to the Alps. The perception of harmony in Alpine skiing was part of the fabric of Alpine modernism in the decades before World War II, but it held particular sway through the late 1910s as a response to fin-de-siècle social and cultural conditions. Although it continued to influence skiers' perceptions of their sport into the 1920s and 1930s (as reflected in discussions about the *Skiparadies* and a second *Heimat*), events and the unstable dynamics of Alpine modernism itself shifted the emphasis of the sport, leading Alpine skiers to speak less of their harmonious relationship with nature and more of the conquering power of speed.

FIVE

Ecstasy in Speed

MARKETING VELOCITY

Italy has been a destination attractive to tourists since the Grand Tours that began in the late seventeenth century. But how was Italy, a latecomer to Alpine skiing and to serving Alpine tourists more generally, to stimulate Alpine tourism after World War I, when well-established competitors in Switzerland, France, and Austria already dominated the business? Most of Italy's tourist business was based on its historical treasures, which afforded little benefit to remote Alpine regions. After Benito Mussolini rose to power in 1922, he engaged in a concerted program to develop Alpine tourism to improve the physical and moral health of Italians as well as to maximize the value of the mountainous regions along Italy's northern border.

To expand Italy's share of the burgeoning ski-tourism market, officials at the Italian National Tourism Agency (Agenzia Nazionale Italiana del Turismo, or ENIT) turned their attention northward to the German-speaking denizens of the eastern Alps. ENIT commissioned a poster from Franz Lenhart, a young Austrian artist from Tirol, to promote winter sport in Italy (figure 10). The font traces sinuous curves through the words *Winter-Sport,* imitating the fluid kinaesthetic of skiing, while the off-kilter lean of the letters *a* and *e* and the sharp peaks of the letters *I, t,* and *l* in *Italien* evoke the jagged peaks of the Italian Alps. Yet nothing in the poster associates the skier with any recognizable Italian landscape: there is no outline of the iconic, crooked summit of Cervinia (the Matterhorn), which lies along the border with Switzerland, nor of the needle-sharp peaks that characterize the Dolomites of northeastern Italy. According to ENIT's advertisement, skiing in Italy bore no relationship to any specific landmark; nor did it seem

FIGURE 10. German-language poster by Austrian artist Franz Lenhart advertising winter tourism in Italy, 1930. Courtesy of the Beekley Family Foundation, Hartford, CT.

to cultivate an appreciable relationship to nature. Rather, winter sport in Italy consisted of speed, pure and simple. The skier's forward lean and blurry outline indicate the rapidity of his descent. This poster, circulated in the 1930s, advertised a new age of Alpine skiing, one in which the celebration of speed outweighed a harmonious relationship with the landscape. These design choices reveal ENIT's efforts to align Italy with the current practice of the sport, making Italian resorts appear more modern and desirable than sedate, traditional ski destinations such as Davos, Chamonix, and St. Moritz.

The end of World War I signaled great changes in nearly every aspect of European society. Skiing was no exception, as the conflict punctuated subtle changes already in motion within the sport. The war calls to mind images of soldiers bogged down in the trenches of northern France, but, as Tait Keller has shown, some of the fiercest and most active fighting occurred on the Alpine front between Italy and Austria-Hungary.[1] The Great War had two major effects on the practice of Alpine skiing. First, the Germans, Austrians, French, and Italians all expanded their ski battalions (as did the Swiss, to patrol their neutral borders), developing training programs based on the technique first systematized by Georg Bilgeri in 1910.[2] The ski battalions laid the foundation for an immense growth in the numbers of leisure skiers in the 1920s and 1930s by introducing soldiers to the sport.

The cultural effects of war also had a tremendous influence on the meaning of Alpine skiing. As a variety of scholars have argued, World War I represented "the birth of the modern age" and validated speed as a cultural value.[3] Similarly, the destruction of the war and the cascading political, economic, and social crises of the interwar era suggested the powerlessness of the individual and led many to lionize war heroes, politicians, athletes, and movie stars as embodying the agency of individuals in a tumultuous time. Celebrations of skiers as conquering heroes stretched back as far as Fridtjof Nansen's Greenland traverse in the late 1880s, but such messages possessed greater resonance in the interwar tumult, and in the 1920s and 1930s, speed and mastery triumphed over the harmonious kinaesthetic of the previous decades.

THE ALLURE OF SPEED

Tourists and mountain climbers had long taken to the Alps to experience the beauty of nature, but skiers, aided by the natural force of gravity and the low friction of snow, introduced a novel and volatile element into the landscape: speed. Although speed was initially interpreted as a harmonization of human action with the natural environment, skiers in the 1920s and 1930s increasingly understood their manipulation of speed as a heroic domination of nature, significantly altering the cultural meanings of the sport.

In the abstract, speed can be described as a dynamic, mutually dependent relationship between space and time.[4] Modern technologies and modern thought blurred the boundary between these two dimensions of human experience. In the modern era, speed is more than a metric: according to one succinct formulation by Jeremy Millar and Michiel Schwartz, "Speed is not so much a product of our culture as our culture is a product of speed."[5] Since the mid-eighteenth century, Western cultures have been defined by a logic of acceleration: speed has become a cultural value with connotations of progress and evolution.[6] Perhaps the most notable celebration of speed in the modern era was futurism, which peaked in the years preceding World War I and helps explain the context in which Alpine skiers' love of speed arose. Filippo Tommaso Marinetti's 1909 "Manifesto of Futurism" declared that "the beauty of the world has been enriched by a new form of beauty: the beauty of speed,"[7] showing how some moderns reimagined speed not as a means to an end but as an end in itself.[8]

In the fin de siècle, inventions such as the automobile and the telephone, as well as the Taylorist acceleration of production processes, had the cumulative effect of democratizing speed, making it accessible first to elites and later to the masses. In the interwar period, speed became a stimulant, consumed by individuals for what Jeffrey Schnapp terms its "erotico-transcendental" effects. And yet, despite its popularity and accessibility, speed still represented the mystical and the supernatural. In short, as Schnapp observes, "speed was the distinctive drug of modernity" from the eighteenth century onward.[9]

Individuals developed profoundly ambivalent relationships with speed. In its industrial and technical manifestations, its dynamics became progressively tyrannical, and the logic of speed and acceleration infiltrated everyday life. For some, the experience of this modern drug was intoxicating; in others, its multiplication of stimuli induced nervousness and panic, making increased speeds a factor in the massive increase in neurasthenia diagnoses during the fin de siècle.[10] Speed thus symbolized both the positive and negative potential of modernity. It could be either a "salubrious lucky charm" or "a sickening virus."[11] Often, in particularly modern fashion, it was both simultaneously. Regardless, speed allowed individuals "to feel modernity in their bones . . . as a physical sensation."[12] Alpine skiers, of course, were among its greatest enthusiasts. Although skiers claimed that they could temper the volatile power of speed by pairing it with nature appreciation, it proved so intoxicating as to alter the meanings and practice of skiing.

Many social commentators associated speed with progressive technological developments such as the train, the automobile, and the airplane. Skiing differed from these innovations, however, in the way that it enabled individuals to experience speed. As Lunn wrote, "Mere speed is not enough. An urchin sliding along on a scooter enjoys a finer thrill than a traveller in a modern aeroplane de luxe which averages more than a hundred miles an hour between Croydon and Paris. To secure the fine unspoiled flavor of pace you must eliminate mechanism, retain the sense of personal control, and preserve the ever-present risk of a fall." As "the simplest of all servants of speed," skis bridged the separation between the individual and the means of locomotion.[13] By harnessing the kinetic potential of gravity, Alpine skiers experienced what the German philosopher Ernst Bloch described in 1930 as "a paradoxically liberated encounter with gravity, a dance of effortlessness" without parallel.[14]

The futurists understood the relationship between the driver and the automobile, or the pilot and the airplane, as transcendent complexes of mechanical and human agency, through which machines were endowed with powers of intuition and moral autonomy.[15] For individuals who were less enamored with technology, however, the dependence of speed on mechanical power proved alienating. In Alpine skiing, this drawback evaporated. Lunn argued that "a man and his horse are two distinct personalities, but an expert ski-runner and his ski form an indivisible unit. The motorist imposes his will through an elaborate mechanism of pedals and levers, but the ski seem to belong to their owner just as wings belong to the bird, so intimate is the connection, so instantaneous their response to the command of mind and body. No form of swift movement gives a sense of personal control so complete."[16] The Frenchman André Teissier echoed Lunn when he averred that Alpine skiing was the most transcendent means of experiencing speed. It produced the sensation of "a force that I bear which seems to emanate from within me, propels me, seizes me, and launches me into space," while simultaneously "[reducing] to a minimum the importance of the auxiliary motor; it eliminates all machinery, nearly all materials outside of ourselves and leaves us alone with speed. . . . The virtuosos attain the speed of a great machine. All thanks to only four or five kilograms of added weight."[17]

Alpine skiers achieved speeds unmatched by any but the most technologically advanced forms of transport, making the skier into a manifestation of what Sigmund Freud termed a "prosthetic God."[18] Generally speaking,

Freud noted that modern technological prostheses were often unwieldy and difficult to control. However, skiers overcame the alienation that Freud considered inherent in modern technology because they were able to handle their instruments without the drawbacks of other means of transport, including pollution and traffic congestion. Alpine skiing offered more than mere acceleration, which could be matched and even surpassed by other forms of transport media: it provided unparalleled individual agency and control.

Because skiers bound themselves to a primitive and relatively natural implement, they regarded the pleasure derived from speed in Alpine skiing as well earned and deeply cathartic rather than alienating. Hannes Schneider and Arnold Fanck asserted in 1925 that Alpine skiers not only equaled the feats of the most advanced technologies but surpassed them: "What no mechanical device can achieve, is achieved by human beings simply standing on their two legs on such a primitive invention as two boards curved upward at their points. *In the ski-runner is embodied the triumph of the living trained body over mechanical matter*" (emphasis in original).[19] With only their courage to guide them and two planks of wood lashed to their feet, Alpine skiers tamed time and space. Arnold Lunn wrote in 1925:

> The worst and best moments in skiing are often separated only by seconds. You are standing at the top of some fierce slope which you have vowed to take straight. You look at the line and observe with sick disgust that the change of gradient is abrupt at the bottom, and that the slight bump half-way down will probably send you into the air. . . . And then suddenly, before you quite realize what has happened, you are off. The wind rises into a tempest and sucks the breath out of your body. . . . Your knees are as wax, and your stomach appears to have been left behind at the top. . . . And now comes the supreme crisis—the run-out where the gradient suddenly changes. You throw your weight forward, and mutter "Hold it, hold it." You clench your teeth, and make strange noises as the shock drives up through your legs . . . and you realize to your intense astonishment that you have not fallen. The pace relaxes. The hurricane dies away. You are drunk with the wine of speed, and you marvel at the faint heart which so nearly refused the challenge. You glory in the sense of control which you have recaptured over your ski, no longer untamed demons hurrying you through space, but the most docile of slaves. You are playing with gravity. You are the master of the snow. You can make it yield like water or resist like steel.[20]

"Drunk with the wine of speed," Alpine skiers could fulfill Charles Baudelaire's early modernist prescription for coping with the pressures of modernity: "One must always be drunk."[21] The skier was an alchemist who mastered nature without subjugating it, developing the courage and will-power that had atrophied in the relative security of modern life. Skiers could thus experience a healthy and liberating form of intoxication. Such senti-ments were not mere philosophical abstractions. In 1934, Nellie Friedrichs wrote of her experiences on vacation in Misurina, Italy, a short distance from the popular Alpine center of Cortina d'Ampezzo. Echoing Lunn, she noted that "the descent was very thrilling for me. I often feel maniacal here, but it's fun all the same."[22]

And yet, as Friedrichs's ambivalent tone suggests, there was something uncanny and unsettling about this speed. Many noted that its effects in Alpine skiing were not uniformly positive. If speed was "the newest God of modern man," as Henry Hoek wrote in 1933, it was not always benevolent but instead could be "a God of incorruptible, soulless, and entirely inhuman numbers." The God of Speed was "insatiable . . . feed him 100 kilometers per hour, and he will want to have 120 at once."[23] Like modernity itself, the dynamics of speed in Alpine skiing obeyed a logic of acceleration. As with other drugs, the human body and mind quickly acclimated themselves to the experience of speed, requiring higher and higher levels of stimulation.[24]

The experience of speed in skiing made everyday life appear dull and empty by comparison, and skiers had to attain higher speeds and experience greater danger to feed their addiction. As early as 1912, the German guide-book authors Carl Luther and G. P. Lücke recognized that the "ecstasy of speed" often created a false sense of security. This in turn "produce[d] an enthusiasm that leads to carelessness" and resulted in spectacular crashes, from which Alpine skiing gained a reputation as a daredevil sport of shat-tered limbs.[25] In theorizing the addiction to speed, Jeffrey Schnapp argues that the crash plays a necessary role by legitimizing speed, marking its abso-lute limit.[26] For some skiers, this risk heightened the erotico-transcendental thrill of Alpine skiing, whereas for others it sapped the joy from the sport. Those who probed the limits of the sport most often, downhill ski racers, were also most familiar with the "comedown" of speed intoxication. Arnold Lunn's son Peter, a ski racer, noted in 1935:

> Gradually . . . the skier becomes hardened to the thrill of speed, and he must ski ever faster if he wishes to enjoy it. Thus the minimum speed at which he begins to be interested by, and to draw active pleasure from, ski-ing becomes steadily higher. . . . [T]he minimum speed at which a skier can enjoy ski-ing increases more rapidly than the maximum speed at which he can ski without

being frightened. As soon as the day comes that the minimum speed at which he begins to draw pleasure from ski-ing is faster than the maximum speed at which he can ski without being frightened, he will cease to enjoy ski-ing.[27]

The stimulation of speed not only produced individual euphoria and terror in equal measure; it also created new ways of seeing and altered the perception of the Alps. Countless skiers described how speed increased the beauty of the landscape. For climbers, reaching the summit of the mountain was the zenith of their encounter with the Alps; the descent was marked by knee-straining, brain-jarring boredom. In skiing, the joy of the descent created a more satisfying dramatic arc to the day's activity in which the anticipation and exertion of the ascent gave way to the cathartic ecstasy of the descent. Arnold Lunn, an avid mountain climber until a fall in 1909 permanently damaged his leg, believed that skiers experienced the Alpine landscape as no one else could. He wrote in 1925: "When every pulse is throbbing with the thrill of a swift descent on ski, the mind is alert to observe and to record a thousand delicate beauties which are missed in a weary tramp [downhill]. . . . [The landscape] never seems more beautiful than when it borrows from the ski something of the ski's own magic motion."[28] Nellie Friedrichs echoed Lunn's sentiments. On one occasion, she relished the distorted optics of sun and snow, describing her descent from the Schöntaufspitze above Sulden as particularly "thrilling, because one could not differentiate highs and lows [in the terrain] in the diffuse light." On another tour, the otherworldly, godlike perspective afforded by a "heavenly descent" overwhelmed her. She breathlessly wrote, "This flight downhill in high snow, and right and left, ahead and behind, the grandiose peaks of the Dolomites . . . is indescribably beautiful."[29]

For Lunn and Friedrichs, speed sharpened the mind and the senses. Skiers' heightened perceptions revolutionized the panoramic landscape aesthetic that first developed among train travelers, Alpinists, and other mountain tourists in the nineteenth century.[30] But whereas train travelers passively observed the landscape from crowded railcars, and Alpinists trudged slowly through it, the Alpine skier experienced what Enda Duffy has termed an "adrenaline aesthetics," in which levelheaded objectivity recedes in favor of pleasure "that is effected first on the body and its sensorium."[31] Skis allowed individuals to enjoy the sensual kinetic experience of speed simultaneously with Romantic panoramas. This euphoric combination of modern speed and timeless nature epitomized Alpine modernism.

Although access to technology had democratized speed in the early twentieth century, skiers believed that their personal control of speed, and the danger this entailed, differentiated them from the urban masses. Many cultural modernists and political and social elites understood political democratization and the commodification of culture as deleterious modern trends.[32] In response, they nurtured a cult of individual heroism.[33] By exerting free will and performing heroic acts, the modernist individual illustrated the transcendent possibilities of the human being. Some imagined that the control of speed endowed skiers with superhuman powers.[34] Stefan von Dévan, a German guidebook author and skiing enthusiast, argued in 1938 that by constantly commanding speed, Alpine skiers grew "beyond the capabilities of average men and can accurately be regarded as supermen [*Übermenschen*]" who welcomed danger and transcended the mundane through the force of their will.[35] The use of the term *Übermensch* evokes Friedrich Nietzsche's criticism, developed in *Thus Spake Zarathustra,* of the decadence of modern civilization and the passivity of the individuals it nurtured. Through their courage and their will to power, Alpine skiers abandoned the prosaic practices of the metropolis to refashion themselves through speed (figure 11).

The experience of speed in Alpine skiing, fueled by the proliferation of ski lifts in the Alps in the 1930s and the wider popularization of "heroic" modernism that both reflected and informed the rising popularity of fascism in Europe, led skiers to understand their sport in new ways. Nietzsche's *Übermensch* escaped the "muddy stream" that was common humanity not by seeking out harmony, but by mastering himself and the world around him through the exercise of his will.[36] Increasingly, skiers understood Alpine skiing not solely in terms of synthesis and harmony but as a process of mastery and domination of the dangerous Alpine winter landscape. Alpine skiers disciplined their bodies and minds not only to survive the Alps but also in an attempt to overcome the apathy and torpor of modern urban life. By the beginning of World War II, mastery dominated both the discourse and practice of Alpine skiing. Mastery in skiing began with mastery of the self. Pierre de Coubertin's early advocacy of modern sport celebrated it as a practice that would harmonize body and mind (see chapter 4), but his later views evinced the same ambivalence and contradiction as Alpine modernism. Coubertin averred in 1935 that sport allowed individuals "to defend man and to achieve self-mastery, to master danger, the elements, the animal, life."[37] Thus athletes

FIGURE 11. Toni Schönecker, *Heimkehr in die Stadt* (Return to the city), 1924. *Der Winter* 18 (1924–25): 144.

towered over what Nietzsche derisively termed "the last man": the apathetic, decadent, overly secure modern individual. Through sport, and especially the test of courage and the will in Alpine skiing, moderns could master themselves and achieve heightened powers of body and mind.

Alpine skiers experienced an even more profound sense of mastery through their domination of external conditions. In the modern era, new technologies and cultural changes were seen as "annihilating" time and space.[38] Marinetti and the futurists proclaimed that "Time and Space died yesterday. We already live in the absolute, for we have already created velocity which is eternal and omnipresent."[39] Although skiers relied on snow, steep slopes, and the force of gravity to achieve their conquest, the sheer mass of the Alps and the millennia of cultural memory that identified the Alpine winter with danger and primitivity only enriched the rhetoric of mastery.

Many Europeans viewed the mountains in winter as the last remaining frontier on the continent. Alpine enthusiasts were dispirited when, in 1890, two Austrian climbers summited what many considered to be the last great unconquered peak in the Alps, the Fünffingerspitze of the South Tirolean Dolomites.[40] The Alpine winter, however, was still a heroic landscape in which individuals could prove their mettle and pioneer new ways of living and perceiving the world.[41] In 1930, the German ski enthusiast Kurt Seeger contended that the skier "uncovers and obtains virgin soil, and in doing so he becomes a discoverer, a trailblazer, a pioneer—a ski-Columbus, a ski-Viking."[42] Paul Dinckelacker, a successful German industrialist as well as an avid skier and mountaineer, argued in 1933 that the skier "experiences something that was beyond the grasp of all preceding generations." The intense pleasure derived from this act of discovery allowed skiers to "reconcile [their] existence with these oppressive times."[43] Commentators increasingly described the heroism of Alpine skiing as a cultural necessity, shifting away from the earlier emphasis on reconnecting modern individuals with nature. By the 1930s, that connection to nature was implied, and Alpine skiers understood their sport as a salubrious and vital act of self-assertion.

SKIING AND MASS CULTURE

Whereas skiers had long been forced to construct analogies to automobiles and airplanes to describe the sensation of skiing, by the interwar period the basis for comparison had shifted. A 1925 advertisement shows Mercedes-Benz invoking the cultural cachet of Alpine skiing and the feeling of mastery experienced by Alpine skiers to market its new cars (figure 12). If skiers were "drunk with the wine of speed," then Mercedes-Benz automobiles afforded the same rush of pleasure and the intense sensation of personal control over time and space.[44] Alpine skiing and Alpine modernism, once the province of the elite, were becoming part of the vernacular of modern mass culture, while paradoxically symbolizing luxury (particularly when paired with the automobile).

FIGURE 12. E. von Offelsmeyer Cucuel, "Herrscher über Raum und Zeit" (Master over Space and Time), advertising poster for Mercedes-Benz, 1925. Courtesy of the Beekley Family Foundation, Hartford, CT.

This vernacularization illustrates further tensions in Alpine modernism. Although many Alpine skiers and other modernists denounced mass culture as an affront to *Kultur,* skiing (like other modernist-inflected cultural and political movements) benefited immensely from its symbiotic, though con-flicted, relationship with mass culture. The sporting press reported on ski races, club events, and Alpine resorts, while advertisers flooded the print media with announcements of new hotels, expanded rail services, and skiing equipment.

Skiers' obsession with speed found its ideal expression in another modern medium: film. Whereas Alpinists found writing and still photography

FIGURE 13. Film still from *Der weiße Rausch,* 1931. Archive of the Deutscher Alpenverein, Munich.

suitable means of describing their relationship with the landscape and of illustrating climbing techniques, Alpine skiers often struggled to evoke the ecstasy of speed in these static media.[45] The development of skiing films illustrates the mutually beneficial relationship between these two forms of modern mass culture.[46]

Beginning in the 1920s and accelerating in the 1930s, ski films emerged as a popular offshoot of the *Bergfilm* genre.[47] Together the German director Arnold Fanck and the Austrian ski instructor Hannes Schneider produced numerous ski films, including *Das Wunder des Schneeschuhs* (1920), *Der heilige Berg* (1926), and *Der weiße Rausch* (1931). *Der weiße Rausch* is an action comedy that culminates in a dramatic and elaborate chase scene in which Schneider and a young Leni Riefenstahl flee dozens of black-clad pursuers on skis (figure 13). During the chase, Riefenstahl (wearing a blouse helpfully monogrammed "LR," lest we forget who is the star) grins in ecstasy. The striking mountain scenery surrounding St. Anton am Arlberg (Austria) is no more than a backdrop, and Fanck largely avoids panoramic shots. He pulls the camera in tight to focus on the glory of movement and speed and the athletic prowess of Schneider, Riefenstahl, and their pursuers. Fanck employs rapid cuts, dramatic angles, and ski-mounted cameras to depict the unique kinetics of Alpine skiing. The skiers, not the mountains, are the stars. The celebration of speed, the cult of the movie star, and the glorification of the transcendent athlete displayed in ski films helped shape the interwar era of heroic modernism in mass culture.

Leni Riefenstahl's star turn in *Der weiße Rausch* also speaks to the way that women came to symbolize the symbiosis of Alpine skiing and mass culture. The number of women skiers grew as the sport increased in popularity and winter vacations became more common among Europe's middle classes.[48] The physical mechanics of skiing continued to make it acceptable in ways that other athletic pursuits were not: for example, women could ski in Fascist Italy without provoking confrontation because Fascist officials and common Italians did not understand the sport to be particularly strenuous.[49] Such beliefs also enabled women skiers to take part in competitive races much earlier than in other sports. British clubs permitted women to race alongside men in the 1920s, the Fédération Internationale de Ski staged women's races at the first Alpine World Ski Championships in 1931, and Alpine skiing events for both men and women were added to the Winter Olympics program in 1936. By contrast, women were not allowed to compete in Nordic ski races until the 1952 Olympics, and even this race (at ten kilometers) was shorter than men's Nordic competitions. Across the Alps, many of the gendered assumptions and moral debates surrounding women's participation in the sport receded in the interwar years. As the German author Hans Fischer noted in his tongue-in-cheek anthropological study of "ski bunnies," published in 1935, men no longer concerned themselves with a woman's dress on the slopes; they only cared whether she was a capable skier and a good comrade in possession of a "true sporting spirit."[50]

Thanks to its symbiotic relationship with mass culture, skiing popularized the ideal of the "strong-willed" New Woman, in contrast to the delicate, "nervous pixie" archetype.[51] Even before World War I, women skiers had been able to challenge constricting fashions (and the culture that upheld them) on the basis of their impracticality in the mountains. The *Bergfilm* director Luis Trenker argued that women's engagement with sport in the previous decades had formed the basis for the aesthetic and morality of the New Woman. As skiers proved, "A woman wants to have freedom of motion, she wants to be as equal as possible with men and with her sporting comrades; out in the mountains, she wants to be not a wife and a mother, but only a woman or a girl."[52] As a result, athletic exploits such as skiing played a vital role in the push for political rights and social equality for women by demonstrating their passion, commitment, and strength.[53]

Nevertheless, the gender dynamics of interwar skiing were not as radically egalitarian as Fischer and Trenker implied. Fischer followed up his celebration of the unaffected relations between men and women on ski tours with an injunction that "sport should never masculinize women."[54] While he accepted women's participation, he disparaged their abilities, averring that one could only marvel at women's achievements in the sport given their less "developed" bodies. He also noted that their equipment was "smaller and daintier" than that of men. The very concept of the "ski bunny" emphasized that women were sexual beings, to be hunted by men on skis.[55] Fischer further proclaimed that on long ski tours, "the man is the leader, the woman is the dependable and true comrade." When they settled into a ski hut at night, the "ski bunny" was expected to transform herself by exhibiting her "unrivaled [mastery] of the arts of the housewife" and "whizz about" between the table and the stove.[56] Even in the egalitarian mountain air, Luis Trenker wrote, "the skiing woman must never forget . . . that she is and should be a lady."[57]

The paradoxical intersection of the New Woman, changing gender dynamics, and the sport of skiing was manifested in a flood of advertisements featuring women. Johann Maier's 1927 poster for the Munich sporting goods store Sporthaus Schuster features the New Woman to great effect (figure 14). Posing with skis, the model wears form-fitting, practical clothes and exhibits the slender and athletic physique associated with the active, independent New Woman. And yet Maier depicts his subject in a moment of inactivity to avoid the perception that sporting endeavors might masculinize her. The poster also eroticizes its subject. Her posture, turned slightly toward the viewer with one hand flirtatiously placed on her hip, accentuates the curves of her body, while her flushed cheeks (whether from athletic activity or makeup) accord with prevailing standards of beauty. By using such images of women, advertisers associated their business with the progressive, exciting novelty of both the New Woman and Alpine skiing. To do so, however, the advertisements continued to depict women as objects of consumption: ravishing ski bunnies to entice men and fashionistas whom women would wish to emulate. Cultural representations objectified women skiers as sexual, physical beings, while their male comrades often displaced them into passive roles.

The depiction of the virtues of Alpine skiing in mass culture could also be turned toward political ends. In 1937, the Fascist regime in Italy circulated a photograph of Benito Mussolini posing shirtless on a ski outing at Mount Terminillo outside Rome (figure 15).[58] The photograph highlighted Il Duce's

SPORTHAUS SCHUSTER
MÜNCHEN, ROSENSTR., 6 NÄCHST DER MARIENPLAT.

FIGURE 14. Poster by Johann B. Maier advertising the Schuster sporting goods store in Munich, 1927. Archive of the Deutscher Alpenverein, Munich.

masculinity while implicitly associating the dictator with the qualities associated with skiing (despite the fact that he poses with ski poles but no skis): mastery, discovery, and decisive action. It shows Mussolini not communing harmoniously with nature but rather dominating the elements and displaying his virility. Even to those who did not ski, the association with ski imagery presented Il Duce as powerful, youthful, instinctive, and commanding. The non-Alpine setting highlights the decisive shift in Alpine modernism away from the celebration of the mountain landscape and toward a placeless mythologization of speed.[59] If an aging politician (who was by all accounts a

FIGURE 15. Benito Mussolini on skis outside Rome, 1937. *Rivista mensile del Club alpino italiano* 56, no. 3 (1937).

poor skier) could reap the benefits of the cultural associations of skiing, then surely Alpine modernism no longer required the Alps or even skiing itself to transmit its cultural messages.[60]

SYNTHETIC LANDSCAPES AND VERNACULAR MODERNISM

The spirit of Alpine modernism united skiers of all backgrounds: philosophers and tourists, young and old, men and women, Fascist dictators and

Jewish teenagers. Rachel Josefowitz Siegel was born in Berlin in 1924 and lived in Switzerland until her family emigrated to New York in 1939. In her memoirs, she recalled a ski trip with her older brothers in the Plessur Alps around Arosa in the late 1930s, where Arthur Conan Doyle had first skied some forty years earlier. This tour was a rite of passage for Siegel, who recalled that she was "proud, oh so proud, to be allowed on this advanced excursion. No more kiddie slope for me." After climbing for some time, Rachel and her brothers shared a chocolate bar to recover some energy and prepared themselves "for a quick run down the slope, nearly blinded by virgin snow." Reflecting on this descent some seven decades later, she remarked, "The feeling of elation and control is with me still. The memory is in my bones and in my heart. I feel the wind on my face and relive the brilliant reflection of sun on fresh snow. My knees and legs remember the tension of dipping to the right, then to the left, guiding the skis with the weight of my body. The alp was mine, the wind my very own, mine and my brothers' as they whizzed by, shouting for joy. I was queen of the mountain."[61]

Siegel's description incorporates all the aspects of Alpine modernism defined by the likes of Carl Luther and Arnold Lunn, demonstrating how these prominent intellectual proponents of the sport gave a philosophical, learned gloss to universal experiences. Siegel's memories of the downhill run are not only intellectual but vividly sensory, confirming the sport's ability to unite physical activity with mental engagement. Skiing made this young teenage girl, a Jewish immigrant to Switzerland, a ruler of the mountain and master of the forces of nature. Every skier could be her own ski-Viking and ski-Columbus.

The tension between harmony and mastery is central to Alpine modernism.[62] It suited the needs of modern individuals, many of whom wished to experience both a stronger connection with nature and a sense of discovery, empowerment, and speed. Taken in isolation, both speed and Alpine aesthetics were immensely pleasurable. In concert, they produced feelings of transcendence, ecstasy, and intoxication, and as the German historian of skiing Erwin Mehl later observed, "the joy of skiing is the joy of the mountains multiplied by the joy of the downhill."[63]

For skiers, the mountains provided a space in which the many, often antagonistic, ideas and trends of modern society could be reconciled and synthesized. But the Alps were also synthetic in another sense: they constituted a fabricated space—a cultural landscape—that moderns invented and elaborated. Alpine skiers sought to cope with modernity not by fleeing from it entirely but by developing a more humane and nuanced form of modernity in the blank canvas of the Alpine winter. Once there, they found that Alpine skiing allowed them to realize the goals of liberation and transcendence not by slowing down the pace of life but by accelerating it and harnessing that speed.

Alpine skiers thus vernacularized modernism, enacting its ideals in everyday life by glorifying speed, articulating new practices and identities, and transcending national divisions. Because cultural modernism was generally inflexible and doctrinaire, it remained quarantined in the realm of "high culture." Less-committed individuals saw the futurists' responses to modern life as excessive and radical; they combined an embrace of modern technology with aggressive misogyny, glorification of violence, and antibourgeois diatribes, demanding a complete rejection of cultural tradition in their pursuit of utopia.[64] The phenomena that constituted Alpine modernism, including the skiing kinaesthetic, the joy of speed, and the discourses of harmonization and mastery, allowed Alpine skiers to create a more accessible form of modernism, one that they formulated and participated in rather than passively observed. By grounding modernist ideals in the vast and timeless Alpine landscape, Alpine skiers grafted avant-garde modernist sentiments onto the perceived authenticity of nature. Skiing's ability to reconcile various dichotomies—nature/culture, mind/body, modern/traditional, and emotional/intellectual—thus positioned it as an ideal response to modern conditions.

In idealizing their sport, skiing advocates minimized the tensions and divisions among skiers. The universalizing rhetoric of Alpine modernism ignored the sport's inherent elitism and the continued subordination of women. If skiing was a panacea in the years before World War II, it was a panacea defined largely by the perceptions of middle-class men. This relatively narrow outlook helps to explain the shifting meanings of the sport between 1900 and 1939 and the increasing valorization of speed, mastery, and heroism.

Alpine modernism made skiing a sport ideally suited to the twentieth century. British sports such as rugby, soccer, and cricket, which spread across the globe in the nineteenth century, reflected the concerns of contemporary British middle classes. These were team sports with ethical aims, meant to inculcate teamwork, camaraderie, and the spirit of fair play along with militarism, masculinity, and muscular Christianity.[65] By contrast, Alpine skiing and many other sports that blossomed in the twentieth century were defined by "aestheticization, eroticization, and the celebration of the body," a shift that paralleled trends in art.[66] Alpine modernism was as different from the nineteenth-century sporting ethic as the futurist aestheticization of speed was from nineteenth-century Romantic landscape paintings. The British middle classes may have invented modern sport in the nineteenth century, but continental Europeans, and skiers in particular, modernized sport by aestheticizing it. The subjective and individual nature of Alpine skiing also attuned it to the commercialist mass culture of the twentieth century.[67] As Alpine skiing became more popular and more focused on a celebration of speed, it transformed the practice of the sport and inspired dramatic changes in the Alpine landscape. Its rapid popularization and expansion after World War II demonstrates that Alpine modernism appealed not only to intellectually minded skiers but to skiers from a wide array of social backgrounds.

SIX

Modernity in Sport

AN ARCHAIC CONTEST

On the morning of January 30, 1924, thirty-three racers representing eleven different countries assembled at the Olympic Stadium in Chamonix, in the shadow of Mont Blanc, to take part in the first-ever Olympic ski race. Surrounded by a small but enthusiastic crowd at the Olympic stadium, the racers took to the course at one-minute intervals beginning at 8:37 A.M. The 50-kilometer (31.1-mile) course began in the Olympic Stadium in central Chamonix and traced a circuit through small villages such as Argentière and Les Praz before returning to the stadium. The racers climbed nearly 2,700 feet to the highest point of the course at Charamillon. A thirty-one-year-old Norwegian, Thorleif Haug, won the gold medal, with Norwegian competitors also taking silver and bronze.[1]

The skiing events at Chamonix had the trappings of modernity, with meticulous timekeeping measures, a series of fourteen control stations connected by a telephone line laid by the French army, and rules defined and enforced by the International Olympic Committee (IOC). The format and structure of the races, however, made them seem outdated in an era of mass sporting spectacles. Despite the rapidly growing popularity of Alpine-style skiing, competitive skiing remained under the firm control of Norway and Sweden until the early 1930s. As a result, the racers at Chamonix competed only in established Nordic events—the 18-kilometer race, the 50-kilometer race, and ski jumping—which had little relation to the contemporary practice of skiing in the Alps and did not fulfill modern spectators' tastes for speed and excitement. The long, relatively flat courses gave most spectators only two chances to view the action: when skiers began the race and when they crossed the finish line. Given that Haug, the fastest skier in the world, completed the 50-kilometer course in three hours, forty-four minutes, and thirty-two seconds, spectators had to divert themselves in the interim with a three-hour brunch indoors.

The increasing popularity of sport beginning in the late nineteenth century depended not only on rising middle-class incomes and status or the growing appreciation of physical activity and competition but also on the rise of spectatorship. Modernist values were most effectively vernacularized through mass-cultural spectacles—and not avant-garde art—because sporting competitions allowed even nonathletes to partake of the action, whether in person or through the media.[2] The combination of speed and nature appreciation in Alpine skiing proved as addictive to spectators as it did to practitioners. The short, steep courses of Alpine races allowed spectators a good view of the event and a chance to delight at the skiers' speed. The skiing events at Chamonix, by contrast, revealed that competitive Nordic skiing held limited appeal to onlookers who were not already devotees of the sport. Similarly, the goals of the two forms of competition varied. The Nordic skiing tradition tested endurance more than skill or technique, and in the era of the airplane and the automobile, the relative lack of speed and obvious danger made Nordic skiing less viscerally appealing to most spectators than the Alpine variety.

If Alpine modernism was the message, competitive modern sport was the medium. Just as skiing in the Alps demanded a reassessment of Nordic practices and motivations, it also demanded an alternative to sober Nordic races to better accord with the goals of skiers and the desires of spectators. The popularization of Alpine skiing as a competitive spectator sport brought the sport millions of new converts and implanted it firmly in European mass culture as spectators attended races, viewed newsreels, and read coverage of the sport in the press. For many skiers, however, this growth came at the expense of skiing's innate charms. In the early twentieth century, Alpine modernism offered a fusion of Romantic and modernist elements. The immense appeal of this aesthetic paradoxically catalyzed a process that undermined its countermodern worldview by introducing the modern sporting values of bureaucracy, rationality, and quantification.[3] The increasing bureaucratization and standardization of skiing for the sake of competition removed much of the local and regional flavor of the sport, remaking previously mystical mountains as generic sporting landscapes engineered to suit the modern lust for speed. Competitive skiing was a devil's bargain: it made the sport more popular and yet, in the minds of many, less meaningful.

Looking back on the formative years of competitive Alpine skiing in the 1920s and 1930s, Arnold Lunn noted with characteristic mischief that "it was the British who first had the eccentric idea that the best way to test downhill skiing was to race downhill."[4] With the benefit of hindsight in the early 1970s, Lunn's good friend and the founder of the Swiss Academic Ski Club, Walter Amstutz, highlighted the revolutionary quality of Lunn's contribution to the development of skiing: "When Newton's apple happened to fall on Sir Arnold Lunn's head, 'gravity ski racing,' as it is commonly practiced today, was born." Those who practiced the sport in what Amstutz designated the "gravity countries" of the Alps quickly improved their technique and differentiated themselves from their Nordic counterparts.[5] The comparison with Isaac Newton, of course, had also been applied to another Alpine skiing pioneer, Mathias Zdarsky (see chapter 3).

This comparison has a number of intriguing implications. Like Newton's elaboration of the mechanical laws, Lunn's "discovery" of competitive Alpine skiing was an innovative reconception of the physical world. Lunn's innovations appear similarly self-evident in hindsight, but established authorities, many of whom considered Lunn to be the leader of a band of heretics, greeted them with deep skepticism. The ski laws developed by Lunn and his Alpine coterie forever altered the practice of skiing, as well as the Alpine landscape, just as Newton's laws of motion revolutionized perception and produced significant material change. The rift between Alpine skiers and Nordic skiers became a full-fledged chasm in the 1920s and 1930s, and the international skiing community came to be defined by a certain geographical determinism. By the early 1930s, Nordic and Alpine enthusiasts agreed that their preferred forms of skiing had evolved to suit differing landscapes. The two sides reached a cautious truce as they realized that their goals, methods, and landscapes were largely incompatible, and in response, the international skiing community became increasingly bifurcated.

Since the beginning of the twentieth century, skiers throughout Central Europe had endeavored to create a form of competition that reflected Alpine modernism. The earliest competitions involved climbing to the top of steep slopes before racing down. Arnold Lunn described this form of competition as a "bastard of a race [that] tested neither Langlauf [Nordic] technique nor Downhill skiing, for it was impossible for a good Downhill racer to make up the time lost on the ascent against a tough skier with lungs and legs of iron."[6]

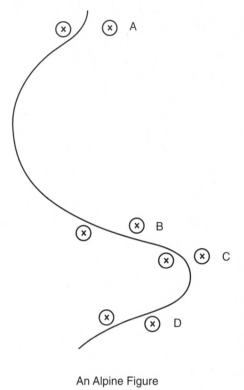

An Alpine Figure

FIGURE 16. Arnold Lunn's slalom. Diagram after an undated illustration prepared for *British Ski Year Book*. Arnold Lunn Papers, GTMGamms143, Georgetown University Library Special Collections, Washington, DC. Image prepared by Scott Warren, Arizona State University.

Whereas Nordic skiing was a slow-burn discipline that favored endurance and an economy of energy allocated over the course of many hours, Alpine skiing, in true modernist form, was marked by virtuosic technique and a short burst of controlled, violent energy.

Around 1910, Lunn set about developing a new form of competition that would test and encourage the development of Alpine technique, which he named the slalom (figure 16). He adopted this term from the Norwegian *slalåm* (which, ironically, described a relatively undemanding slope). Skiers were required to turn around flags placed at irregular intervals to demonstrate their prowess in making turns of varying sharpness and speed.[7] Concurrently, Lunn and others developed a parallel variety of Alpine competition known simply as the "downhill," which reduced the number of flags placed on the course to allow for greater speeds.

These embryonic forms of competitive Alpine skiing accorded much better with modern aesthetic tastes than imported Nordic practices did. In 1909, Pierre de Coubertin's journal *Revue Olympique* defined the Olympic movement's modernist kinaesthetic of sport, which closely paralleled Alpine modernism. The unnamed author (likely Coubertin himself) described modern sport as consisting of rhythm and speed, the tension of which produced "sporting satisfaction." The sensation of rhythm, argued the author, comprised "the strongest and healthiest of sporting joys," but this sensation could be "obliterated" if speed and rhythm were out of balance. Although pure speed could be viscerally stimulating, it was "much less sound, much less refined, and less perfect" than a speed checked by rhythmic movements. Excessive speed was "very monotonous," and the beneficent effects of rhythm could not be realized "without moderated speed."[8] Lunn's slalom, which forced racers to control their speed and develop a rhythm of broad, sweeping movements, accorded with the many manifestations of this modern kinaesthetic.[9] Although a straight downhill schuss was exciting for the skier, it was not particularly aesthetically pleasing to the spectator or a good test of competitors' technique.[10] The synthesis of rhythm and speed in the slalom added to the allure of a sport that already reflected the "hectic pace, the agitation, and the 'nervousness' of modern life."[11]

As Alpine competitions grew in number after World War I, a new manifestation of the Alpine-Nordic dispute developed. Whereas the fin-de-siècle conflict had divided Central European skiers, the new dispute pitted Alpine skiers hailing from Central Europe against Scandinavian Nordic enthusiasts. In the wake of the disappointing skiing competitions at Chamonix, Arnold Lunn and his allies began to push the IOC and the newly constituted Fédération Internationale de Ski (FIS) to adopt Alpine skiing in international competitions. As chairman of the Technical Committee of the Ski Club of Great Britain, Lunn wrote to the Swiss secretary general of the IOC, Albert Berdez, in 1926: "The Ski Club of Great Britain is anxious that the races at the next Winter Olympic Games should not be confined to long distance races, as a long distance race is an overwhelming and an unfair advantage for those teams who can devote the entire winter to training among the mountains. . . . There appears to be no logical reason for excluding a Downhill Race, which, unlike the Long Distance Race, is primarily a test of technique rather than of physical strength and endurance."[12] It was certainly apparent that the current form of competition favored Scandinavian skiers: the eight Scandinavians in the 50-kilometer race at Chamonix took the top eight places, followed by an Italian skier who finished twenty-six minutes off the winning pace.[13] Lunn suggested that an Alpine competition would offer a test of skiing technique rather than general fitness.

Lunn, who had been a proud "Norwegian" during the Zdarsky-Paulcke debate, now argued that "the immense prestige of Norwegian skiing had an effect analogous to the immense prestige of Aristotle in the Middle Ages," choking off all debate and innovation.[14] The resulting schism pitted a vision of skiing rooted in centuries of tradition against one that stressed its dynamic modernity. Moreover, each school resented the other for attempting to enforce the practice of a form of skiing unsuited to their local landscape and sporting ideals.

Lunn's proposal unsurprisingly met great resistance from the Scandinavians, who considered themselves to be the guardians of a sacred legacy that extended beyond mere sporting competitions. Much of the Alpine-Nordic friction in the 1920s and 1930s arose from attempts by Scandinavian skiers to check the ambitions of "faddish" Alpine skiers and reassert control over what they regarded as their patrimony. The annual Holmenkollen winter games staged in Oslo beginning in 1892 (with origins dating back decades earlier) were as much a patriotic celebration as a sporting competition, and many Norwegians refused to condescend to the Alpine dilettantes who claimed to have developed a new and improved form of their national heritage. A prominent Norwegian opponent of Alpine skiing and of foreign influence in Norway's national sport in general argued that it would be disastrous for Norwegians to "subordinate" themselves: "We must not forget that skiing emanated from here and that we understand these things better than foreigners." It was unthinkable that the Norwegians would allow themselves to be "dictated to by Central Europe."[15]

Other Scandinavians offered more measured responses to Alpine skiing, although they, too, failed to grasp its appeal. Writing to Arnold Lunn in 1927, the Swedish secretary of the FIS, Carl Hamilton, argued that the Alpine-Nordic division was a matter of demographics: "Why downhill races are of so little interest for us in Sweden is, that they can only be arranged in the least or not-at-all inhabited parts of the country, which would be too expensive and which hardly would meet with any appreciation."[16] Like Lunn and Coubertin, Hamilton implicitly recognized that sporting competitions had to challenge competitors while also attracting spectators, and the geography of Scandinavia shaped the preferences of both.

By the mid-1920s, the antagonists in the dispute agreed that different landscapes produced different sporting practices. In 1930, the Swedish president of the FIS, Colonel Ivar Holmquist, disputed the notion that there was an irreconcilable division between Alpine and Nordic skiers. He argued that the sport was always fundamentally the same but varied slightly according to the terrain. Still, Holmquist believed that "downhill races do not interest the Scandinavians," who preferred races that, in the words of the Norwegian FIS vice president Nicolai Östgaard, "develop vigor, tenacity, abnegation, and force of character." Holmquist conceded that downhill events such as the slalom were "magnificent," but in the end, he dismissed them as a mere "specialty."[17] Nordic skiers adhered to a traditional vision of the sport that involved not only descents but also climbs and traverses. Theirs was as much a fight against the specialization of functions that attended modern sport and society as it was a doctrinal debate with Alpine skiers.

In the 1920s and early 1930s, Alpine skiers began to push for a formal division between the two schools in competitions. In 1926, the Ski Club of Great Britain, in an effort spearheaded by Arnold Lunn, published a pamphlet of Alpine racing rules that also defended Alpine skiing as a competitive sport on topographical grounds: "The *Langlauf* [the long-distance Nordic race] developed logically from the type of country around Oslo: small undulating hills which naturally lend themselves to short spurts of uphill racing; but we do not understand why this type of race, indigenous to Norway, should be the only form of race which receives international sanction. Alpine skiing is essentially a matter of long, unbroken descents, and it is absurd to exclude from International Meetings held in the Alps a form of race which is eminently suited to Alpine ground."[18] The authors quoted disparagingly from an instructional pamphlet published by the Norwegian Ski Association that devoted only one short passage to the downhill, simply advising that "when going downhill one should regain breath and rest as much as possible. Avoid falling as it both fatigues and lowers the spirits."[19] To Alpine skiers, who considered downhill runs to be "the Alpha and Omega" of skiing and not a mere interlude for rest, the contrast between each region's competitive skiing ethos could not have been more stark.[20]

Lunn and other British and Swiss Alpine enthusiasts took the first step in rebelling against the Scandinavian-dominated FIS when they founded the Kandahar Ski Club in Mürren, Switzerland, in January 1924, while the first Winter Olympics were taking place across the border in Chamonix. This club, which was unaffiliated with either the Swiss or British national ski clubs but nevertheless included many prominent members of both, lobbied both the national ski clubs and the FIS to include Alpine events on the international competition program. Lunn made an important ally in the Austrian skier Hannes Schneider, who was an international skiing celebrity even before he costarred in *Der weiße Rausch*. In March 1928, after the IOC and FIS once again failed to include any Alpine skiing events at that year's Winter Olympic Games in St. Moritz, Lunn and Schneider staged an Alpine race known as the Arlberg-Kandahar.[21] This immediately became the premier international Alpine skiing event and created a visible split in the culture of skiing.

The FIS recognized that it could either continue to ignore Alpine skiing and see itself marginalized, or it could welcome Alpine skiers into the fold and reap the benefits of the sport's popularity. At the FIS Congress in St. Moritz in 1928, delegates first recommended the inclusion of Alpine disciplines in competitions, but the conservative FIS was not yet ready to concede. Instead, the federation agreed to allow Alpine races to be staged as exhibition events at the 1929 FIS championships in Zakopane, Poland. The growing success of the Arlberg-Kandahar, which in 1929 nearly tripled its number of competitors from 45 to 130, left many Alpine skiers frustrated with the intransigence of the FIS.[22] In 1929, Walter Amstutz argued that if the FIS was truly international in character, then it must end the dictatorship of the Nordic members and hold the needs of its Central European members in equal regard. If it refused to do so, Alpine skiers were prepared to organize to represent their own interests. While conveying respect for their Nordic cousins, they argued: "We do not wish to strap a fetter [*Hemmschuh*] on the development of skiing out of mere piety and will not allow ourselves to be dictated to by a group that today no longer possesses a majority and that also no longer unconditionally possesses the leading role."[23]

In asserting their independence from the often-patronizing authority of Nordic skiers, Alpine skiers claimed to represent the future of the sport. A 1929 British editorial cautioned that the Norwegians were "in danger of isolating themselves" if they continued to impede the international recognition of Alpine skiing: "The Norwegian dictatorship must cease. There is no longer any reason to justify the omnipotence of the Northerners in international skiing. The South can today contribute quite as much as the North to the further development of skiing on an international basis."[24]

Many Nordic skiers first saw Alpine skiers in action in the late 1920s and 1930s, demystifying what many had assumed to be an incomplete and frivolous interpretation of their beloved national sport. In winter 1930–31, Arnold Lunn invited a prominent Norwegian skiing advocate, Captain Christian Krefting, to Mürren. After skiing with Lunn, Krefting observed, "the name 'downhill racing' . . . gives an average Norwegian a very faulty conception of what happens. This is natural as we conceive of hills as hills and not practically vertical drops. . . . To get down in our usual Norwegian way was quite out of the question—that would be tempting Providence too much."[25]

As Alpine skiers became more intransigent and their numbers swelled, both camps acknowledged that Alpine skiing and Nordic skiing were fundamentally different and that the interests of both would be best served by allowing for separate competitions. The FIS sanctioned the first Alpine skiing championships for men and women in 1931, and the Alpine events were added to the Olympic program at the 1936 Winter Games in Garmisch-Partenkirchen.

In 1937, Nicolai Östgaard described the division within skiing as a separation between the "classical" and the "Alpine" forms of the sport.[26] Implicit in this dichotomy is a division between the classical and the modern. In the debates over the inclusion of the Alpine disciplines in international competition, the association of the Alps with modernity was a constant subtext. For Alpine skiers, the virtue of Alpine skiing lay in the modern balance of rhythm and speed, whereas their Scandinavian antagonists, for whom skiing was a long-established marker of identity and tradition, proved deeply suspicious of the same modernity.

Spectators voted with their feet and flocked to Alpine skiing competitions. The 1936 Winter Olympic Games, staged by the Nazi regime in Garmisch-Partenkirchen, illustrated the rise of Alpine skiing as a mass cultural event. The downhill race drew 8,813 spectators; the slalom race attracted 15,895, exceeding the stadium capacity by 70 percent. The event was so popular that spectators spread out into the hills and climbed trees to get a better view.[27] A French reporter marveled at the massive, raucous crowd swarming at the edges of the piste, their anxious excitement palpable as they viewed the precipitous angle of what he termed the "infernal course." (figure 17) As the athletes hurtled down the slope, the crowd roared in approval. The slopes were lined with representatives of the emerging mass society. Judges and timekeepers observed the competition; mass-media journalists, photographers, radio reporters, and camera operators recorded and broadcast the events worldwide; sausage vendors, cigarette sellers, and paperboys attended to the needs of the mass of spectators. As the competitors approached, the crowd heaved forward, pressing postcards and photographs into their hands in the hope of an autograph. The spectacle of skiing truly made it the "King-sport of the Winter Games."[28]

The universalizing and internationalizing trends in Alpine skiing gained impetus from similar currents in mass culture, allowing the sport to appeal

FIGURE 17. Finish area of the men's downhill race, Fourth Winter Olympics, Garmisch-Partenkirchen, Germany, 1936. International Olympic Committee, Lausanne.

to practitioners and spectators alike. In contrast, its claims to modernity and novelty offended Scandinavians who adhered to the traditionalist, Romantic practice of *Skiidrett.*

SPEED AND SPECIALIZATION

Citius, altius, fortius (Faster, higher, stronger) was not only the motto of the Olympic movement but also the manifesto of modern sport. This doctrine pushed Alpine skiers—and particularly competitive racers—to strive toward ever-greater achievements.[29] Like industrial culture, modern sport valued quantification, speed, and performance. These animating principles came to exert increasing influence over the popular practice of skiing, leading to the development of increasingly specialized skills.

The young Swiss skier Walter Amstutz helped push the sport into a new era in the late 1920s. Obsessed with determining exactly how fast an Alpine skier traveled, Amstutz conducted clumsy speed trials at Mürren, Switzerland, timing himself with a stopwatch in his pocket and later having his good friend Arnold Lunn serve as a more reliable timekeeper. After some abortive attempts, Amstutz acknowledged a number of deficiencies in his experiment: stopwatch timing was notoriously inaccurate, and the chosen slope on the Allmendhubel was too short and too gentle to allow for great speed. "In short," he wrote at the end of his life, "I did not dispose of the means or the support I needed to tackle the problem in a professional manner."[30]

In 1929, however, after taking up the position of spa director in St. Moritz, Amstutz had the technical and environmental resources at his disposal to carry out his experiments. He decided to broaden his investigation to determine the fastest Alpine skier in the world, a quest that would appeal to the modern taste for spectacle and garner publicity for the town. In 1930, with the sponsorship of the Swiss Academic Ski Club and the local Ski Club Alpina St. Moritz, he established a speed-skiing competition known as the *Kilometer-lancé* (translated into English by the race organizers as the "Flying Mile").

The organizers corrected many of the deficiencies Amstutz had identified in his earlier attempts to measure his own speed. All the skiers traversed an identical segment of the Corviglia slope on uniform, hard-packed snow. Under the direction of a local scientist, Professor Richard Straumann, who specialized in aerodynamics and the developing field of chronometry, the race organizers marked off a 150-meter course (all subsequent courses in the yearly competition were 100 meters long) and tested the racers sequentially in order to obtain consistent data. The Austrian Gustav Lantschner (who played a supporting role in *Der weiße Rausch*) won the contest with a speed of 105.7 kilometers per hour (65.7 miles per hour).[31]

The St. Moritz Tourism Board staged the *Kilometer-lancé* annually from 1930 to 1938. At the 1932 competition, another Austrian racer, the twenty-year-old Leo Gasperl, obliterated Lantschner's record, reaching a top speed of 136.3 kilometers per hour (84.7 miles per hour). His feat created a sensation. Many commentators saw in his achievement the validation of human potential in an industrial age, echoing the heroic ideology of Alpine modernism. Luis Trenker observed that Gasperl was "simply a bold man on two slats" who, "without a motor," had reached speeds previously achieved only with advanced technology.[32] In photographs, the competitors at St. Moritz resemble ace pilots and race-car drivers with their protective helmets and goggles. Many skiers, including Gasperl, used fin-like prosthetic attachments to improve aerodynamics, giving them the appearance of alien beings or scientific test subjects. Their technique also departed dramatically from that of common skiers: Gasperl clutched straps attached to the skis to hold his body in a tightly tucked

FIGURE 18. Austrian Leo Gasperl at the *Kilometer-lancé* speed skiing competition, 1933.

aerodynamic position while he streaked downhill (figure 18). Because such a posture left skiers vulnerable to falling if they encountered any bumps or changes in snow consistency, course organizers tended to the piste by packing down the snow and clearing the terrain of rocks, roots, and divots.

By the end of the decade, speed skiers abandoned the St. Moritz competition because of the limitations of the terrain. Straumann estimated that even in ideal conditions, skiers would not be able to exceed one hundred miles per hour at St. Moritz because the course was too short and not steep enough: indeed, Gasperl's 1932 record held through the Second World War. After the war, speed records climbed steadily as scientists worked with skiers to perfect equipment and technique and to engineer the landscape and snow. The current records for speed skiing were set at Les Arcs, France, in 2006; Simone Origone of Italy holds the men's record at 251.4 kilometers per hour (156.2 miles per hour) and Sanna Tidstrand of Sweden holds the women's record at 242.6 kilometers per hour (150.7 miles per hour).[33]

To place these figures in perspective, Walter Amstutz observed that "a free-falling body under normal atmospheric conditions near sea level," falling in a nonaerodynamic, spreadeagle position, attains a speed of 192 kilometers per hour (119.3 miles per hour).[34] When the Italian skier Pino Meynet set a new world record at 194.4 kilometers per hour (120.8 miles per hour) at Cervinia in

1975, he skied faster than a free-falling human. By the 1930s, speed skiers were distancing themselves from the common practice of the sport, engaging in a highly specialized activity that depended on cutting-edge scientific innovations to produce infinitesimal improvements in performance. These innovations took shape not on Alpine slopes but in controlled wind tunnels; increasingly, the skiers themselves were little more than test subjects manipulated by scientists. In the late 1980s, Amstutz described the appeal of this quasi-sport to the skier:

> Traveling at high speed is something intoxicating that holds a magic spell over man, whether it is performed by him or by beast, or whether it is attained by muscular or mechanical power or by the force of gravity. It is a test of courage and prowess, and it may be that on such occasions the racer will also meet his alter ego. In any case it is a prerequisite for him that the speed of his mind is a match for the speed of his body, as alertness is required in order to hold a straight course, which is a tricky concern at maximum velocity. For, once he has passed the 185 kph [115 miles per hour] speed mark, he so to speak takes to the air, i.e. his skis partly lose contact with the piste and float on a thin cushion of air, which has been wedged in between his skis and the race track.[35]

By the early 1970s, then, speed skiers not only attained velocities on par with modern machinery, but they were quite literally flying, translating the rhetorical flourishes of Alpine modernism into reality.

Although speed skiing became a fringe activity, it represents the zenith of the Alpine modernist obsession with speed and the influence of trends in modern sport on Alpine skiers. Because modern sports are united by "an empirical, experimental, mathematical worldview," as Allen Guttman has observed, the roles and functions of athletes became progressively specialized, as did the goals and nature of competition.[36] The fetishization of speed in the *Kilometer-lancé* demonstrates how the quest for records led to increasingly narrow specialization. Yet in the 1920s and 1930s, thanks to the mutually constitutive development of Alpine modernism among leisure skiers and the increasing visibility of skiing as a competitive modern sport, speed skiing represented the essence of Alpine skiing.

FROM AESTHETICS TO TECHNICS

Practices and techniques from competitive skiing increasingly pervaded leisure skiing. Inspired by the feats described and pictured in the mass media, recreational skiers sought to emulate the technique of elite athletes. Skiing competitions proliferated at all skill levels, particularly in the postwar era. In the early 1950s, there were approximately 1,900 competitions annually in West Germany alone. Alongside approximately a dozen large events, such as the German national championships and international events, there were nearly 400 events organized by district, region, or skiing association, and another 1,500 small events staged by towns or local clubs.[37] As competitive Alpine skiing became popular, the border between leisure skiing and competitive sport blurred.

As all skiers endeavored to emulate the most accomplished racers, technique became highly standardized. Skiers who had once celebrated the way that skiing called upon mystical, organic instincts now generally agreed that these instincts had to be actively trained and paired with a rigorously tested technique. The natural and transcendent associations of early Alpine modernism shifted to assimilate the rational values of modern sport: every action had to have a purpose. At the 1936 Winter Olympics in Garmisch-Partenkirchen, the electronic equipment that timed Alpine races was accurate to one-fifth of a second.[38] As Alpine skiers increasingly obsessed over these fractions of time, subjective, aesthetic appreciations of skiing began to be displaced by a more objective, scientific practice.

Improvements in performance increasingly required the skier's use of the most modern, finely tuned equipment. Édouard Frendo, who taught elite French skiers after World War II, argued that superior skiing depended on three factors: technique, audacity, and equipment. Whereas the first two requirements were well established, Frendo's intense focus on equipment was novel. He believed that "the requirements of this new technique are such that, without perfectly adapted equipment, skiers who wish to master it risk wasting their time in sterile efforts and in undisciplined trials."[39] In the early 1930s, ski manufacturers had begun to respond to the demand for dependable racing skis by offering skis with metal components.[40] Wooden skis were prone to splitting, rendering them unreliable in high-speed turns.[41] After World War II, the popularity of skiing and the high demand for innovation allowed manufacturers to attract accomplished engineers in Europe and beyond. Particularly notable was the use of plastics to make skis simultaneously stronger and more flexible, an innovation that was introduced by the American aeronautical engineer Howard Head, whose 1946 ski model revolutionized both competitive and leisure skiing.

Skiing techniques and instructional methods, too, became more rationalized and technocratic. Édouard Frendo noted that the postwar French success in Alpine skiing depended not on skiers' inherent talents but instead on turning the mountain slopes into a "laboratory" for the perfection of skiing technique. He freely admitted that he was not himself a skiing champion but rather a "technician" who optimized his students' performances.[42] In the 1930s and early 1940s the Third Republic and the Vichy government both supported Frendo's initiatives to establish a nationally funded and operated school for skiers (the École Supérieure de Ski) and another for instructors (the École Centrale de Formation de Moniteurs). These investments bore fruit: the French dominated postwar international competitions, along with the Austrians, who had also invested heavily in rationalizing instruction and technique. The Swiss skier Philippe Baehni opined that "without a shadow of a doubt, the Austrians are not better skiers than their adversaries, but their training is better conceived, allowing them to win tenths of a second here and there." The Austrians trained rationally, repeatedly practicing specific turns and movements to gain a slim advantage. Baehni summarized the outlook of the era when he wrote that "sport has become a science" that required insights from doctors and psychologists as well as highly trained ski instructors. As a result, even an individual sport such as skiing became a team activity. In this technocratic age of modern sport, he wrote, "It is truly rare that an athlete achieves an exceptional performance solely by his own wherewithal."[43]

Thus skiing became not a matter of instinct and innate talent but a mechanical problem to be solved. The Swiss ski pedagogue Josef Dahinden wrote in 1935 that "skiing is a science; unlike walking, it is not an unconscious instinct. . . . We require mechanics; this [mechanics] is and remains the basis, the great law, around which all else is grouped." The autodidactic skiing genius celebrated by early Alpine modernists was extinct; as Dahinden himself wrote, "No master falls from heaven."[44] Any such master would in any case still require intensive training to attain international standing. Skiing expertise had to be informed by scientific precision, and the best racers mastered an "energy economy" by eliminating all extraneous movements that wasted precious time and energy.[45]

This new kinaesthetic of Alpine skiing mirrored the pragmatic ethos of sport and modernity. The sociologist of sport Henning Eichberg has observed that in order to improve performance, the modern athlete "moves in a straight line in a universe of right angles." Any extraneous movement is counterproductive, ornamental, and wasteful, "the expression of primitive premodernity, or even a crime against modernity."[46] To maximize speed, Frendo created a technique that abandoned the "stem" turn favored by skiers in the decades before World War II, in which the tips of the skis form a V shape. He replaced it with the parallel turn, a style that minimized friction and was "the only turn that could be executed at great speed." He described this innovation as reflective of the peculiarly French "taste for clarity in the simplicity and the elegance of movement."[47] In a postwar update to his original musings on ski technique, Josef Dahinden promoted a technique that he described as a "natural commodity." By focusing on elasticity and movements that began in the body's center of gravity in the hips and moved out to the shoulders, arms, and legs in responsive countermovements, Dahinden elaborated a "natural" kinaesthetic in line with Alpine modernism.[48]

Like early Alpine modernists, Dahinden and other ski instructors and pedagogues from the 1930s to the 1950s stressed fluidity, rhythm, and holism. The new experts were not, however, concerned with rehabilitating modern individuals by altering their physical movements. Instead they focused on improving performance, drilling and practicing turns until time-saving gestures became instinctive.[49] The sport that had once offered the promise of managing the stresses of modern life now incorporated the Taylorist productivism of modern society. The competitive mindset came to dominate the practice of leisure skiing, making movement a means to an end.

The methodical pursuit of rationality and constantly improving performances led to excesses that provoked criticism. In January 1938, an FIS-sanctioned international event in Garmisch-Partenkirchen ended in tragedy when an Italian racer, Giacinto Sertorelli, lost control on the icy course and slammed into a tree, dying on impact. Sertorelli, a pupil of the Austrian speed skier Leo Gasperl, had won silver medals in the downhill event at the 1936 and 1937 FIS World Championships. Nor was Sertorelli the only victim that day: another Italian skier was paralyzed below the waist, the four-time Austrian world champion, Anton Seelos, dislocated his shoulder, and the German national champion, Rudolf Cranz, broke his leg. A French skiing journal published an editorial lamenting that this "most noble of human games" had descended to the realm of "brutal sport" because of decadent "excess" in the racing world. "Skiing has lost all its beauty and all its nobility," it declared, because international sporting circles viewed the competitive skier as little more than a "ski jockey" who existed solely to generate profits for the tourism industry and to bring glory to managers and trainers.[50] Skiers, managers, and race organizers were all complicit in the carnage on the slopes of Garmisch-Partenkirchen because of their quest for records, glory, and profit. As a result of incidents like these, the Alpine modernist celebration of salutary speed faded away.

For many skiers, the lust for records transformed the sport from a liberating and relaxing pastime into a constraining and alienating practice. Arnold Lunn, echoing Oswald Spengler's declensionist model of history, lamented: "Downhill racing is approaching the final phase of the culture cycle, through which every great culture is doomed to pass, the creative spring-time, the summer of perfected achievement, the autumn still glorious with deciduous coloring, and the winter in which the frosts of scientific technique destroy the last flowering of inspiration."[51] Lunn encapsulated the sentiments of many Alpine skiing pioneers, who were at first overjoyed at the popularization and international recognition of the sport but quickly became unnerved by its trajectory. Inevitably, Lunn argued, due to the competitive instinct, all sports were doomed to engage in a cycle that "ends in joyless over-specialization."[52] Alpine skiers were no longer the plucky upstarts who had challenged the stale orthodoxy of their Nordic cousins and presented a countermodern vision of life. Instead, Alpine modernism came to reflect the rationality and obsession with order that its first practitioners had rejected.

Skiing also began to lose its reputation as a therapeutic, restorative activity. Critics echoed the French hygienist Philippe Tissié's 1919 opinion about sport: "The athlete is a sick person."[53] The sporting mindset appeared detrimental to character development and personal happiness, and many agreed that "poorly understood sport does more harm than good" by leaving athletes exhausted and dedicated to the hypertrophic development of a highly specialized skill. Sport correctly practiced, the Swiss physician Rudolf Campell averred, fostered "relaxation, versatility, and harmony," the core tenets of Alpine modernism.[54] Incorrectly practiced, it became a career. These dangers were reflected in the views of Stefan von Dévan, who argued that "skiing demands the entire being," and therefore skiers must submit to "regular, systematic training" year-round. Optimum performance depended on committed attention to nutrition, sleep, and even "the strictest self-mastery in sexual life," and skiers should avoid other sports because they needed time to rest their bodies and recover their nerves.[55]

These concerns reached their ironic climax in the run-up to the 1968 Winter Olympics in Grenoble, when the French trainer of the British Alpine team introduced his charges to yoga and meditation. The British press described the novel training methods as "a rather elaborate back-to-nature mechanism. Alpine ski racers are now as stressed and strained as industrialists and senior civil servants, and further success obviously requires some kind of psychological antidote."[56] A sport that had once helped individuals cope with shattered nerves now exhausted its competitive practitioners physically, mentally, and emotionally.

SEEING THE ALPS THROUGH SPORT

Changes in the practice and motivations of Alpine skiing also began to affect the relationship between noncompetitive skiers and the mountain environment. In 1940, the German ski-touring enthusiast Heinz Dramsch asserted that the "devil" of records endangered the sport. Writing of his beloved peak Marmolada, in Italy's South Tirol, Dramsch observed that its slopes, which took a capable skier some four hours to climb without mechanical assistance, could now be descended in two to four minutes under ideal snow conditions. The obsession with speed led every skier to consider himself an "ace" and to comport himself like a racer. As a result, many a "harmless and staunch ski tourist and enemy of all sporting quests for records has allowed himself to be trapped by the Moloch speed." Dramsch acknowledged the seductiveness of speed: "He almost caught me, the demon of speed, the Moloch of all nature appreciation, the Satan who degrades men into muscle machines."[57] If speed was the distinctive drug of modernity, the average skier's relationship with the stimulant was shifting from recreational use toward dependency.[58]

Dramsch presented a contrasting vision of skiing. Whereas record seekers slavishly obeyed the stopwatch—"the demon speed squats inside and ticks and ticks"—Dramsch and his band of ski tourists went "as fast as we like," absorbing the beauty of nature at their leisure.[59] They practiced the sport as a means of relaxing and fostering a connection to nature. According to Dramsch and countless other skiers like him, the pulsing hordes of Alpine skiers pursued speed for speed's sake, lacking any more profound motivation. The lust for records, the intrusion of sporting practices, and the growth of tourism (Dramsch expresses his disdain for "the bronzed ones") all conspired to desecrate *his* majestic and meaningful Marmolada, making it little more than a sterile, placeless stage for speed—what John Bale has described as a "sportscape."[60] The skiers who crammed Marmolada's slopes could just as well have been skiing on any other mountain with steep descents and convenient transportation connections.

Nevertheless, Alpine skiing was not a sport that was once in tune with nature and later became alienated from it by speed and sport; its transformation reflects an ideology in flux. Skiing mediated the relationship between skiers and the Alps, with practices and perceptions shifting over time. Early Alpine modernism celebrated a flowing kinaesthetic and harmony with nature before shifting to emphasize speed and the conquest of natural forces. The growth of competitive skiing helped bring about this shift, and yet the rhythmic kinaesthetic remained important in competition, albeit in the instrumental form of efficient ski technique. As the complaints of Heinz Dramsch, Arnold Lunn, and others indicate, Alpine skiing remained a contested practice, marked by vibrant debate.

PART THREE

Landscapes of Leisure

SEVEN

Consuming Alpine Skiing

ELITE SPORT AND MASS CULTURE

The camera alights on a futuristic compound perched precariously atop the Schilthorn in the Swiss Alps. Inside, James Bond has been busy investigating a plot by the devious villain Blofeld to brainwash a group of beautiful women to sterilize the world's food supply. After uncovering the conspiracy, Bond, played by the British model George Lazenby in his only turn as the iconic secret agent, dons a form-fitting, powder-blue ski suit, slips on a hat and goggles, and steps into skis before slipping out the back door. As Bond skis away from the compound, Blofeld's henchmen catch sight of him and scramble a team in pursuit. The chase is on. Bond executes a wide array of impressive turns and jumps to avoid the machine-gun-wielding minions. The director uses skiing camera operators and rapid cuts to convey the speed of the chase and the danger facing our hero. After crashing to dodge a hail of gunfire, Bond continues down the hill on a single ski, executing a number of acrobatic maneuvers to outwit his pursuers, who crash into trees and careen over cliffs.

For today's filmgoing public, skiing in a Bond film is unremarkable; it is merely another indication, alongside his penchant for sports cars, supermodels, and gambling, that Bond is masculine, dangerous, skilled, and desirable. But when *On Her Majesty's Secret Service* appeared in theaters in 1969, James Bond's first appearance on skis reflected important changes in the practice and meaning of skiing.

Portrayals of skiing in popular culture in the early decades of the twentieth century emphasized its exoticism and elitism. When Mercedes proclaimed skiers and drivers as "master[s] over space and time" in 1925, they appealed to a coterie of elite consumers through the contemporary association of both skiing and driving with luxury and mastery. Similarly, a number of popular ski films from these decades, including Arnold Fanck's *Der weiße Rausch,* highlighted the curiosity and exoticism of this relatively new leisure activity. Fanck's film was a spectacle with little appreciable plot, echoing an earlier era of film that, as a "cinema of attractions," had much in common with circus shows and cabaret.[1] In contrast, the skiing scenes in *On Her Majesty's Secret Service* excite the viewer without evoking the same sense of the foreign and exotic that undergirds *Der weiße Rausch,* as the sport had become accessible to Europe's growing middle class. Skiing is simply a part of James Bond's cosmopolitan lifestyle, something for postwar Europeans to aspire to, in a film in which he also cavorts on Portuguese beaches and drives an Aston Martin.

In the middle of the twentieth century, a new paradox replaced the tensions between nature and speed, harmony and mastery in skiing. As the Bond film shows, the sport continued to symbolize luxury and cosmopolitanism—but it was luxury in a form accessible to millions. As had so often been the case in the development of Alpine modernism, these contradictions only bolstered the popularity of the sport. The act of skiing conveyed elite luxury, but it also became a marker of middle-class status. The burgeoning middle class not only took ski vacations but also consumed Hollywood films depicting skiers, viewed ski races on television, and purchased products endorsed by skiers.

Whereas the enjoyment of travel and tourism had once been secondary to the experience of speed and movement in Alpine modernism, they became central to its meaning in the second half of the twentieth century. The Alps remained a "modern space of experience," but the nature of that experience and its constituency changed as skiing was taken up by a broad swath of the middle class.[2]

The intersection of middle-class tourism and popular culture transformed Alpine modernism in three important ways. First, it became more broadly social, making skiing less a sign of individual virtue than a symbol of middle-class identity. Second, although skiers still rhapsodized speed and nature, the public imagination of the sport emphasized touristic consumption — flashy hotels, all-inclusive vacations, and celebrity-endorsed products — above all else. Third, changing skiing practices and patterns of consumption, in concert with the rising influence of competitive skiing, shifted the implications of Alpine modernism away from a countermodern reinvention of the world and instead turned it into a vector of modern mass culture as middle-class tourists sought out new experiences and exhibited their social status. If the interwar period laid the groundwork for the growth of Alpine skiing by popularizing the sport and by making it an object of consumption, the rapid expansion of the middle class and the economic boom of the 1950s brought the sport firmly into the realm of mass culture, exponentially increasing tourist visits to the Alps.

FROM AMATEURISM TO PROFESSIONALISM

When he became president of the International Olympic Committee (IOC) in 1952, the American Avery Brundage began a concerted project to rein in commercialism at the Olympics, and Alpine skiing drew his particular ire. Alpine skiing competitions drew huge crowds (including television viewers) and became the cornerstone of the Winter Olympics, but tension between the sport's rampant commercialization and the IOC's strict amateur statutes was increasing. Brundage, who had long expressed doubts about the legitimacy of Alpine skiing as an Olympic sport, made his position known preceding the Grenoble Winter Olympics of February 1968. He stated pointedly that Pierre de Coubertin, the founder of the modern Olympic movement, "did not dream that governments, instead of using sport for educational purposes, would make it their business to develop an elite class of athletes to promote tourism and the sports equipment and clothing business. Are we to sit idly by and see the Olympic Movement, the most important social force in the world today, swamped in a materialistic tide of commercialism and nationalism?"[3]

The line between competitive skiers and business interests had always been a fuzzy one, given the variety of equipment and clothing skiers required and the sport's relationship to the tourism industry. In the postwar period these connections multiplied at a rate that unsettled many sporting purists. Brundage was a particularly dogmatic believer in amateurism who believed that if the IOC did not police professionals, the Olympic Games would become little more than a commercial pageant, an affront to his belief that "the moral and spiritual values of fair play and good sportsmanship ... are essential for a better world." [4] Brundage's position reflected his generation's interpretation of sport as an avocation with ethical ambitions, a belief informed, whether consciously or subconsciously, by social prejudices against those who used their athletic prowess for personal gain. So vehemently did

Brundage oppose the participation of quasi-professionals in Alpine skiing that he advocated devious tactics to combat it. In 1952, he contacted the president of the Fédération Internationale de Ski (FIS), Marc Hodler, to ask for his assistance in rooting out professionalism in Alpine skiing. Brundage suggested that public examples be made in order to create a chilling effect:

> Skiing is suffering from the same difficulties that we had here in the United States with Track and Field Athletes, Swimmers, etc. twenty years ago. Every time one violation of the rules occurs and is not stopped it leads to a score of others. The manner in which we managed to prevent practices of this kind was by suspending two or three prominent athletes who were involved, some of them innocently. . . .
>
> In skiing there has been so much laxity and so much commercialization in the past that I am afraid drastic measures will be needed to stop these practices. The newspapers will not give you much publicity unless some prominent skier has been suspended. If you take this action in some of the aggravated cases it will be brought to the attention of the public and the skiing world, and if the statements that are released are carefully worded, I think most of your troubles will be over.[5]

The commercialization of Alpine skiing, the increased visibility offered by television, and the connections between the sport and the tourism industry came to a head in the case of the Austrian Alpine skier Toni Sailer, giving the IOC and the FIS a very public chance to "make an example" of Alpine skiing. The "Blitz from Kitz" (Sailer was a native of the Austrian town of Kitzbühel who first skied at age two) swept the gold medals in the Alpine events at Cortina d'Ampezzo, Italy in 1956. The Italian Zeno Colò, gold medalist in the downhill at the 1952 Winter Olympics in Oslo, described Sailer as the embodiment of the modern competitive skier: "His every movement is controlled, not by reason, but by lightning subconscious reflex. In the language that the skis talk through the feet, to the legs and body. It is a language unknown to most men and women, but it is the whisper Sailer understands best."[6] Coincidentally, the Cortina Games were the first televised Winter Olympics, and the telegenic Austrian positioned himself as a lucrative property. Crowds of admirers mobbed him as he finished his medal-winning run, hoping for an autograph or at least a brush with greatness. Here was "a 20-year-old Austrian who combines the muscles of a champion with the sensitivity of an artist and the glamour of a movie star."[7]

Sailer quickly parlayed his newfound celebrity into a variety of business ventures. He starred in two skiing-themed movies that attained wide inter-

FIGURE 19. A Polish-language poster advertises Toni Sailer's film *Der schwarze Blitz* (Black Lightning), 1958. Courtesy of the Beekley Family Foundation, Hartford, CT.

national distribution in 1958, *Ein Stück vom Himmel* (A Piece of Heaven) and *Der schwarze Blitz* (Black Lightning) (figure 19). A 1959 profile in an American skiing magazine described Sailer as "a public idol . . . a fashion model for a German skiwear firm . . . a Kitzbühel hotel owner and business-man." He supplemented these ventures with a singing career (he was particu-larly popular in Japan), a memoir, and advertisements for Italian textiles, German ski apparel, and Austrian fashion.[8] Sailer's activities quickly caught the attention of both the IOC and the FIS.[9] In Austria, Sailer was "bigger than James Dean." He defended himself against his critics, exclaiming, "I am a free man. . . . I can buy a business, *nicht?* . . . Why shouldn't an amateur skier make an investment? An investment makes money. And a skier has to have money or he can't ski!" The IOC and FIS were especially concerned by his ownership of a hotel in Kitzbühel. Sailer contended that a parcel of land had been given to him as a gift by the city of Kitzbühel and that the Austrian Ski Association had raised no protests when informed of the gift.[10]

The Sailer case exposed the tension between rules that were defined at the turn of the century, when competitive sport was largely an affair for established elites, and the growing commercial interest in Alpine skiing.[11] Sailer did not consider himself a professional athlete because he had not been paid to race; rather, he earned money as an ancillary benefit. The land he owned in Kitzbühel was a gift from his hometown, the film studio paid for his acting in his two films and not for his skiing, and he sold his image for clothing advertisements. In the end, the IOC and the FIS ruled that Sailer would not be allowed to ski in the 1960 Winter Olympic Games in Squaw Valley, California. He was forced into a lucrative retirement from international amateur racing in 1959, at the age of twenty-four.

Making an example of Sailer did not root out professionalism in skiing, however, because the distinction between amateurs and professionals was increasingly irrelevant. Elite Alpine skiers like Sailer could capitalize on their fame in ways that would have been unthinkable to proponents of amateurism at the turn of the century. Much of Brundage's frustration arose from his inability to adapt his strict definition of amateurism (he was a former amateur athlete who had competed at the 1912 Olympic Games in Stockholm) to the celebrity status of prominent athletes from the 1950s onward.

The 1968 Winter Olympic Games in Grenoble confirmed Brundage's worst fears. The commercialization of Alpine skiing had expanded from a handful of successful racers capitalizing on their celebrity to the pervasive commodification of the sport as a whole, and the administration of the IOC was unable to single out particular racers to blame. Because French law at the time did not allow the IOC to protect Olympic images and logos, French companies appropriated them to sell a wide range of products.[12] Feudor sold an Olympic-themed lighter, "the Olympic flame," Lafuma marketed luggage embossed with the Olympic rings, and Crédit Commercial de France became "the official bank of the tenth Olympic Games." Companies also used Olympic imagery to sell champagne, beer, and, cigarettes.[13] The state-run

FIGURE 20. French advertisement for Winter Olympics–themed cigarettes, 1968. Comité d'Organisation des Xèmes Jeux Olympiques d'Hiver, *Xèmes Jeux Olympiques d'Hiver/Xth Winter Olympic Games: Official Report* (Grenoble, 1969), 133.

tobacco monopoly, the Société d'Exploitation Industrielle des Tabacs et des Allumettes (SEITA), distributed half a million packs of commemorative cigarettes at home and abroad through state entities such as Air France, the French Tourism Board, and the Foreign Office.[14] The packaging featured Alpine skiing iconography in the form of skis, poles, and flags, and SEITA produced two distinct varieties to publicize the Winter Olympics: "Grenoble," which had an "American taste," and "Isère," with "French taste" (figure 20). Thus both public and private interests appropriated the prestige of the Olympics and the cultural meanings associated with winter sports for commercial purposes.

The advertising blitz surrounding the Grenoble Games constituted a concerted effort by French tourism interests to bolster receipts at Alpine resorts. A German journalist described the event as little more than "a mammoth advertisement for France's seriously ill tourism industry."[15] Alpine skiing was a particular target for advertisers because, in the words of the FIS president Marc Hodler, Alpine skiing "is executed by an overwhelming majority of the people taking interest in it . . . and [is] not just [watched] by spectators." This highly participatory sport required expensive travel, equipment, and accommodation, with the consequence that "business has taken great interest in skiing and in the skiers."[16] Brundage concurred that Alpine skiing posed a unique problem, writing to Hodler in 1950, "I am quite willing to recognize that there is a distinction between swimming, gymnastics and skiing as exercises and as competitive sports."[17]

By 1968, the commercialization of Alpine skiing had become a major irritant to the IOC and to Brundage in particular. Because Alpine skiing drove much of the winter tourism industry, it was in the interests of both individual skiers and the countries they represented to capitalize on victories in international competitions. In 1966, Brundage anticipated the challenge that Alpine skiing would pose in Grenoble two years later: "In Alpine countries . . . a large proportion of the national income from tourism and manufacturing comes through the sport of skiing, and the result is that Olympic champions are national heroes like the two French sisters after Innsbruck who were taken on a triumphal tour to meet the President and were loaded with presents and gifts. Anyone who seeks to enforce amateur regulations in these countries is an enemy of the state and is soon sidetracked."[18] The sisters in question, Christine and Marielle Goitschel, each won two medals at the 1964 Winter Olympics in Innsbruck and were welcomed in their hometown of Val d'Isère with a parade, a banquet, and a gift of forty-nine acres of land from the commune.[19]

This generosity was made possible by the income that skiing generated for Alpine communities. Karl Gamma, the director of the Swiss Association of Ski Schools (Schweizerische Skischulverband) argued that, given the secondary effects of sporting successes on tourism numbers, "a gold medal in skiing is of far greater use in Switzerland than a World Cup title in football."[20] Great skiers became associated not only with the brands of skis and bindings that they used but also with their hometowns and the mountains where they trained. French racing successes in the 1960s produced a wave of economic effects, allowing French manufacturers to monopolize the domestic equipment market while also increasing their international market share. Similarly,

French Alpine resorts cemented their popularity among domestic vacationers and began to appeal more directly to foreign tourists, including Swiss and Italian skiers across France's southeastern borders.[21]

A synergistic, triangular relationship thus developed among world-class skiers, equipment manufacturers, and tourism interests. All Alpine nations vied for influence in the lucrative winter-tourism and ski-equipment industries. For countries like Austria and Switzerland that depended on revenues from Alpine tourism, race victories on the international stage were more than a matter of prestige: they could have a profound effect on the country's economic well-being. These connections offended Brundage's amateur ethos, leading him in 1970 to condemn the commercialization of skiing as "a poisonous cancer" that "must be eliminated without further delay."[22] Brundage and the IOC kept thick files of advertisements and newspaper clippings that exemplified amateurism violations, and in 1971 Brundage circulated an internal report of some twenty-six pages listing the connections between Alpine skiers and advertisers.[23] Unsurprisingly, Switzerland (with 23 offending skiers), France (22), and Austria (16) registered the most violations, as these countries housed the best competitive skiers and were also the most prominent winter tourism destinations.[24] The connections between competitive skiers and the businesses and governments that benefited from the sport were legion but often difficult to disentangle, creating endless frustration for Brundage and the IOC.

Before Brundage stepped down from the IOC presidency in 1972, he campaigned unsuccessfully to remove Alpine skiing from the Olympic program because of the sport's commercial connections. Indeed, Brundage attempted to eliminate the Winter Olympics entirely on the grounds that they were not of "universal interest."[25] His futile struggle against Alpine skiing illustrates the sport's fundamental transformation from a loosely organized leisure pursuit to a highly integrated, multibillion-dollar industry.

ADVERTISING SKIING

In 1968, the French skier Jean-Claude Killy followed in the tracks laid down by Toni Sailer in the previous decade. Killy grew up in the French commune of Val d'Isère, a skiing mecca in which his father operated a hotel. At the 1968 Grenoble Olympics, Killy swept all three Alpine events, just as Sailer had, earning a rapturous response from his countrymen. Recognizing that he could make a much better living as a celebrity than he could toiling away as an amateur skier in the

World Cup series, Killy signed with the International Management Group, a premier sports management agency, in May 1968. Like Sailer, Killy effectively retired from amateur skiing at the age of twenty-four. He quickly signed a number of lucrative endorsement deals, and in 1969 the journalist Hunter S. Thompson followed the Frenchman, Chevrolet's general manager John Z. Delorean, and the recent Heisman Trophy winner O. J. Simpson on a Chevrolet advertising tour across the United States. Thompson marveled at Killy's "publicity juggernaut," writing that his "career reads as if his press agent had written the script for it—a series of spectacular personal victories, climaxed by the first triple-crown triumph in the history of skiing while the whole world watched on TV." Here was a handsome young pitchman for the television age.[26]

What made Killy a particularly useful celebrity endorser was the manner in which his image and achievements aligned with the aspirations of consumers. According to Thompson, the seemingly endless economic growth of the postwar decades "produced a sassy middle class with time on its hands." In an age when satellites beamed Winter Olympic coverage from the French Alps to households in Los Angeles and London, when moviegoers could watch James Bond's ski acrobatics in cinemas from Tokyo to Toronto, the proclivities of this global middle class varied little. As Thompson wrote, "Skiing is no longer an esoteric sport for the idle rich, but a fantastically popular new winter status-game for anyone who can afford $500 for equipment."[27] As skiing became a totem of the cosmopolitan middle class, it became possible for a young skier from a small village in the French Alps to become a global icon.

In light of these powerful market forces, it became impossible to separate the sport of Alpine skiing from the business of Alpine skiing. The luxurious and modern image of skiing promoted the sport itself, boosting sales of equipment, hotel accommodations, and lift tickets, but it also endowed a wide array of unrelated products with its aura of modern luxury. Thus the sport helped to define postwar popular culture; and, conversely, Alpine skiing became closely entwined with broader trends in Western culture.

As one German observer put it, Alpine skiing became "a preoccupation of the masses, a fashion sport."[28] As the ranks of the middle class swelled after World War II, many Western Europeans defined their identity not through work, as had long been the case, but rather through leisure, and particularly skiing.[29] Alpine skiing symbolized cosmopolitanism, youth, and heightened sexuality.

Representations of female sexuality were a common theme in postwar Alpine skiing advertisements not only because advertisers followed the "sex sells" mantra, but also because women could be used to highlight the luxurious

FIGURE 21. Advertising poster by Arnaldo Musati for Cervinia (the Matterhorn) and Breuil, in Italy's Valle d'Aosta, 1953. Photo © Christie's Images/The Bridgeman Art Library.

associations of the sport. Advertisers depicted fashion-conscious women in Alpine milieus, surrounded by skiing iconography, to emphasize the sport as an element of a modern, cosmopolitan lifestyle.[30] This leisured femininity characterizes Arnaldo Musati's 1953 poster advertising the Italian resort village of Breuil at the base of Cervinia (the Matterhorn) (figure 21). The poster depicts a beautiful woman in a rapturous pose. The subject sports fashionable clothes

FIGURE 22. *Das Skimagazin* and the sexualization of Alpine skiing, 1969. *Das Skimagazin*, no. 7, vol. 4, (1969), issues 1 and 2. Photographs courtesy Deutscher Alpenverein, Munich.

that emphasize her sexuality, including a modish halter top (a hint at the abundant sunshine that Italian resorts promoted heavily as an advantage over more northerly Alpine destinations). Although the woman is certainly the focus of the advertisement, elements of the background signal that Breuil is a ski paradise: her ski poles and fuzzy mittens suggest that she has been skiing (without masculinizing her by showing her in action), and the legendary form of Cervinia looms in the background, with gondolas rising from the Alpine village below.

The use of female sexuality in the commodification of Alpine skiing proved highly malleable to shifts in popular attitudes toward sex. Beginning in the 1960s, some advertisers made the connection between sex and skiing more obvious and graphic. For example, in the late 1960s and early 1970s, the editors of the German-language quarterly *Das Skimagazin* attempted to differentiate their magazine from a crowded market of German ski periodicals by adorning the cover with scantily clad female models posing with skis (figure 22). The magazine's articles were relatively standard for the ski publishing industry, but the covers branded *Skimagazin* as youthful, exciting, and transgressive—a symbol of the Alpine lifestyle in the swinging sixties.

Advertisements suggested that escape to the mountains and away from the formality of everyday life would induce a sense of the exotic that allowed tourists of both sexes to celebrate their carnal nature in the Alps.[31]

PLANNING A VACATION

The ultimate goal of ski advertisements, regardless of their iconography, was to convince consumers to purchase goods and services. The economic benefits of Alpine tourism spread downward from the peaks to Alpine villages and into the metropolises of the lowlands, generating "fertilizing" economic effects that few other sectors could replicate.[32] Because tourism is not a single product but rather, as scholars of tourism have described it, "a pastiche of heterogeneous elements amalgamated by advertising and marketing," ski tourism created a tight, finely tuned web of economic activities.[33] Skiing both supported and depended on a wide array of other industries, including hotels and restaurants, equipment manufacturers, agricultural producers, and transportation and communications services.

In the postwar years, sport and tourism, and in particular the beneficent combination of the two in Alpine skiing, were not only tools of economic development, but social necessities. As the head of the French National Olympic Committee, Count Jean de Beaumont, averred in 1968, "Modern man is beset more cruelly each day in his struggle for existence."[34] The French author Samivel concurred in his summary of modern civilization: "No air, no space, no sun, no silence, no contact with the living world, suppression of cosmic rhythms, no possibility of free action or adventure." Mountains and the outdoor sports they hosted, wrote Samivel, were a necessary "counterweight" to modernity, and as a result, they were a matter of "public interest."[35] Both states and citizens conceived of tourism and sport as important to public well-being and social stability.

To trace the myriad economic and social effects of this once-simple sport, let us imagine a well-to-do German family of four living in Munich in 1964. The father, Herr Schmidt, was a successful businessman who benefited from the German *Wirtschaftswunder* and had begun to collect many of the markers of middle-class status—a refrigerator, a television, and, as a proud Bavarian, a BMW sedan. Many of his friends had taken up Alpine skiing, and using his hard-earned, state-guaranteed vacation time, he hoped to escape the city with his wife and two children over the winter holidays.

As Herr Schmidt began to plan his ski holiday, he considered Alpine destinations both in and outside Germany. As John Urry has observed, the tourist consumes *places* as much as goods and services, making tourism a uniquely spatial form of consumption.[36] As tourism infrastructure spread in the postwar era, the sport could be practiced easily outside the Alps—in the Pyrenees or the German *Mittelgebirge,* for example—but the selling point of Alpine skiing was not the sporting act alone. Rather, winter tourists consumed the Alpine landscape and skiing services simultaneously.

Tourists not only consumed places, they redefined them. Orvar Löfgren refers to tourism as "a transnational mode of production" and Dean MacCannell as "a concrete form of the internationalization of culture."[37] Ski tourism had long possessed an international character: resorts such as Chamonix and St. Moritz attracted skiers from around the globe. A full 50 percent of tourists in Austria before World War II were foreign, and after the war, tourists from the other Alpine nations, England, and the United States flooded Austria's western Alpine states.[38]

Herr Schmidt's vacation research confirmed the international character of ski tourism. The German Automobile Club (Allgemeiner Deutscher Automobile Club, or ADAC) published periodic encyclopedic surveys of European skiing destinations. The author of the 1956 edition noted, however, that secondary ski areas such as the Schwarzwald in Germany could not be covered because the book included only the resorts that could be said to belong in "the crown of the Alps."[39] A 1958 inventory of the "one hundred most beautiful downhills in the Alps" reflected this transnational worldview, presenting the locations on maps that did not show political borders. The author proceeded roughly from west to east, moving between countries as necessary.[40] This organizational scheme implied that political boundaries had little influence on the choice of a ski destination and that tourists would make decisions based on price, accessibility, amenities, and quality of skiing. Indeed, as for Nellie Friedrichs in the 1930s, an international destination was often more desirable than a domestic one, as it had the cachet of exotic luxury.

While pondering his options, Herr Schmidt recalled watching the first-ever internationally televised Winter Olympics, broadcast from Cortina d'Ampezzo, Italy, in 1956. The combination of speed and landscape in Alpine skiing made for an impressive television spectacle. The Italians, like most hosts of the Winter Olympics, saw in the Games an excellent chance to advertise the venue as a world-class winter tourism destination. The Italian

National Olympic Committee spent some 3.2 billion lire (U.S. $5.12 million in 1956, or U.S. $43.9 million in 2013) to construct stadiums, coordinate services, and advertise the Games, while the Italian government spent a further 460 million lire (U.S. $736,000 in 1956, or U.S. $6.3 million in 2013) to improve infrastructure in the area, including roads, railways, sewage systems, street lighting, and parking lots.[41]

In the midst of a long and dreary German winter, the Schmidts leaped at the chance to spend a week in the Italian Dolomites, known for good snow conditions, clear blue skies, and Mediterranean warmth. The improvements at Cortina to prepare for the 1956 Olympics had made the Italian village into an international-class resort. By the mid-1960s, Cortina offered some 15,000 tourist beds, more than other world-class destinations such as St. Moritz (12,000), Davos (11,000), Garmisch-Partenkirchen (10,700), and Chamonix (10,000).[42]

But the Schmidts had to make many preparations before traveling to Italy, starting with the purchase of skis. Most skiers, even beginners like Herr Schmidt, demanded equipment of the highest quality, and many sought out the brands promoted by world-class skiers like Jean-Claude Killy, who signed a massive endorsement deal with the American company Head Skis upon retiring from amateur competition in 1968.[43] The cost of equipment rose even as skiing became more popular. In 1955, a German ski magazine determined that outfitting an Alpine skier with equipment and clothing of average quality cost 327 deutsche marks (US$78, or US$610 in 2013).[44] By the mid-1960s, the cost had risen to one thousand marks (US$400 in 1966, or US$2,210 in 2013).[45] The editorial staff of *Der Winter* lamented in 1967 that "skiing has become a *Volkssport,* [and] the *Volk* has become affluent. Thus, skiing has become a sport for the affluent *Wirtschaftswundermenschen,* nothing for poor wretches" (figure 23).[46]

For men like Herr Schmidt, however, the high cost of a skiing holiday served as a marker of status, and the sport held great appeal precisely because it was both widely popular and a highly conspicuous form of consumption. Whereas some of his coworkers could only afford to take their families on day trips to the nearby Bavarian Alps, he relished the chance to splurge on a luxurious Italian holiday. Skiing destinations, like other vacation spots, carried varying amounts of social prestige, and each became a brand in its own right.[47] Similarly, the choice of skis and the brands and fashions of ski clothing differentiated the burgeoning ranks of skiers.[48]

Herr Schmidt implicitly recognized Urry's argument that tourists established "extensive distinctions of taste . . . between different *places. . . .* Part of

FIGURE 23. A German magazine diagrams the cost (in deutsche marks) of outfitting a skier, 1955. "Kleinigkeiten gross geschrieben," *Ski* 8 (1955): 56. Photograph courtesy Deutscher Alpenverein, Munich.

what people buy is in effect a particular social composition of other consumers."[49] In Cortina d'Ampezzo, the Schmidts would ski among a cosmopolitan middle class from across Western Europe, surrounded by shopping and entertainment opportunities that could be matched only by other high-class Alpine winter resorts. In the 1960s, when the ranks of skiers grew annually in Germany by 250,000 and in France by 200,000, *Der Winter* observed that a skier like Herr Schmidt would pay "a lot, relatively, but happily, in order to do something for his prestige."[50] In the postwar era, when leisure time came to be understood as a human right throughout Western Europe, ski tourism presented many opportunities for the conspicuous demonstration of social status.[51]

To access Cortina from Munich, the Schmidts had the choice of rail or automobile travel. The desire to win what one French businessman called "the battle of winter sport [tourism]" and pressure from business interests led governments to undertake massive transportation projects to connect the Alps to the lowlands.[52] The efforts of the French government to close the gap between French winter resorts and their rivals in Switzerland and Austria for tourist visits reveal an alliance between public and private actors that typified the development of skiing. In 1945, French winter resorts organized a trade association (Comité des Stations Françaises de Sports d'Hiver) to lobby the government, improve cooperation and coordination between private and public actors, and advertise French tourism. Their efforts led to a number of state-led initiatives. The state railway company (Société Nationale des Chemins de Fer Français) altered its train schedules to better accommodate tourists traveling to the Alps from major urban areas such as Paris and Marseille, and the state engineering corps (Ponts et Chaussées) completed projects to widen roads, build bridges, and dig tunnels to allow more efficient car and rail transport in the mountains. Local commune governments also got in on the action, upgrading and coordinating services such as water, sewage, electricity, snow removal, and fire and emergency services.[53]

The 1963 completion of the Europabrücke, a 2,549-foot-long, 620-foot-high bridge traversing the steep Wipptal south of Innsbruck, Austria, made it possible for the Schmidt family to travel to Cortina by car. The Europabrücke provided an efficient north-south road link between Germany and Italy, thus confirming Alpine Austria as an important transportation corridor.[54] The construction of the Europabrücke and its celebration by the Austrian Olympic Committee, which was preparing to host the 1964 Winter Games in Innsbruck, illustrates how Alpine skiing stimulated infrastructure development in the postwar era and how these state-directed projects in turn accelerated the development of Alpine tourism.[55]

Upon the Schmidts' arrival in Cortina, their activities supported a wide range of occupations and industries, as they needed to be housed, fed, and entertained. On the mountain, they paid to use the network of chair and cable lifts that took skiers from the center of the town into the surrounding mountains. Beginners like the Schmidts also required ski instruction, itself a developing industry. Each Alpine state tested and certified its ski teachers in much the same way as doctors and lawyers. This process began in the 1920s, when Swiss cantons funded the training of ski instructors and then issued them permits allowing them to teach in the canton.[56] Swiss tourism interests considered the resulting lack of consistency in instruction to be a liability and believed that a standardized, easily taught and learned technique would help brand Switzerland as a ski paradise and eliminate confusion among customers. Thus, in fall 1934, varied tourism interests, including the Swiss Federal Railways, the Swiss Tourism Association, the Swiss Hotelier Society, the Association of Swiss Transport Establishments, and the Swiss Center for the Promotion of Tourism formed the Association of Swiss Ski Schools (Schweizerische Skischulverband) to standardize instruction across the country.[57] Austria began regulating ski instructors in 1928, and France followed suit in 1948.[58]

Alpine skiing produced economic benefits across a wide array of industries. Skiers like the Schmidts could expect to spend 1,500–2,000 deutsche marks (US$375–$500 in 1966, or US$2,690–$3,590 in 2013) annually on equipment, transportation costs, and room and board for one week's stay at an average winter resort, and the figure could quickly increase if skiers chose more expensive equipment or more prestigious destinations.[59] Alpine skiing allowed members of the middle class to display their wealth and establish gradations of status through choices such as the location of their resort and the types and the brands of equipment and clothing they purchased.

ATTRACTING TOURISTS

Winter tourism became a matter of great interest not only for Alpine communities and private businessmen, but for national governments as well, as the example of postwar Austria demonstrates. Before World War I, the Austro-Hungarian Empire included some of Europe's largest oil fields in Galicia, important industrial zones surrounding Prague, Budapest, and Bratislava, and significant ports on the Adriatic, including Trieste and Split. After World War II, Austria consisted of the ruined metropolis of Vienna, a collection of agricultural and industrial lowlands to the east, and Alpine terrain in the west that, while aesthetically beautiful, offered few resources useful to an industrial economy.

It was in the Alpine hinterland, however, that the Austrian government charted a path toward economic viability. The politicians in Vienna recognized that the new Austria would wield far fewer industrial resources than before, whether as the political and cultural center of the Austro-Hungarian Empire or as a part of Hitler's Reich. In search of an economic model, they turned their attention to Austria's First Republic, which had faced similar economic challenges after World War I. In the face of the massive decline in productive capacity effected by the dismantling of the Hapsburg Empire, the interwar Austrian government invested heavily in tourism infrastructure. With the help of extensive advertising, Austria quickly became a summer and winter vacation destination on a par with Switzerland, particularly for visitors from Central and Eastern Europe.

At the end of World War II, many Austrian hotels and railways were either badly damaged or entirely destroyed. The government scrambled to rebuild and modernize Austria's tourist infrastructure in order to compete with the long-established and undamaged resorts of Switzerland and nascent Alpine destinations in France and Italy. The Tourism Section of the Federal Ministry for Commerce and Reconstruction was formed to direct the rebuilding program. The Tourism Section estimated that it would cost some 100 million schillings (US$3.86 million in 1955, or US$33.6 million in 2013) to repair and restock existing hotels, rebuild roads and railways, and advertise that Austria was prepared to welcome tourists again.[60]

Early reconstruction efforts focused on restoring basic services, and it was not until the establishment of the European Recovery Program (the Marshall Plan) by the United States in 1947 that the Austrian government was able to devote significant funds to the development of tourism. It focused its efforts and resources on the French- and American-occupied zones in western Austria, with the Alpine states of Tirol, Salzburg, and Vorarlberg receiving nearly 62 percent of the total Marshall Plan funds dedicated to tourism (though they accounted for only 49 percent of the Austrian population).[61] From 1950 to 1955, the Austrian government funneled some 525 million schillings (US$20.25 million in 1955, or US$176 million in 2013) into the Alpine tourist economy. This figure included 404 million schillings to modernize hotels, 28 million schillings for international advertising, and 93 million schillings for the construction of chair and cable lifts.[62] Although the Austrian monarchs had neglected the Alpine regions of their empire for centuries, the Alps now constituted a significant competitive advantage in the tourism market.[63] Alpine Austria was reconceived as a prime tourist destination thanks to a combination of state investments and private initiatives.

In France, the expansion of the ski industry was notable for the way that skiing destinations were created ex nihilo. The developers of postwar French resorts prided themselves on identifying and satisfying tourist desires. A 1956 guide to ski destinations in the Alps described the ideal characteristics of a winter resort as "first-class motorways that are also cared for in winter; high-altitude winter sport centers that are assured of snow; treeless, long, obstacle-free downhills; groomed slopes in combination with all sorts of mountain railways and ski lifts; [and] modern, well-managed hotels."[64] Although the German author of this text believed that these attributes were most readily found in Switzerland, it was the French who worked most feverishly to create the perfect ski tourism experience.

The new French resort was a product of public-private cooperation and planning initiatives that had begun before World War II. The French enthusiasm for skiing lagged significantly behind that of the Germans, Austrians, Swiss, and British. A senator from Savoie, Antoine Borrel, argued in 1934 that if France could create modern, desirable winter resorts, ski business would follow. The contemporary clientele wanted state-of-the-art hotels with a "gay and lively" atmosphere, alongside modern amenities such as good transport connections and telecommunications. To achieve these ends, Borrel argued, the French needed a master plan to raise capital and direct development.[65] The fall of France to the Nazis in 1940 in fact benefited the development of French winter resorts immensely, as the Vichy government, which ruled over France's Alpine regions until the Italians occupied them in late 1942, endeavored to exploit the Alps economically to compensate for the loss of German-occupied northern France. By the end of the war, significant plans were in place, and, as in Austria, the French viewed the expansion of the winter tourism industry as a way to stimulate the postwar economy.[66]

The opening of the resort of Courchevel in 1946 typified the technocratic French approach to ski tourism. Courchevel was the product of a plan by an engineer, Maurice Michaud, and an architect, Laurent Chappis, under the direction of the elected assembly of Savoie. Such management also occurred at the national level. The French government's Commission Interministérielle d'Aménagement de la Montagne (CIAM) was created to study potential tourist sites and to coordinate the efforts of private developers. In 1964, CIAM announced "Plan neige," a project to add 150,000 tourist beds in French winter resorts between 1965 and 1975. The goal was met through heavy government investment.[67]

The French model highlighted the self-sufficiency of the winter resort. French ski villages lay at high elevations and were largely isolated from established communities in the Alpine valleys. They catered to tourists' every need, offering skiing, hotels, restaurants, shopping, and entertainment.[68] This model generated immense profits while simultaneously fulfilling the desire of postwar winter tourists for all-inclusive, luxurious experiences.[69] It reached its apex in winter 1956, when Club Méditerranée opened its first vacation centers. Club Med operated three villages: two in the Swiss village of Leysin and one at Monêtier-les-Bains, France. Visitors were provided with skis, equipment, lessons, lift tickets, and evening social activities as part of the vacation package.[70] In short order, this all-inclusive model, based on what one French observer called "an artificial developed city in the heart of the white desert," was exported throughout the Alps.[71] In the following decades, Club Med added many more all-inclusive villages across Alpine France, Italy, and Switzerland to meet demand from skiers across the globe.

The French model transformed Alpine tourism. The French discovered, according to one German observer, that Alpine skiing, at its core, was a matter of "taste and money." By constructing hypermodern resorts in "snow deserts," French developers and government agencies could engineer the ideal modern skiing experience without having to adhere to the staid architectural traditions and conservative ethos of earlier winter resorts.[72] As a result, France emerged as the originator of "touristic avant-gardism," erecting massive "ski precincts" marked by their "modernity and diversity."[73]

By the 1960s, the combination of modern resorts and the success of French racers in international competitions made France the premier ski destination. The author of a 1967 German skiing guide lauded these developments, writing: "France has the highest ski slopes, the newest ski venues, the most original ski lifts and the perkiest ski bunnies. Skiing in the French Alps is chic, sporty, expensive. Skiing in France is a budding sport that is without unnecessary conventions and that is growing extremely fast."[74] Whereas the defining trends in Alpine skiing culture in the first half of the twentieth century were elaborated in the Eastern Alps by Anglo-German skiers, in the postwar era the geography of influence shifted markedly. The number of French ski resorts grew from thirty in 1945 to two hundred in 1975.[75] Italian resorts were quick to imitate them. Postwar technocrats improved the ski industry for consumers by facilitating access to the mountain and offering a wide array of services, while the tourism industry benefited from increasing profit margins.

Through winter tourism, a peripheral practice and a marginal landscape became central to European modernity. The French innovations in Alpine tourism signaled a dramatic reconception of the relationship between skiers and the Alps. Skiers had long adapted their sport to the climate and terrain of the mountain landscape at hand, focusing on areas that had already been popularized by summer tourists. After the war, tourism advocates oriented new developments entirely around the needs of the burgeoning middle class. In turn, skiing became a vital part of middle-class identity and modern consumer culture. This reconception of Alpine skiing would extend even further as tourism developers sought to remake the Alps themselves as a more profitable leisure landscape.

EIGHT

The Pursuit of White Gold

MANUFACTURING MIRACLES

In early January 1964, the Austrian federal minister Heinrich Drimmel faced a seemingly impossible challenge. In his secondary appointment as president of the Austrian Olympic Committee, Drimmel was responsible for ensuring the smooth functioning of the 1964 Winter Olympic Games in Innsbruck. For Austria, which had endeavored since the end of World War II to rebuild its economy while steering a neutral path between the Soviet Union and the United States, the Winter Games were a prestige project meant to showcase a modern, cosmopolitan, affluent nation to the world. Unfortunately for Drimmel, years of organizational meetings and infrastructure development and over one hundred million schillings' (US$25.84 million in 1964, or US$194 million in 2013) worth of investment could not guarantee a resource vital to the event: snow. The eastern Alps experienced an unusually warm and dry winter in 1963–64. Photographs from December 1963 depict verdant hills, a catastrophe for the Games set to begin late the following month. Whereas ice rinks could employ modern refrigerant technologies to host events like skating and hockey, the telegenic and wildly popular Alpine skiing events were at the mercy of natural conditions.

With the success of a televised global spectacle at stake, on December 30, 1963, the Austrian Olympic Committee voted to implement emergency measures for the preparation of the skiing pistes outside Innsbruck.[1] On January 9, Alois Lugger, the mayor of Innsbruck, initiated a dramatic project: hundreds of army reservists, deployed under Drimmel's authority as federal minister, began transporting snow to the competition sites from the snow-rich Gschnitztal, twenty to twenty-five miles away along vertiginous Alpine

FIGURE 24. The "miracle of Innsbruck": Austrian army reservists transport snow before the 1964 Winter Olympic Games. Organisationskomitee der IX. Olympischen Winterspiele in Innsbruck 1964, *Offizieler Bericht der IX. Olympischen Winterspiele Innsbruck 1964* (Innsbruck: Österreichische Bundesverlag für Unterricht, Wissenschaft und Kunst, 1967), 78.

roads.[2] Over the next three weeks, 950 soldiers, policemen, and firemen were mobilized to load 115 trucks with snow and distribute it on the downhill course at Patscherkofel and the slalom course at Axamer Lizum (figure 24). Combined, they worked 113,000 hours to cover the courses in a six- to eight-inch layer of snow. In total, the men transported 9,000 cubic meters of snow to Patscherkofel and 6,650 cubic meters to Axamer Lizum.[3]

The work of the organizers was not yet finished, however. The snow that now blanketed the Alpine skiing courses was in no condition to serve as a track for world-class skiers whose speeds approached eighty miles per hour. A team of "piste gardeners" sprayed the snow with water (44,000 gallons at Patscherkofel alone) to create a course of uniform depth and firmness, a feat that was "rarely managed on natural snow," to allow skiers to race in speed and safety.[4] The preparation of these pistes came to be known as the "miracle of Innsbruck," a logistical feat that assured the success of the Games.

More generally, this man-made miracle epitomized a significant postwar shift in the relationship between skiers and the Alps. Although it began as an improvised reaction to mitigate the inadequacies of natural circumstances, he end result was a piste that was in fact better suited to competitive Alpine skiing than even the best natural snow conditions could be.[5] Whether for elite competition or leisure skiing at resorts, snowfall was often unreliable, and fallen snow tended to melt, refreeze, and be blown by the wind into bumps and troughs. After World War II, race organizers and resort operators increasingly manipulated the snow to maintain uniform pistes.

Although Alpine skiing had originated as a means of appreciating the "natural" mountain landscape as a refuge from modern, mechanized civilization, new converts to the sport tended to be less willing to trudge uphill for hours for an ecstatic ten-minute descent. In the postwar era, French tourism advocates referred to the snow as "white gold." The Alpine states quickly recognized that "white gold resists devaluation and converts easily to currency," and the mountains came to be seen as a natural resource to be exploited, managed, and developed, not an object of spiritual devotion.[6] Alpine modernism in this era was less about individuals seeking transcendence than about different groups seeking to accomplish material goals. States attempted to increase national economic production and to benefit the physical and mental health of their constituents; Alpine communities sought to become economically viable year-round and to attain a higher standard of living; corporations and joint-stock companies attempted to realize the potential for great profits; and a rapidly expanding body of skiers sought to enjoy the sport with all the trappings of modern luxury and convenience. The interests of these disparate groups aligned in such a way that all parties promoted the transformation of the Alpine landscape to render it more responsive to the rational and orderly dictates of modern sport and commercial tourism.

LIFT INFRASTRUCTURE

Before nature could serve as a refuge from modern urban life, paradoxically, it had to be commodified, marketed, and made accessible.[7] To many skiers of the early twentieth century, their sport offered an escape from the technical manipulation of the Alpine landscape wrought by the pressures of modernization.

For all of the rhetoric about its organic simplicity and primitive origins, skiing had always depended heavily on technological innovations, such as

Alpine railways that brought skiers from the cities and new technologies that made skis and bindings safer and more responsive.[8] Before the late 1920s, however, the ski slopes themselves had been left more or less untouched. With the construction of the first rudimentary cable lifts in the late 1920s and their proliferation in the 1930s, the sport and the relationship between skiers and the landscape underwent a critical shift. No longer was the Alpine landscape simply to be tackled by skiers as they encountered it. Rather, it became an environment engineered for speed, ease of access, and safety.

Spatial arrangements, as Richard White has written, "reveal the social arrangements that help produce them," and the reshaping of the Alps for the sake of tourism and sport suggests that the image of the Alps as an Arcadian refuge coexisted uneasily with the rationalist dictates of capitalist modernity.[9] The modern cultural appeal of Alpine skiing was, as the term itself implies, highly dependent on a sense of place. But as it grew in popularity, public authorities and private business interests refashioned wide swaths of the Alps to create what John Bale terms "sportscapes," or "monocultural sites given over solely to sport, rather than multifunctional landscapes."[10] A given Alpine landscape might once have accommodated diverse activities such as skiing, hiking, hunting, nature appreciation, and preservation. But the demands of Alpine skiers for cleared slopes and groomed snow overrode these other uses.

The growth of skiing both depended on and gave rise to the development of Alpine infrastructure, the backbone of which was an increasingly dense network of lifts. Charles Viard, a successful French lift developer of the 1930s, argued that investments in lifts would allow the French ski tourism business—disadvantaged from the outset by having fewer domestic skiers than Germany, Austria, and Switzerland—to become more competitive. Viard recognized the intense competitiveness of the tourism industry, writing: "For a tourist resort, not to advance is to regress." In 1927, Viard traveled to successful Swiss, German, and Austrian resorts to identify their advantages and to determine whether they could be replicated in France. Viard noted that the reason for their success was obvious upon arrival: "All had been created for skiers, in the form of cable cars, funiculars, [and] transport installations that, in eliminating the fatigue of reascent, permitted easier access to the snow fields at high altitude." The result was a "double profit" for the stations: the lifts attracted skiers to the resort, and the resort could stay open longer because the lifts transported skiers to higher altitudes where the snow cover lasted late into the spring.[11]

Until the late 1920s and early 1930s in Switzerland, Austria, and Germany, Alpine skiers mostly depended on funicular railways that had been constructed in the late nineteenth and early twentieth centuries to ferry summer tourists to panoramic vista points.[12] In Alpine France and Italy, where even summer tourism lagged behind that of the Germanic eastern Alps, developers recognized that by installing mechanical lifts, they could turn an Alpine wasteland into a profitable ski paradise almost overnight. Cable lifts, quicker and cheaper to construct than funicular railways, allowed skiers to ascend the mountain quickly in order to descend it on skis even more rapidly. According to one French ski magazine, the "vogue for the downhill" and the construction of lifts were "parallel" developments that increased the popularity and profitability of the sport.[13]

The opening of the winter resort in Sestriere, in northwestern Italy, in the winter of 1934 provided a model that challenged Swiss and Austrian supremacy in the competition for tourist visits. Sestriere was the first successful resort created solely to serve Alpine skiers. Built under the direction of Giovanni Agnelli, the head of the Milan-based Fiat automobile company, this development optimized access to the snow via an integrated transport network. Skiers arrived by means of an extension of the autostrada from Milan and a purpose-built train station. By 1938, three lifts provided access to seventy-four downhill runs. Agnelli's project was qualitatively different from earlier attempts to develop ski infrastructure around existing Alpine villages such as Davos and Chamonix. At Sestriere, lifts, accommodations, and entertainment operated under centralized ownership in a previously uninhabited landscape. The French followed this blueprint in creating their own winter resorts.

Consumers and producers of skiing alike delighted in this new paradigm of winter tourism, demonstrating that even as late as World War II, many Europeans believed that the technological development of the Alps complemented rather than disfigured the beauty of nature.[14] French and German commentators marveled at how the construction of lifts at Sestriere, paired with two immense, modernist hotel towers, transformed the barren Alpine "snow desert" into a ski paradise.[15] Other Alpine villages that aspired to develop winter tourism facilities viewed Sestriere as a shining example of "the industrial revolution on the mountain." According to one French reviewer, the Italian resort succeeded because it installed the infrastructure that allowed Alpine skiers to indulge in "their élan for the descent," which itself suited "the accelerated rhythm of modern life."[16] Carl Luther agreed, writing that rather than emulating the austerity and seriousness of Swiss-style winter resorts, which existed to train the will and the body, Sestriere was a "winter playground" that allowed the masses to enjoy the simple thrills of the sport.[17] Recognizing that concerted investments along the Italian model would allow French destinations to compete with the Swiss standard-bearer resorts for customers, a collection of French state and private tourism interests formed the Syndicat National des Télépheriques et Téléskis (STT) in 1938 to coordinate efforts to construct more lifts.[18]

Experienced skiers, too, generally welcomed these developments. One French skiing journal contended that the cable lifts served as "an excellent means of propaganda in favor of the mountain and of skiing."[19] Henry Hoek argued that ski lifts were a "logical and necessary" spur to the further development of winter resorts that was needed to cater to "the will of the masses."[20] Both sources reflect the contemporary belief that democratizing access to the mountains would benefit society as a whole. Even the German Alpine Association (Deutscher Alpenverein), which lamented the profusion of ski lifts as "a further step towards the mechanization of the mountain world," conceded that given the "stampede" of skiers congregating on popular slopes, opponents had to accept the construction of further lifts in the Alps.[21]

The popularity of lifts was self-perpetuating. A network of lifts became a necessity for a truly modern ski resort, and the number of lifts in Alpine countries multiplied rapidly. A 1954 advertisement for Conca di Pila in Italy's Valle d'Aosta illustrates how winter resorts used lifts to market their services and also how this technological innovation fused with existing discourses of modernity and luxury (figure 25). The advertisement highlights colorfully dressed, fashionable, and attractive men and women posing in ski clothes on a balcony, while a lift carries other happy couples upward. The text describes the lift network that connects the ski slopes at Conca di Pila with the Alpine villages below. Lift infrastructure takes center stage in this advertisement: skiers are barely visible in the background. What is being advertised is not Alpine skiing itself, nor the Alpine landscape, which serves as a mere backdrop to the action, but rather the modern infrastructure and cosmopolitan clientele of the Valle d'Aosta, indicating an important shift in consumer demands.

Lift operators and winter stations charged a hefty fee for rides on ski lifts, but the secondary economic benefits were even greater. For winter resorts and businesses in Alpine villages, lifts defined spatial boundaries for Alpine skiing. In the era before lifts, skiers took to the mountains surrounding established Alpine villages, skied until they grew tired, and then returned to their hotels and chalets. The bounded mobility afforded by the ski lift turned

FIGURE 25. Poster by F. Romoli advertising Italy's Valle d'Aosta, 1954. Photo © Christie's Images/The Bridgeman Art Library.

Alpine space into an object of capitalist consumption, a reconception of the natural environment that rivaled the nineteenth-century commodification of mountain air.[22] Keeping skiers tethered to a network of lifts created a captive market for hotels, restaurants, and other services.[23] This trend has continued: half a billion passengers per year rode ski lifts in the Alps by the year 2000.[24]

For skiers, lifts made the sport more attractive by removing some of the mental and physical barriers to practicing the sport. Before the proliferation of ski lifts, Alpine skiers understood their sport as heroic and adventurous, an act of exploration with its roots in Fridtjof Nansen's Greenland traverse. The sense of mobility and liberty provided by skis constituted one of the major attractions of the sport. For the less adventurous majority, however, these attributes made skiing appear arduous and dangerous. The construction of lifts effectively defined the terrain as safe and suited to skiing. The presence of state-certified ski instructors and meticulously groomed pistes classified by skill level suggested that Alpine skiing was a sport for all ages and ranges of experience. Further, by eliminating the need for a taxing uphill climb, lifts made skiing considerably easier and thus substantially more attractive and accessible. Ski pistes were analogous to highways; both drivers and skiers enjoyed freedom and autonomy in motion, but that motion was bounded by the routes laid out for them.

In 1943, Arnold Lunn summarized the attraction of lifts to both producers and consumers, writing that "ski-lifts have not only multiplied manyfold the aggregate of downhill skiing on any particular day; they have also increased the number of days on which skiing is practicable. At Adelboden [Switzerland] a snowstorm confined us to the practice slopes, and even when the snow had ceased falling it was often too soft and too deep for a long climb, but the modern skier is almost independent of weather."[25] Whereas an enthusiastic skier might have climbed and descended ten thousand meters and traveled a distance of fifty kilometers on skis in a single season before the construction of lifts, a competent and enthusiastic skier aided by lifts could cover the same amount of terrain in a single day.[26]

The construction of ski lifts accentuated the conquest of time and space that had made Alpine modernism so popular. In 1950, the German Alpinist and ski enthusiast Fritz Schmitt contended that Alpine skiing in the era of the lifts suited modern inclinations, writing that "the man of our time no longer wants to walk and climb, he wants to ride."[27] Another commentator, W. L. Steinberger, contended that "in an era in which the hands of the clock race inexorably in the background, it is understandable that we leave no stone unturned to allow us to fully exploit as many of our fast-evaporating leisure hours as possible." The point of the lifts, argued Steinberger, was not to "save hours," but rather to "gain time," and they contributed to the postwar skier's sense of mastery.[28]

LANDSCAPE MODIFICATION

Changes to the Alps to cater to skiers did not stop at the creation of an increasingly dense lift network; they extended to the modification of the terrain itself. The Nazi organizers of the 1936 Winter Olympics in Germany acknowledged that there was nothing natural about the pristine aesthetics of the downhill and slalom courses near the Alpine village of Garmisch-Partenkirchen. To create safe, fast courses, the officials had removed "dangerous" and "troublesome" rocks, bridged streams, and cleared away trees.[29] By the 1964 Games in Innsbruck, world-class Alpine skiing competitions demanded a highly uniform piste. Even before they began trucking in and grooming snow on the racing slopes, Austrian officials had cleared the existing landscapes of their "defects." To prepare the slalom courses at Axamer Lizum, the organizers felled 3,600 trees and used eleven thousand kilograms of Donarit explosive to clear the trails. A group of eighty-four soldiers put in over 146,000 hours of labor pulling roots and stumps; clearing, blasting, and grooming the trails; and building irrigation systems, access trails, and bridges.[30]

The international regulations governing Alpine skiing races codified these engineering efforts. By the early 1980s, the FIS required that the terrain be "completely cleared of stones, stumps and such obstacles, in order to eliminate all objective danger for the competitors, even when the snow on the course is scarce" and stipulated that the piste should have a minimal number of bumps and no major ledges that would force the racer to leave the ground. Further, for safety, "the course must . . . become wider with increasing speed." In the highly technical slalom, the competition was to be held on snow that was "as hard as possible." Should snow begin to fall during the race, the chief of the course was required to pack it down or have it removed.[31] All of these rules aimed to control and rationalize nature. What resulted was not an artificial space but a managed natural one that offered, as John Bale observes, "a blending of humanity and nature."[32]

Skiers' opinions about landscape modification varied. Some celebrated the new, intensely managed pistes, arguing that they offered the best opportunities for refining one's technique. The Frenchman Marcel Ichac averred in 1934 that "to train on a piste is to train with security and efficiency; it is to grow accustomed to direct descents, to turns at great speed, to all the delicacies of technique. It is, in a word, the acquisition of style."[33] In purely sporting terms, then, the piste was a positive development equated with progress, a necessary precursor to the postwar technical revolution effected by Édouard Frendo and others.

Because landscape modification before World War II was limited to world-class racing pistes, there were few objections raised. After the war, as sporting practices began to influence not only the technique of leisure skiers but the mountains on which they skied, commentators bemoaned the homogenizing and taming of the Alpine landscape. In the early 1970s, the Swiss sports journalist Karl Erb traced the parallel modifications in skiing and the Alpine landscape in the quarter century after World War II. He described a series of revolutionary changes that resulted from the fundamental incompatibility between elite "stadium sport" and nature. In order to fashion the Alps in the image of sport, "piste architects" besieged the Alpine landscape with "enormous machinery . . . turn[ing] the mountain into a construction site and transform[ing] it according to their desires and dogmas." As a result, the skier "must grapple with nature no longer." The reshaping of the Alps to conform to the ideal notion of a ski piste was an unfortunate byproduct of the "perfectionism of the twentieth century." According to Erb, modern technology had made the landscape artificial and predictable, and the sport had become thoroughly detached from nature. This standardization of the environment reduced downhill races to "aerodynamic tests at hundred-kilometer tempo" and the slalom to "a trapeze act for balance-artists and ski acrobats." The modern skier, a "thoroughbred" and a "scientifically constructed apparatus," had become as rational, uniform, and replaceable as the environment through which she skied, and neither the rationalized landscape nor the modern, sport-minded skier could exist in a vacuum.[34]

The relationship between skiing and the landscape shifted as business interests and sporting bureaucracies defined ideal conditions and engineered the terrain to achieve their goals. For business operators, the primary goal was to increase profits by broadening access to the Alps and improving safety. For sports officials, the paramount concerns were safety and fairness in competition. The public generally supported these developments. Lifts made leisure skiing more accessible, affordable, and suited to the vogue for the downhill; piste management for ski competitions made for exciting, telegenic contests.

SNOW MANAGEMENT

Snow was both a blessing and a curse for the postwar ski industry. It needed to fall in the right places and at the right times in order to sustain the massive capital investments in infrastructure and the service sector. The technological manipulation and eventually the production of snow made ski conditions more reliable for operators and consumers alike.

Though valuable, snow could be too much of a good thing. Avalanches—the "white death" of the Alps—posed a particular danger to resort infrastructure as well as to individual skiers. Abnormally warm and wet weather triggered a series of destructive avalanches across the Alps in the first months of 1951, remembered as the "Winter of Terror." On January 20, the Swiss ski center of Andermatt suffered six avalanches in an hour, destroying countless homes, restaurants, and hotels, a devastating blow to a community dependent on regular tourist visits. Throughout the Alps, over 250 people lost their lives.[35] As investments in the Alpine landscape multiplied, state officials and private business interests began to engineer the Alpine landscape to minimize the probability of and damage from avalanches. These groups expressed optimism in the ability of technology to "tame" the winter landscape.[36] Resort operators and state officials employed both offensive and defensive strategies to manage the destructive power of snow and the mountains, and in many ways the Alpine landscape came to resemble a war zone. On the pistes themselves, resort operators employed tank-like grooming machines. In packing down the snow to make a more uniform surface, these machines also decreased instabilities that could trigger avalanches. Armies in the Alpine lands began to use explosives—dropped from helicopters or fired by mortar or cannon—to trigger small, preventative avalanches and thus reduce the probability of a larger and more destructive avalanche. But it was the defensive approaches to avalanche management that truly gave the landscape the look of a battlefield. Locals had long planted lines of trees on the outskirts of Alpine villages to reduce the destructive power of avalanches, but resort operators redoubled these defenses by erecting fences and buffer walls to channel and arrest the flow of snow. These bore a distinct resemblance to the buffer walls and tank traps constructed in the Second World War: many of the structures would not have been out of place on the beaches of Normandy.[37] The fear of avalanches led to coordinated efforts to manage the landscape and defuse its immense destructive potential, but many critics lamented the effect of avalanche defenses on Alpine aesthetics (figure 26).

If too much snow could prove lethal, too little threatened financial disaster. Developers could construct massive hotels, new lifts, and excellent transportation connections, but as the Austrian Olympic Committee had learned, without abundant "white gold" on the slopes, all of these investments were worthless. The ski industry became so lucrative and highly capitalized that a warm winter created an economic catastrophe on a par with a harvest failure.[38] The operators of a new lift in Chiemgau, a town in the foothills of the

FIGURE 26. Alpine avalanche barriers in the mid-1960s. Source: "Lawinenverbauungen," *Der Winter* 54 (1966–67): 304, 306.

Bavarian Alps, learned this lesson in the winter of 1971–72. The new lift up the local Hochfelln mountain cost its operators some eleven million deutsche marks, but it sat unused due to a particularly poor winter. For the lift operators, who had hoped to pay down their debt with profits from the new lift, the lack of snow proved ruinous.[39]

Winter resorts had to demonstrate "snow security" to convince Alpine skiers to make advance reservations and pay high prices in the increasingly crowded winter tourism market. On this count, the consistently cold weather of the Alps offered a distinct advantage over other European ski destinations, such as the Pyrenees. However, there was great variation in temperature and snowfall within the Alps. The southern Alps of France and Italy experienced Mediterranean warmth in fall and spring, making their ski season two to four weeks shorter than that of the northern Alps. The northwestern Alps of French Savoie and the Swiss Bernese Oberland enjoyed particularly long and reliable ski seasons because of their sustained exposure to cold, wet storms arriving from the Atlantic Ocean.[40]

Equally important in determining snow coverage was elevation. Throughout the Alps, a resort at six thousand feet could typically open two weeks earlier and close four weeks later than one at four thousand feet.[41] Tourism operators thus endeavored to develop ski areas at higher elevations. Resort operators studied snow security obsessively, as slight variations in snowfall could mean the difference between profit and economic disaster. Actuaries agreed that a ski area could be viable economically only if it averaged "a minimum cover of 30–50 cm (12–20 inches) on at least 100 days in 7 out of 10 winters, from 1 December to 15 April." For the joint-stock companies such as the French Compagnie des Alpes that invest in and operate ski resorts, snow security protects profits and determines where to invest.[42]

Unsurprisingly, ski resorts were not inclined to leave snow security up to nature, and they began to invest in systems for producing snow on demand. The so-called snow cannon, an apparatus that combines water and highly pressurized air to spray artificial snow across a ski slope, was invented in 1950 and held out the promise that nature's deficiencies could be mitigated through human ingenuity.[43] Over subsequent decades, engineers tinkered with snow cannons to make them viable on the massive scale needed at Alpine ski resorts, and they began to be installed widely in the 1980s. The resort of Les Menuires in Savoie typifies the wholesale adoption of snow cannons in Alpine resorts. Beginning in the 1980s, an automated system coordinated 188 snow cannons arrayed between elevations of 5,600 feet and 7,400

ENNEIGEMENT
Un fonctionnement simple...
Sur ce dessin futuriste, tout paraît simple : à la sortie de
la salle des machines, l'air et l'eau sous pression sont
refoulés dans des tuyauteries enterrées le long de pistes.

FIGURE 27. An artist's sketch from the late 1980s depicts the potential of snow cannons to transform the ski industry. Courtesy Nivéales Médias.

feet. Snow production at Les Menuires was remarkably resource-intensive, requiring a reservoir containing 53,000 cubic meters of water and a central power station that produced 1,320 kilowatts per hour. It allowed the operators to manufacture snow to cover eight kilometers of piste, thus guaranteeing snow security and lengthening the season perceptibly.[44] By 2006, approximately 30 percent of all ski slopes in the Alps could be treated with manufactured snow, and at many of the largest and most profitable resorts, more than 80 percent of slopes could be maintained in this manner.[45]

Arnold Lunn once trumpeted the transformative nature of ski lifts, but it was when ski lifts were combined with snow cannons that Alpine skiers truly became "almost independent of weather." Ski lifts and snow cannons combined to prolong the ski season by connecting the winter stations at lower elevations with the snow at higher elevations at the beginning and the end of the season (figure 27). Although weather conditions could still harm business, improved access to higher elevations through ski lifts and the ability to produce snow "à la carte" placed the ski industry on firmer financial footing.

Many viewed the wave of infrastructure development in the Alps with a sense of foreboding, however. By the end of the twentieth century, investments in the winter tourism industry were so massive that in the Alps that an alternative economic path was, in the words of one Swiss observer, "no longer imaginable."[46] In wide swaths of the Alps, tourism interests engineered the landscape to ensure the maximum productivity of the ski industry.

Viard's maxim that a failure to advance is tantamount to regression suggests a capitalist tendency to continually streamline and rationalize products and services to increase profits. In the case of Alpine skiing, however, the alteration of the material landscape and skiers' perception of it was not simply a matter of a high-modern domination of nature. Although snow cannons covered pistes with manufactured snow, the success of the postwar ski industry also relied on a deep understanding of natural processes, including avalanche conditions, climate patterns, and elevation-related variations in snowpack. The sport remained as dependent on natural conditions as ever before.

RETROFITTING THE ALPS

Prior to World War II, Chamonix had been the jewel in the crown of the French Alpine resorts and the only French destination that could compete in prestige with Swiss resorts such as St. Moritz and Davos. After the war, the turn-of-the-century charm of Chamonix could not compensate for the fact that the village no longer met modern standards for an Alpine ski destination: it lacked the amenities of Sestriere and other purpose-built Alpine resorts. Chamonix had originally emerged as a winter resort in the early twentieth century, when the sport was not dependent on lifts and the most common practice was ski touring. The steep and varied terrain surrounding Europe's highest peak, Mont Blanc, allowed courageous skiers to test their skill while enjoying the mountain's majestic aesthetics. As lift-fueled downhill fever swept Europe from the 1930s onward, Mont Blanc and its challenging terrain became liabilities. The ski slopes were widely dispersed, and the lifts that provided access to the Alpine slopes were insufficient, forcing skiers to endure long waits before ascending the mountain.[47] New skiers flocking to the Alps found the steep slopes around Chamonix too difficult. They were also too dark: the shadow of the massive form of Mont Blanc prevented ski tourists from acquiring a much-coveted winter suntan. To solve this dilemma and to win the battle "against shadows and against the slope," developers in the mid-1950s began "to search at 2,000 meters [6,562 feet] for what was lacking below: easy and sunny ski terrain."[48] They constructed a world-class system of cable lifts connecting Chamonix, at 3,500 feet, to more suitable ski terrain—"Super-Chamonix," at 8,000 feet—where the skier could access a dozen different ski runs within twenty feet of the lift.[49]

The construction of the new lifts solved Chamonix's problems in one fell swoop. By the end of the decade, the lifts made a further six square kilometers of skiable terrain available to skiers and transported them out of the shadow of Mont Blanc, making Chamonix an appealing hybrid of a picturesque Alpine village and a sunny, modern ski resort. At the higher elevations snow security was vastly improved; some parts of the resort could serve skiers year-round. Finally, the landscape satisfied the needs of modern leisure skiers, who could ski freely "without running the risk of jumping a rocky ridge or of striking a tree, without the nagging worry of executing a turn at all costs to avoid a dangerous drop, because everywhere the terrain is largely cleared."[50]

The explosive growth of Alpine skiing and winter tourism after 1930 transformed the sport from a rather diffuse recreational activity into a multibillion-dollar industry. In Austria alone, the number of overnight stays in winter grew from just over 2 million in 1937 to an astounding 39.8 million in 1980. By the end of the twentieth century, the Alps counted some twelve million residents but welcomed at least ten times that many tourists annually. The region possessed beautiful vistas, steep and challenging terrain, high levels of snowfall, and geographic proximity to Europe's metropolises. But before skiing could become a pillar of the modern Alpine economy, the landscape, too, had to be modernized. To satisfy skiers' demands for both speed and safety, tourism advocates built lifts, blasted terrain, and managed snow resources. Alpine modernism thus shifted markedly over the course of the twentieth century. An aesthetic that had once advocated bridging the modern divide between nature and culture by mastering natural forces and harmonizing with the natural landscape had now evolved into a doctrine of development that served a wide range of constituencies, from Alpine skiers and mountain dwellers to hoteliers and investors. For both producers and consumers of Alpine skiing, the landscape was a means to an end, leading to variety of projects that recast the Alps as a hybrid of nature and human technologies.

Epilogue

DEBATING ALPINE MODERNITY

The material changes in the sport of skiing and the Alpine landscape during the twentieth century are indisputable. We return now to the question of meaning. Was Alpine skiing a beneficent force that promoted individual health, cultivated social intercourse, and modernized the Alpine economy, as Andrzej Ziemilski argued in 1959? Or, as Arnold Lunn averred in 1941, had it come to cater to the philistine urges of "mass man" by using technology to render the mountains more accessible, a process that stripped them of their natural grandeur and rendered them artificial? The sport had always inspired panegyrics and polemics in equal measure, and the perception of Alpine skiing as a transcendent art that allowed for self-expression and feats of courage sat uncomfortably with the commercial promotion of ski racing and the role of skiing in the winter tourism economy. Lunn's view of skiing as art clashed with Ziemilski's vision of skiing as a practice to be scientifically mastered as a means to an end, whether that end was individual health, social stability, mass entertainment, or economic development. The ability of the sport to be all things to all people was the antinomial appeal of Alpine modernism, but to purists like Lunn and Heinz Dramsch, Alpine modernism had shifted too far in favor of pragmatists who sought to use the sport to achieve other ends. As the transformative power of competitive sport and winter tourism accelerated in the 1930s, criticisms of the direction of the sport became more vociferous.

As the synergistic relationship among mass culture, competitive sport, and winter tourism blossomed, Alpine skiing both symbolized and helped to construct the postwar leisure society. Producers and consumers of Alpine skiing alike benefited from the critical mass of skiers. However, to a small but vocal group of critics who expanded on the wartime critiques, the mass expansion of Alpine skiing represented the culmination of the destructive potential within the sport and of modern inclinations toward rationalization and commodification: it created a Faustian narrative arc in which the persistent and repeated actions of a wide array of actors to improve the human condition—by enjoying leisure activities or rendering the "snow desert" economically viable—ended by debasing both skiing and the Alps.

This heterogeneous group of critics comprised nature enthusiasts, conservationists, Alpinists who felt that the mountains had been disfigured to suit the needs of lazy skiers and avaricious business interests, and old-guard members of the media, many of whom had begun skiing before the profusion of ski lifts and denounced the sport's increasing artificiality and alienation from nature. The introduction of ski lifts in the late 1920s and early 1930s provoked immediate criticism, as some members of each of these groups considered any technical interventions that aided leisure as perversions of the landscape or the ethos of Alpine skiing. Others perceived lifts as merely an annoyance that could be easily avoided. When the number of lifts and hotels multiplied exponentially as the French model of development swept the Alps, the chorus of criticism grew louder. Detractors complained that the expansion of lifts crowded out the traditional practice of skiing and that lifts and hotels alike ruined the aesthetics of the mountain for everyone. Most of these critics came from Germany, Austria, and eastern Switzerland, where Alpine skiing had much stronger connections to the "back to nature" movements of the fin de siècle.[1] These critics protested the influence of French and Italian technocrats and businessmen on the Alpine landscape, complaining that these latecomers treated the Alps as a commodity to be bought and developed, not a landscape to be revered and protected. In the end, however, these sharp criticisms had little effect, and the bulk of middle-class skiers in the postwar era welcomed the changes.

Skiers had always connected skiing with art in explicit and implicit terms. In an early debate on the practice and ideological orientation of skiing, Lunn criticized Mathias Zdarsky for failing to recognize that Alpine skiing was "an art, and a beautiful art."[2] Alpine modernists explained their relationship with the Alps through the vocabulary of aesthetics and concepts drawn from art, arguing that the unique relationship between skiers and the Alps produced transcendent effects that went far beyond mere leisure. Indeed, art criticism presents a useful lens for understanding the development of Alpine modernism. The emergence of Alpine skiing as an industry exposed it to market forces and, in the minds of detractors, reduced the sport and the landscape to kitsch—a concept popular among modernist cultural critics in the 1920s and 1930s who lamented the effects of the twin evils of mass culture and mass production on art.[3]

The American art critic Clement Greenberg differentiated kitsch from art in a 1939 essay: "Kitsch is mechanical and operates by formulas. Kitsch is vicarious experience and faked sensations. Kitsch changes according to style, but remains always the same. Kitsch is the epitome of all that is spurious in the life of our times. Kitsch pretends to demand nothing of its customers except their money—not even their time."[4] This definition has relevance for Alpine modernism. As skiing became a cultural commodity and an industry, the serious philosophical and aesthetic engagement implied by early Alpine modernism faded from importance. Where the original aesthetic had celebrated speed and adventure in the stark landscape, postwar Alpine modernism stressed consumption and experience, reshaping skiing as a means of middle-class identity formation and economic development. The mutually advantageous relationship between producers and consumers of Alpine skiing produced "snow à la carte," the all-inclusive experiences of Club Med, and the capitalist synergy of James Bond on skis. It was in the Alps, the German essayist Gerhard Nebel argued in 1950, where "the destructive strength of tourism" was made most explicit and where "the European disease breaks out in a chain of abscesses."[5]

Critics of postwar Alpine skiing argued that whereas earlier skiers were active agents who attempted to reshape modernity in their own image, contemporary skiers were unthinking consumers of an inauthentic sport and an artificial landscape. Greenberg wrote that art in the age of mass culture had been "capitalized at a tremendous investment which must show commensurate returns; it is compelled to extend as well as to keep its markets."[6] Winter tourism, likewise, commodified and marketed the formerly transcendent in conformity with the logic of expansion. Greenberg averred that kitsch in art showed no "regard for geographical and national-cultural boundaries. Another mass product of Western industrialism, it has gone on a triumphal tour of the world."[7] Alpine skiing followed the same pattern, as developers applied models that demanded the alteration of the landscape to homogenize the practice of the sport throughout the Alps. As the German Alpinist Henning Bohme wrote in 1983, "Ski fanaticism annihilates the landscape with technical brutality. . . . That which is possible is done—because it brings profit."[8] The Alps, once imagined as an escape from urban problems, became a landscape marked by pollution, overcrowding, and environmental damage on a par with the metropolises of the lowlands.

Even the greatest proponents of Alpine skiing harbored fears that their beloved sport would degenerate to the realm of kitsch. In 1959, when Ziemilski asked rhetorically whether skiing was merely a passing fad along the lines of the hula hoop and rock and roll, he acknowledged that for non-skiers and critics, there was little to differentiate postwar Alpine skiing from these heavily marketed "mass hysterias."[9] Indeed, Alpine skiing could be fused with a wide array of disposable trends: a 1958 German instructional guide associated the kinaesthetics of Alpine skiing with the momentary mambo craze.[10] Later, in the 1977 film *The Spy Who Loved Me*, Roger Moore's James Bond made a perfunctory descent of the Austrian Alps accompanied by a period-specific, disco interpretation of the film series' iconic theme. These amalgamations of Alpine skiing with passing fads echo Greenberg's assertion that "when enough time has elapsed the new is looted for new 'twists,' which are then watered down and served up as kitsch."[11]

In the early twentieth century, Alpine modernists interpreted skiing not as antimodern but instead as particularly and unconventionally modern. Later, Alpine skiing came to reflect and indeed create postwar modernity in ways that many critics found disturbing. The Austrian Gustav Prerowsky noted in 1960 that moderns are "inundated with stimulation" and argued that as a result, Alpine skiing had been influenced by the impersonal social forces that defined postwar societies: speed, haste, mechanization, and rationalization.[12] The ski boom reflected the desire of moderns to escape the demands of the working world, but Alpine skiing itself came to be imbued with the modern regard for productivity and efficiency. In 1951, the German Helmut Sohre claimed that the axiom "Time is money" had come to dominate Alpine leisure as it did everyday life, and as a result, the material manifestations and ideological principles of capitalism had colonized the Alpine landscape.[13]

The democratization of leisure that began in the interwar era and accelerated after World War II led to overcrowding on the slopes and disillusionment among ski enthusiasts. The general secretary of the Deutscher Skiverband, Hansheinrich Kirchgessner, wrote in 1955 that mountain railways and ski lifts, which were created to allow modern individuals "to reach the heights faster in order to indulge in relaxation through sporting activity up in God's free nature," instead alienated skiers by forcing them to endure long journeys to the ski slopes and "hours-long queueing" for the lifts. The vogue for lift-supported skiing, wrote Kirchgessner, "only furthers massification and the commotion of everyday life."[14] Alpine skiing had originally been an elite practice, undertaken by those who had the time, money, courage, and physical toughness to confront the Alps in winter. The spread of lift infrastructure, argued the German Alpinist Franz Grassler, submitted this formerly elite sport to "the herd instinct." Skiing on heavily groomed pistes carried all of the nobility of mass transit.[15] As Grassler implied and a 1942 German editorial stated explicitly, the newcomers to the sport did not possess the necessary moral development and mental fortitude to understand that "the downhill is a spice, with which one should not spoil the good taste of snow and winter."[16] A 1952 French editorial lamented that "the exhilaration" of speed had become "too easily accessible to too many people."[17] This small group of skiers and Alpine enthusiasts echoed a longstanding elite criticism of mass culture, that democratization inevitably led to philistinism and the popularization of the frivolous tastes of the masses. In short, the avant-garde aesthetic of Alpine modernism became disposable kitsch.

Many of these failings were blamed on faddish youth in particular. In 1950, the author of a German editorial traced the decline of traditional skiing practices to the younger generation's compressed relationship to time, writing that the older generation "either has [more] time or a different sense of time" than the youth. The lift-aided piste rider was "a child of his era, anxious and quick." Young people's desire to amass as many experiences as possible in a short amount of time alienated them from nature, the appreciation of which demanded patience and contemplation.[18] In an article in *Der Winter,* Friedl List argued that the relationship between youth and nature "no longer exists at all." Because youth were "overfed daily and hourly with ersatz experience through cinema, radio, and cheap literature," they viewed nature as dull and inert.[19] For these critics, the discursive category of "youth" encapsulated a wide range of fears about democratization and mass culture. Postwar societies across Europe placed great hope in the regenerative potential of youth but also feared that a rebellious youth would not uphold the morals of previous generations.[20] Serious Alpine skiers feared that the hedonistic urges of "the youth" would irrevocably change both the sport and the Alpine landscape through the exclusive practice of downhill skiing, at which point the easily distracted youth would discard Alpine skiing as an outdated fad and move on to their next ersatz experience. Nature, which for the older guard was imbued with moral meaning, was to the nebulous youth but a platform for speed trials and a realm of impulsive consumption.

This distaste for postwar skiing practices and their cultural meanings led some to call for the abandonment of lift-aided downhill piste skiing in favor of traditional Alpine touring outside the confines of the winter resorts. Arnold Lunn declared in 1943 that lifts undermined the pleasure of skiing because they "stale the thrill of those moments when the skis gather speed on the first downward dive of the day."[21] Through Alpine touring, which required climbs and horizontal traverses as well as downhill runs, Alpine skiing critics embraced slowness. The German Alpinist Konrad Klärner believed that the fast, "carefree" nature of the downhill suited postwar youth, whereas Alpine touring was the sphere of the mature skier. Ski touring, argued Klärner, was delightfully "unmodern," freed from "the shackles of technology" and "the hands of the clock."[22] The German Werner Toth-Sonns characterized climbing the mountain under one's own power as "a first release from technical slavery" in a highly mechanized age. For those ascending the mountain on skis, the sport and the landscape once again became pleasingly "unmodern."[23] The German skier Georg Frey concurred, arguing that ascending the mountain allowed the skier to contemplate nature and to experience "the joy of discovery" that once defined Alpine skiing. For "the person of refined tastes" who resisted the lure of the lifts, a climb was not an onerous trudge but "an aesthetic pleasure."[24]

Touring, these critics argued, would return the sport to its imagined organic simplicity and strip it of its kitschy associations with luxury and commercialism. If kitsch "replaces ethics with aesthetics," as Modris Eksteins has observed, then this plea to revive Alpine touring represented an attempt to resurrect the ethical bearing of early Alpine modernism. It called on skiers to rediscover pristine nature and to restore the downhill to its role as merely a component of the Alpine skiing experience.[25] In short, critics lamented the hypertrophic aestheticization of speed and cosmopolitan luxury in skiing and romanticized forms of the sport that they believed better balanced aesthetic pleasure with an ethical commitment to nature and the edifying potential of sport.

The revival of Alpine touring, which German Wolf Burger classified as "old and at the same time modern," was not an escape from modernity but an attempt to escape the decadence that had corrupted Alpine skiing.[26] In the years before the technologization and democratization of the sport, Alpine skiing was consistently described as exceptionally and thrillingly modern. But for these postwar critics, the balance between nature and modernity had been upset: the millions of new skiers meant that nature and modernity could never again be amalgamated as they had been in the early years of the sport.

Whereas some blamed the degradation of moral values for the changes, others attributed them to the incursion of industrial capitalism. In 1955, in an article condemning the commercialization of the mountains, the German Alpinist Hermann Kornacher connected the feverish construction of ski lifts to the progressivist, competitive ethos that characterized both sport and the tourism industry, invoking the Olympic motto: "Fortius (i.e., more rash and more ruthless), citius (i.e., faster and more rational, more profitable), altius (i.e., higher, more advertising power, more sensational)!"[27]

The arrival of purpose-built winter resorts triggered a flood of criticisms of kitsch. The tourism director of the Swiss village of Saas-Fee argued in 1971 that tourists demanded a distinctive local atmosphere and contended that "a tourism resort without a partnership with a village will gradually become a soulless ghetto."[28] As the tourism director of Oberstdorf im Allgäu, Germany, contended, "The 'atmosphere' of a winter sport resort cannot be planned in an engineer's office." Instead, successful resorts had to grow "organically" over time so that the residents could develop "a natural relationship with the land and the soil," unlike the purpose-built resorts, which had no permanent residents and became ghost towns in the off-season.[29] Indeed, the hypermodern French resorts had a short life, many doing good business for only five or ten years before visitors abandoned them in favor of more modern resorts at higher elevations. These criticisms illustrate an important point about modern tourism, noted by Dean MacCannell: no matter how heavily planned and capitalized the industry might be, tourism "is ultimately dependent on a non-economic relation."[30] The sense of place provided by historic Alpine villages still mattered to many tourists. Many of the traditional winter resorts such as St. Moritz, Kitzbühel, and the retrofitted Chamonix maintained their popularity throughout the twentieth century, capitalizing on their blend of perceived historical charm and modern amenities.

Alpine skiers and the tourism industry entered into a Faustian bargain when they began engineering the Alpine landscape. The Alpine modernist revolution was driven by tensions and contradictions that came to diminish the pristine aesthetics of the Alps, which for some skiers constituted the primary appeal of the sport. Wolfgang Schivelbusch described a comparable effect created by railroad travel, noting how railroad infrastructure and the democratization of rail travel stripped both the act of travel and the

FIGURE 28. A postwar photograph depicts the effects of skiing on Alpine landscapes Photograph © Jürgen Winkler. Archive of the Deutscher Alpenverein, Munich.

landscape of their "auratic" character.[31] The Alps became a monocultural landscape given over to winter tourism, leading to sprawl, overcrowding, and a placeless, anti-Romantic aesthetic (figure 28). As the continued popularity of the sport illustrates, however, for most skiers, the experience of speed and the appeal of luxury compensated for this perceived loss.

Although the scathing criticisms of Alpine skiing, tourism, and their combined effects on the Alps were never more than a minority viewpoint, they nevertheless led some developers and public officials to reconsider their approach to Alpine development. In 1977, the French president Valéry Giscard d'Estaing admitted that the French approach to Alpine tourism had undercut the Romantic appeal of the landscape. In a speech at the French

Alpine commune of Vallouise, he stated: "If the human wasteland expands, the touristic attraction [of the mountains] will lessen considerably. The urbanite looks to the mountain for contact with untamed nature. But he comes also to visit landscapes shaped by millennia of peasant perseverance and different lifestyles from those of the city. . . . Enough with technocratic visions for development in the mountains. Think of people, think of Mankind."[32]

Such sober analyses of the sport became the norm. By the end of the twentieth century, the number of skiers in Europe's five Alpine nations had grown from a few thousand at the beginning of the century to a total of 18.5 million, a large majority of whom practiced the Alpine style exclusively.[33] This truly extraordinary rate of growth placed immense pressure on the Alpine environment. By the 1970s these environmental effects were evident and well-known, and developers and Alpine communities tallied up the potential environmental effects of winter tourism in required environmental impact statements preceding any additional development.

Discussions about the ethos of Alpine skiing persisted, but they settled into familiar, well-established debates about the proper relationship between nature and culture, tradition and modernity, ethics and aesthetics. Giscard's appeal for moderation in development encapsulates this moment in the making of the modern Alps because he united the promotion of tourism with criticisms of Alpine skiing. Many of the vituperative debates of previous decades moderated from the 1970s forward. In the postwar decades of rapid expansion, the utopian faith in the ability of the sport to engender individual transcendence, social democratization, and uncomplicated economic transformations evaporated. A pragmatic diagnosis of the sport's costs and benefits emerged in its place. By the 1970s, Alpine modernism had transformed from a transcendent, heroic ideology into a considered, mundane calculation that attempted to unite disparate interest groups by balancing access, sustainability, and profit.

MOUNTAINS AND MEANING

The historical development of skiing and the Alps presents a familiar narrative of the relationship between humanity and nature in the modern era. When nature is imagined as a place without humans, any rise in human influence on the environment triggers Edenic narratives about paradise lost through the insatiable appetite for growth and profit. The Alps, long a frontier located at the heart of Europe, have been the subject of many such narratives. Romantics lamented the nineteenth-century vogue for Alpine tourism that led to the development of railways and hotels. Those who saw in the Alps the epitome of the sublime fulminated against mountaineers' races to climb and "conquer" Alpine peaks. When skiers first appeared, Alpinists protested their pursuit of speed at the expense of nature appreciation. As Alpine skiing became increasingly entangled with competitive sport and the tourism industry, early adopters of the sport exclaimed that these developments debased the sport and the landscape. When snowboarding emerged as a countercultural alternative to Alpine skiing in the 1970s and 1980s, many postwar Alpine skiers defended their sport as respectful and contemplative, a marked contrast to the attitude of faddish snowboarders, whom skiers deemed brash and impudent, with no respect for tradition or the grandeur of nature. And on it goes.

The ideology of Alpine modernism was always fluid and dynamic, and no particular iteration of it can be identified as representing the "natural" state of skiing or the "proper" relationship to the Alps. The narrative of the decline and fall of the Alps posits a natural, homeostatic state, devoid of human influence, a pristine landscape that has been disrupted by a decadent modern culture.[34] But such a narrative is inevitably mythical. For centuries, Europeans have projected their values onto the Alps. Generations of Alpine peoples have exploited the environment to make a living, whether by herding livestock to pasture in Alpine meadows or by constructing lifts and hotels to profit from the tourism industry. Similarly, modern individuals have sought to conquer the Alps and to allow the Alps to conquer their souls, whether by climbing up mountains or skiing down them. Perceptions of nature are conditioned by culture, and the Alps are defined as much by the cultural imagination as by geology or geography.

In its various forms, Alpine modernism sought to define the ideal relationship between modern individuals and the Alps. It housed many, often conflicting practices and beliefs. But Alpine modernism was not only a discourse about the relationship between humans and nature: it was an ideology that stimulated the modernization of the Alps. At times this was a project undertaken cynically in the pursuit of profit, but just as often it aimed to achieve humanitarian individual, social, and economic goals. By Andrzej Ziemilski's metric, the postwar democratization of Alpine skiing represented progress, as access to the sport widened considerably. But when it comes to the touristic development of the Alps, one man's progress is another man's poison. The Alps counted forty thousand different downhill ski runs in 1990, prompting the British Marxist critic Martin Kettle to describe the Alps as "a single-commodity colony of lowland Europe."[35] The Alps were appropriated, materially and discursively, to serve the needs of metropolitan civilization. Yet the mountains in turn exerted an effect on Europe's lowland metropolises. Seen through the eyes of Alpine modernists, the Alps became a synthetic landscape, one that attempted to balance nature and culture, creating an idealized, future-oriented society in a landscape once deemed backward.

In the coming decades, as global warming accelerates, Alpine skiing will not disappear, but its practice will shift markedly. Climate models suggest that rising temperatures will harm ski areas at lower elevations (four thousand to six thousand feet), where snow coverage has already declined markedly since the 1980s; resorts at higher elevations will remain viable.[36] However, the proportion of resorts with snow security will decline significantly: by one estimate, a temperature rise of one degree Celsius by 2050 would drop snow security across Europe to 75 percent of medium-sized to large resorts (from the current level of 90 percent). A two-degree rise would drop snow security to 60 percent, and a four-degree rise would leave only 30 percent of resorts snow secure.[37] Despite the argument that Alpine skiing has become estranged from nature, it has remained fundamentally dependent on the environment, in the form of slopes and snow. Technology has altered the sport's relationship to nature, not eliminated it.[38] As the appraisal of the Alps by Giscard and countless others in recent decades suggests, surely we are witnessing the dawn of a new age of Alpine modernism, one in which the reengineering of the mountains for fun and profit is giving way to a more nuanced understanding that stresses the fragility of this massive landform. Even though the Alpine environment and the role of the mountains in European culture have changed immensely since the late nineteenth century, individuals will continue perceive the Alps as they did when young Wilhelm Paulcke received his Christmas gift in 1883 and took to the hills outside Davos: rushing downhill, surrounded by Alpine peaks.

NOTES

INTRODUCTION

1. Fabrizio Bartaletti, "What Role Do the Alps Play within World Tourism?" International Commission for the Protection of the Alps (CIPRA), http://alpsknowhow.cipra.org/background_topics/alps_and_tourism/alps_and_tourism_chapter_introduction.html, accessed August 18, 2013; Kurt Luger and Franz Rest, "Der Alpentourismus: Konturen einer kulturell konstruierten Sehnsuchtslandschaft," in *Der Alpentourismus: Entwicklungspotenziale im Spannungsfeld von Kultur, Ökonomie und Ökologie,* ed. Kurt Luger and Franz Rest, (Innsbruck, 2002), 21.

2. Bartaletti, "What Role Do the Alps Play?"

3. Organisation for Economic Co-operation and Development, *Climate Change in the European Alps: Adapting Winter Tourism and Natural Hazards Management* (Paris, 2007).

4. Thomas Becker, "Harakiri auf der Piste," *Süddeutsche Zeitung,* February 23, 2009.

5. William Cronon, "Introduction: In Search of Nature," in *Uncommon Ground: Rethinking the Human Place in Nature,* ed. William Cronon (New York, 1996), 23–56, esp. 34–51.

6. Andrej Ziemilski, "Der Skilauf in der Zivilisation des 20. Jahrhunderts," *Der Winter* 48 (1960–61), 31–33, 36.

7. Carl J. Luther, "Älter als Methusalem," *Der Winter* 32 (1938–39), 1–3; Roland Huntford, *Two Planks and a Passion: The Dramatic History of Skiing* (London, 2008), 2.

8. Ziemilski, "Der Skilauf," 32, 33.

9. Ibid.

10. Ibid., 36.

11. Ibid., 33.

12. Ibid., 36.

13. Elisabeth Hussey, "The Man Who Changed the Face of Alpine Racing," *Skiing Heritage Journal* 17 (December 2005): 7–12; Edward Smyth, "Sir Arnold

Lunn (1888–1974)," *Alpine Journal* 94 (1989–90): 213–16; "The Sir Arnold Lunn Papers: Collection Description," Georgetown University Special Collections, www .library.georgetown.edu/dept/speccoll/cl143.htm, accessed January 13, 2014. See also Lunn's autobiography, *Come What May: An Autobiography* (Boston, 1941).

14. Lunn, *Come What May,* 297, 299–300.

15. Ibid., 302.

16. On the mapping of Europe in terms of civilizational development, see Larry Wolff, *Inventing Eastern Europe: The Map of Civilization on the Mind of the Enlightenment* (Stanford, CA, 1994).

17. John Urry, *Consuming Places* (London, 1995), 144. For a particularly insightful case study of this phenomenon, see Wolfgang Schivelbusch, *The Railway Journey: The Industrialization of Time and Space in the Nineteenth Century* (Berkeley, 1986).

18. On the varieties and significance of Alpinist cultures, see Rainer Amstädter, *Der Alpinismus: Kultur, Organisation, Politik* (Vienna, 1996); Dagmar Günther, *Alpine Quergänge: Kulturgeschichte des bürgerlichen Alpinismus (1870–1930)* (Frankfurt, 1998); Olivier Hoibian, *Les alpinistes en France, 1870–1950: Une histoire culturelle* (Paris, 2000); Lee Wallace Holt, "Mountains, Mountaineering and Modernity: A Cultural History of German and Austrian Mountaineering, 1900–1945" (PhD diss., University of Texas at Austin, 2008); Tait Keller, "Eternal Mountains— Eternal Germany: The Alpine Association and the Ideology of Alpinism, 1909–1939" (PhD diss., Georgetown University, 2007); Kerwin Lee Klein, "A Vertical World: The Eastern Alps and Modern Mountaineering," *Journal of Historical Sociology* 24, no. 4 (2011): 519–48.

19. Michel Clare, "Préface," in Paul Gignoux, *Ski sur les Alpes* (Paris, 1956), xiv.

20. See Christiane Eisenberg, *"English Sports" und deutsche Bürger: Eine Gesellschaftsgeschichte, 1800–1939* (Munich, 1999); Norbert Elias and Eric Dunning, *Quest for Excitement: Sport and Leisure in the Civilizing Process* (Oxford, 1986); Allen Guttmann, *From Ritual to Record: The Nature of Modern Sports* (New York, 1978).

21. Charles Amorous introduces the term *Alpine modernity* in "L'implantation du ski alpin dans les Alpes françaises: La tradition étayage de la modernité," *Revue de géographie alpine* 88, no. 4 (2000): 9–20.

22. Max Weber most famously developed the argument that modernity is "disenchanted" in *The Protestant Ethic and the Spirit of Capitalism* (Hoboken, 2001). For a historiographical overview of the relationship between modernity and disenchantment, see Michael Saler, "Modernity and Enchantment: A Historiographic Review," *American Historical Review* 111 (2006): 692–716.

23. Marshall Berman, *All That Is Solid Melts into Air: The Experience of Modernity* (New York, 1988).

24. This is not to imply that outdoor leisure and tourism activities before Alpine skiing were somehow less "modern": they depended on a wide array of technological infrastructure, and practitioners of leisure activities such as sightseeing, mountain climbing, and hiking reimagined and recast the world around them, whether consciously or unconsciously. See Thomas Lekan, "A 'Noble Prospect': Tourism, *Heimat,* and Conservation on the Rhine, 1880–1914," *Journal of Modern History* 81, no.

4 (2009): 824–58; Klein, "A Vertical World"; John Alexander Williams, *Turning to Nature in Germany: Hiking, Nudism, and Conservation, 1900–1940* (Stanford, CA, 2007).

25. Recent studies of sport, leisure, and tourism have convincingly argued that these subjects demand critical attention. See Rudy Koshar, *German Travel Cultures* (Oxford, 2000); Shelley Baranowski and Ellen Furlough, eds., *Being Elsewhere: Tourism, Consumer Culture, and Identity in Modern Europe and North America* (Ann Arbor, 2001); Shelley Baranowski, *Strength through Joy: Consumerism and Mass Tourism in the Third Reich* (New York, 2004); Dean MacCannell, *The Tourist: A New Theory of the Leisure Class* (Berkeley, 1999); Orvar Löfgren, *On Holiday: A History of Vacationing* (Berkeley, 1999); Alain Corbin, ed., *L'avènement des loisirs, 1850–1960* (Paris, 1995); Urry, *Consuming Places;* Ellen Furlough, "Making Mass Vacations: Tourism and Consumer Culture in France, 1930s to 1970s," *Comparative Studies in Society and History* 40, no. 2 (1998): 247–86.

26. On "social modernism," see Roger Griffin, *Modernism and Fascism: The Sense of a Beginning under Mussolini and Hitler* (Basingstoke, UK, 2007), 338.

27. This "maximalist" view of modernism is theorized by Susan Stanford Friedman in a series of essays: "Definitional Excursions: The Meanings of *Modern/ Modernity/Modernism,*" *Modernism/Modernity* 8, no. 3 (2001): 493–513; "Periodizing Modernism: Postcolonial Modernities and the Space/Time Borders of Modernist Studies," *Modernism/Modernity* 13, no. 3 (2006): 425–43; "Planetarity: Musing Modernist Studies," *Modernism/Modernity* 17, no. 3 (2010): 471–99. Cf. Peter Wagner, *A Sociology of Modernity: Liberty and Discipline* (London, 1994), and *Modernity as Experience and Interpretation: A New Sociology of Modernity* (Cambridge, 2008).

28. In *History of the Alps, 1500–1900: Environment, Development, and Society* (Morgantown, WV, 2009), Jon Mathieu has noted that from 1500 to 1900, the Alpine regions exhibited economic coherence and were distinct from the lowland areas, because of their shared low levels of urbanization, relatively slow population growth, and dependence on regionally specific industries such as mining. In social and political terms, however, Alpine communities generally identified more with adjacent lowland territories than with one another (224). The popularization of skiing, combined with wider cultural, political, and socioeconomic trends, helped transform the Alps into a coherent region in the twentieth century. On the historical development of Alpine peoples and landscapes, see also Werner Bätzing, *Die Alpen: Geschichte und Zukunft einer europäischen Kulturlandschaft* (Munich, 2003).

29. On the malleability of modernisms outside avant-garde circles, see Maiken Umbach, *German Cities and Bourgeois Modernism, 1890–1924* (Oxford, 2009).

30. Matthew L. McDowell, "Sports History: Outside of the Mainstream? A Response to Ward's 'Last Man Picked,'" *International Journal of the History of Sport* 30, no. 1 (2013): 20.

31. William Cronon, "A Place for Stories: Nature, History, and Narrative," *Journal of American History* 78, no. 4 (1992): 1347–76.

32. E. John B. Allen, *The Culture and Sport of Skiing: From Antiquity to World War II* (Amherst, 2007); Huntford, *Two Planks and a Passion.* Huntford's

monograph extends into the postwar era, but the bulk of his narrative and analysis deal with the years before World War II.

33. David Blackbourn, "Das Kaiserreich transnational: Eine Skizze," in *Das Kaiserreich transnational: Deutschland in der Welt, 1871–1914,* ed. Sebastian Conrad and Jürgen Osterhammel (Göttingen, 2006), 302–24; H. Glenn Penny, "German Polycentrism and the Writing of History," *German History* 30, no. 2 (2012): 265–82.

34. Jennifer Jenkins, "Locating Germany," *German History* 29, no. 1 (2011): 108–26.

35. J. R. McNeill, "Observations on the Nature and Culture of Environmental History," *History and Theory* 42, no. 4 (2003): 35.

36. "Entangled history" is the common English translation of *histoire croisée* or *Verflechtungsgeschichte,* a methodological approach first developed by French and German historians to add depth and nuance to comparative and transnational studies. See the works by Michael Werner and Bénédicte Zimmermann, "Beyond Comparison: *Histoire croisée* and the Challenge of Reflexivity," *History and Theory* 45, no. 1 (2006): 30–50; *De la comparaison à l'histoire croisée* (Paris, 2004); and "Vergleich, Transfer, Verflechtung: Der Ansatz der histoire croisée und die Herausforderung des Transnationalen," *Geschichte und Gesellschaft* 28, no. 4 (2002): 607–36. See also Jürgen Kocka and Heinz-Gerhard Haupt, *Comparative and Transnational History: Central European Approaches and Perspectives* (New York, 2009); Jani Marjanen, "Undermining Methodological Nationalism: Histoire croisée of Concepts as Transnational History," in *Transnational Political Spaces: Agents—Structures—Encounters,* ed. Mathias Albert, Gesa Bluhm, Jan Helmig, Andreas Leutzsch, and Jochen Walter (Frankfurt, 2009), 239–63.

37. Celia Applegate, "A Europe of Regions: Reflections on the Historiography of Sub-national Places in Modern Times," *American Historical Review* 104, no. 4 (1999): 1181.

38. Robert K. Burns Jr., "The Circum-Alpine Culture Area: A Preliminary View," *Anthropological Quarterly* 36, no. 3 (1963): 130–55.

39. On the relationship between marginality and centrality in modernism, see Berman, *All That Is Solid Melts into Air;* Friedman, "Definitional Excursions," "Periodizing Modernism," and "Planetarity."

CHAPTER ONE. AN UPHILL CLIMB

1. Arthur Conan Doyle, "An Alpine Pass on 'Ski,'" *Strand,* July–December 1894, 657, 661.

2. Ibid., 658–61.

3. Ibid., 658.

4. Ibid.

5. Fernand Braudel, *The Mediterranean and the Mediterranean World in the Age of Phillip II,* vol. 1 (Berkeley, 1995), 29.

6. Ibid., 33.

7. Paul Guichonnet, "Le milieu naturel alpin," in *Histoire et civilisations des Alpes,* ed. Paul Guichonnet (Toulouse, 1980), 1:11.

8. Settlements in the early modern era were known for their "Alpine freedoms," a product of their relative geographical isolation and the regional preference for political organization at the communal level. As a result, religious reformers found in the Alps greater tolerance for individual freedoms and a refuge for their heterodox theologies. See Werner Bätzing, *Die Alpen: Geschichte und Zukunft einer europäischen Kulturlandschaft* (Munich, 2003), 110–14.

9. Walter Woodburn Hyde, "The Alps in History," *Proceedings of the American Philosophical Society* 75, no. 6 (1935): 434.

10. Luis Trenker and Walter Schmidkunz, *Berge und Heimat: Das Buch von den Bergen und ihren Menschen* (Berlin, 1933), 61–62.

11. Paul Guichonnet, Elisabeth Lichtenberger, and Brigitte Prost-Vandenbroucke, "L'évolution contemporaine," in Guichonnet, *Histoire et civilisations des Alpes,* 2:252–53.

12. Werner Bätzing, *Die Alpen: Geschichte und Zukunft einer europäischen Kulturlandschaft* (Munich, 2003), 74–79. On the importance of territoriality to states in the modern age, see Charles Maier, "Consigning the Twentieth Century to History: Alternative Narratives for the Modern Era," *American Historical Review* 105, no. 3 (2000): 807–31.

13. Bätzing, *Die Alpen,* 13–14.

14. Max Senger, *Wie die Schweizer Alpen erobert wurden* (Zurich, 1945), 256.

15. Trenker and Schmidkunz, *Berge und Heimat,* 53, 61.

16. Ernst Bloch, "The Alps without Photography," in *Literary Essays* (Stanford, CA, 1998), 440.

17. Letter from Arnold Lunn to his mother, February 15. Sir Arnold Lunn Papers (hereafter ALP), Georgetown University, box 1, folder 1. This letter mentions the recent end of World War I and thus was likely written in 1919.

18. Trenker and Schmidkunz, *Berge und Heimat,* 31.

19. Denis E. Cosgrove, *Social Formation and Symbolic Landscape* (London, 1984), 236.

20. See Edward Dickinson's discussion of the role of the Alps in defining race as an aesthetic rather than a scientific category in late nineteenth- and early twentieth-century German-language discourse. Edward Dickinson, "Germanizing the Alps and Alpinizing the Germans," *German Studies Review* 33, no. 3 (2010): 579–602.

21. Fergus Fleming, *Killing Dragons: The Conquest of the Alps* (New York, 2002), 1–12; Marco Armiero, *A Rugged Nation: Mountains and the Making of Modern Italy* (Cambridge, UK, 2011), 13–26.

22. Arnold Zweig, "Dialektik der Alpen: Fortschritt und Hemmnis," in *Berliner Ausgabe,* 3, no. 4 (Berlin, 1997), 98–99.

23. J. W. Burrow, *The Crisis of Reason: European Thought, 1848–1914* (New Haven, CT, 2000). On the role of art in training the tourist "eye" in the nineteenth century, see Orvar Löfgren, *On Holiday: A History of Vacationing* (Berkeley, 1999), 19–21.

24. J. Schaefler, "Heilige Berge," *Mitteilungen des Deutschen und Österreichischen Alpenvereins* 22 (1896): 184.

25. Bätzing, *Die Alpen,* 16.

26. Bernhard Tschofen, "Tourismus als Alpenkultur? Zum Marktwert von Kultur(kritik) im Fremdenverkehr," in *Der Alpentourismus: Entwicklungspotenziale im Spannungsfeld von Kultur, Ökonomie und Ökologie,* ed. Kurt Luger and Franz Rest (Innsbruck, 2002), 92.

27. On the Austrian *Sommerfrische* as a liberal cultural escape for Viennese intellectuals, see Deborah R. Coen, "Liberal Reason and the Culture of the *Sommerfrische,*" *Austrian History Yearbook* 38 (2007): 145–59. Cf. Alison Frank, "The Air Cure Town: Commodifying Mountain Air in Alpine Central Europe," *Central European History* 45, no. 2 (2012): 185–207.

28. See John Alexander Williams, *Turning to Nature in Germany: Hiking, Nudism, and Conservation, 1900–1940* (Stanford, CA, 2007).

29. Klaus Eckert, *Alpenbahnen* (Munich, 2000), 6.

30. Bätzing, *Die Alpen,* 206.

31. Löfgren, *On Holiday,* 61.

32. Wolfgang König, *Bahnen und Berge: Verkehrstechnik, Tourismus und Naturschutz in den Schweizer Alpen, 1870–1939* (Frankfurt, 2000), 15.

33. Alexander Innes Shand, *Old-Time Travel: Personal Reminiscences of the Continent Forty Years ago Compared with Experiences of the Present Day* (New York, 1904), 138–39.

34. Arnold Lunn, *Mountain Jubilee* (London, 1943), 279.

35. On skiing before the nineteenth century, see Roland Huntford, *Two Planks and a Passion: The Dramatic History of Skiing* (London, 2008), 3–44; E. John B. Allen, *The Culture and Sport of Skiing: From Antiquity to World War II* (Amherst, MA, 2007), 7–35. On the relationship between skiing and Norse mythology, see Gerd Falkner, "Ull und Skadi: Skibrauchtum und Götterglaube," pamphlet accompanying exhibition of the German Ski Museum (Planegg, 2006).

36. Allen, *Culture and Sport of Skiing,* 27–28.

37. Johann Christoph Friedrich GutsMuths, *Gymnastik für die Jugend* (Schnepfenthal, 1804), 386–90.

38. Allen, *Culture and Sport of Skiing,* 39–42, 50–55.

39. The German *Turnen* movement arose in the context of Napoleon's occupation of the German lands, when Friedrich Ludwig Jahn developed a system of noncompetitive gymnastics meant to cultivate healthy bodies and active, disciplined minds while simultaneously promoting German nationalism. In the later nineteenth century, the *Turnen* movement was seen as offering an alternative to the competitive ethos of modern sport.

40. Benedict Anderson, *Imagined Communities: Reflections on the Origin and Spread of Nationalism,* rev. ed. (London, 1991).

41. Huntford, *Two Planks and a Passion,* 65–77. For discussions of the relationship between sport and modernity, see Allen Guttmann, *From Ritual to Record: The Nature of Modern Sports* (New York, 1978), esp. 15–56; Georges Vigarello, "Le temps

du sport," in *L'avènement des loisirs, 1850–1960,* ed. Alain Corbin (Paris, 1995), 193–221.

42. Anton Obholzer, *Geschichte des Schilaufs, mit besonderer Berücksichtigung Mitteleuropas* (Vienna, 1935), 19.

43. Alon Confino, *The Nation as Local Metaphor: Württemberg, Imperial Germany, and National Memory, 1871–1918* (Chapel Hill, NC, 1997). Cf. Celia Applegate, *Nation of Provincials: The German Idea of Heimat* (Berkeley, 1990).

44. On geographical-diffusion theory in sport, see John Bale, *Sports Geography,* 2nd ed. (London, 2003), 52.

45. The German Henry Hoek and the Briton E. C. Richardson remarked on the importance of Norwegian students in bringing skiing to the continent in their early skiing guidebook, *Der Ski und seine sportliche Benutzung* (Munich, 1907), 10.

46. On the role of the German educational system in "institutionalizing" innovation and driving the German challenge to British industrial superiority in Europe in the second half of the nineteenth century, see David Landes, *The Unbound Prometheus: Technological Change and Industrial Development in Western Europe from 1750 to the Present,* 2nd ed. (Cambridge, MA, 2003), esp. 339–48.

47. Carl J. Luther, "Die Anfänge des Skilaufes in Mitteleuropa," *Ski-Chronik: Jahrbuch des Mitteleuropaeischen Ski-Verbandes* 2 (1909–10): 2–3.

48. Quoted in Huntford, *Two Planks and a Passion,* 179.

49. Gerd Falkner, "Wilhelm Paulcke (1873–1949): Initiator der Gründung des Deutschen und des Mitteleuropäischen Skiverbandes," *SportZeiten* 8, no. 1 (2008): 80.

50. Wilhelm Paulcke, *Berge als Schicksal* (Munich, 1936), 32.

51. Arnold Lunn, *A History of Ski-ing* (London, 1927), 23.

52. Fred Rubi, "Der Wintertourismus in der Schweiz: Entwicklung, Struktur und volkswirtschaftliche Bedeutung" (dissertation, University of Bern, 1953), 13.

53. Wolfgang Schivelbusch, *The Railway Journey: The Industrialization of Time and Space in the Nineteenth Century* (Berkeley, 1986), 14.

54. Susan Barton, *Healthy Living in the Alps: The Origins of Winter Tourism in Switzerland, 1860–1914* (Manchester, UK, 2008), 23–28, 52–57.

55. Arnold Lunn, *Switzerland and the English* (London, 1944), 180.

56. Arnold Lunn, *Ski-ing* (London, 1913), 217–18.

CHAPTER TWO. A CIVILIZING FORCE

1. Fridtjof Nansen, *The First Crossing of Greenland* (London, 1890), ix.

2. Ibid., 5.

3. Ibid., 73.

4. On fin-de-siècle spectacles, see Vanessa Schwartz, *Spectacular Realities: Early Mass Culture in Fin-de-Siècle Paris* (Berkeley, 1998).

5. Wilhelm Paulcke, *Der Skilauf: Seine Erlernung und Verwendung im Dienste des Verkehrs, sowie zu touristischen, alpinen und militärischen Zwecken* (Freiburg im Breisgau, 1905), 2.

6. Arnold Lunn, *A History of Ski-ing* (London, 1927), 24.

7. Jules Payot, "L'hiver à Chamonix," *La montagne* 3 (1907): 500–501.

8. The German Alpine Association (Deutscher Alpenverein, founded 1869) and Austrian Alpine Association (Österreichischer Alpenverein, founded 1862) merged into a single German and Austrian Alpine Association in 1873. They remained united until 1938, when Nazi Germany's annexation of Austria led the regime to rename the association Deutscher Alpenverein (DAV) and bring it under the control of the party-state. In 1945, following the defeat of Germany in World War II, Allied officials disbanded the DAV. The Austrian Alpine Association was reconstituted that same year, whereas the DAV reformed with the permission of Allied authorities in 1952. The two associations have remained separate since.

9. Wilhelm Paulcke, "Der Skilauf in den Alpen," *Mitteilungen des Deutschen und Österreichischen Alpenvereins (MDÖAV)* 27 (1901): 18–19.

10. Françoise Rey and Claude Marin, "1924, les Jeux Olympiques de Chamonix," in *La grande histoire du ski,* ed. Musée Dauphinois (Grenoble, 1994), 54–57.

11. Fred Rubi, "Der Wintertourismus in der Schweiz: Entwicklung, Struktur und volkswirtschaftliche Bedeutung" (dissertation, University of Bern, 1953), 14, 17.

12. "Der Wintersport und die Ausstellung 'München 1908,'" *Der Winter* 3 (1908–9), 6.

13. Verwaltungen der k.k. österreich. Staatsbahnen und der österreich. Südbahn, "Wintersport in Österreich" (Vienna, 1914), 84–88 (pamphlet).

14. Carl J. Luther and G. P. Lücke, *Der Skitourist* (Munich, 1913), 18–19.

15. Max Nassauer, *Gebirge und Gesundheit: Hygienische Winke besonders für die Frauen* (Munich, 1908), 6–7, 39.

16. F. Kleinhans, "Alpinismus und Schneeschuhsport," *MDÖAV* 38 (1912): 291.

17. Vera Martinelli, *Zwischen Telemarkschwüngen und Sportkorsetts: Frauen und Skisport; Das Beispiel Schwarzwald* (Schorndorf, 2008), 155; Olive Hockin, "On Women's Clothes," in *Ski Club of Great Britain and National Ski Union Year-Book, 1914,* ed. H. C. H. Marriott (London, 1914), 378.

18. Nassauer, *Gebirge und Gesundheit,* 7, 39.

19. Marie Marvingt, "Les femmes et le ski," in Louis Magnus and Renaud de la Fregeolière, *Les sports d'hiver* (Paris, 1911), 176, 178.

20. Gertrud Pfister, "Gracefully and Elegantly Downhill ... Women and the Sport of Skiing in Germany (1890–1914)," in *Winter Games, Warm Traditions: Selected Papers from the 2nd International ISHPES Seminar, Lillehammer 1994,* ed. Matti Goksøyr, Gerd von der Lippe, and Kristen Mo (Sankt Augustin, 1996), 229.

21. Hockin, "On Women's Clothes," 377, 382.

22. Henry Hoek and E. C. Richardson, *Der Ski und seine sportliche Benutzung* (Munich, 1907), 82–83.

23. Hockin, "On Women's Clothes," 384.

24. Marvingt, "Les femmes et le ski," 180–81.

25. Mathias Zdarsky, 1915, quoted in Erwin Mehl, ed., *Zdarsky: Festschrift zum 80. Geburtstage des Begründers der alpinen Skifahrweise* (Vienna, 1936), 185.

26. Martinelli, *Zwischen Telemarkschwüngen und Sportkorsetts,* 155; Pfister, "Gracefully and Elegantly Downhill," 227.

27. Willi Romberg, "Die Damen und der Schi-Wettlauf," *Der Winter* 3 (1908–9): 2.

28. Martinelli, *Zwischen Telemarkschwüngen und Sportkorsetts,* 155.

29. Quoted in William Sheridan Allen, *The Nazi Seizure of Power: The Experience of a Single German Town, 1922–1945,* rev. ed. (New York, 1984), 17.

30. Stefan Szymanski, "A Theory of the Evolution of Modern Sport," *Journal of the History of Sport* 35, no. 1 (2008): 2. Szymanski locates the dawn of modern, associative sport in eighteenth-century England. Central European skiing in the fin de siècle emulated this example before becoming more closely aligned with the state in the early twentieth century. Szymanski's analysis nicely complements that of Jürgen Habermas, who theorized the role of the public sphere as an alternative to authoritarian state power in the eighteenth century. See Jürgen Habermas, *The Structural Transformation of the Public Sphere: An Inquiry into a Category of Bourgeois Society* (Boston, 1991).

31. Tim Ashburner, *The History of Ski Jumping* (Wykey, UK, 2003), 28.

32. Lunn, *A History of Ski-ing,* 165.

33. Wilhelm Paulcke, *Berge als Schicksal* (Munich, 1936), 50.

34. Christiane Eisenberg, *"English Sports" und deutsche Bürger: Eine Gesellschaftsgeschichte, 1800–1939* (Munich, 1999), 16–17.

35. On Weberian modernity in sport, see Allen Guttmann, *From Ritual to Record: The Nature of Modern Sports* (New York, 1978). Cf. Norbert Elias and Eric Dunning, *Quest for Excitement: Sport and Leisure in the Civilizing Process* (Oxford, 1986).

36. Paulcke, *Der Skilauf,* 178.

37. Indeed, some ski clubs began as sections of national Alpine associations, leading to disputes over the proper role and mission of the Alpine clubs, the use of Alpine huts by skiers, and the relationship between skiers and alpinists more generally. See, for example, Archive of the Deutscher Alpenverein (German Alpine Association—hereafter DAV), Munich, BGS 1 SG/14/1–3, which details a dispute within a Munich-area Alpine club between skiers and Alpinists regarding the use of DAV huts. On the relationship between the German and Austrian Alpine Association and modern leisure and sporting cultures, see Dagmar Günther, *Alpine Quergänge: Kulturgeschichte des bürgerlichen Alpinismus (1870–1930)* (Frankfurt, 1998), 104–49. On its relationship with skiing in particular, see 106–14.

38. Lunn, *A History of Ski-ing,* 163–72.

39. John Allen notes that Schneider had sold 1,350 pairs of skis by Spring 1893. E. John B. Allen, *The Culture and Sport of Skiing: From Antiquity to World War II* (Amherst, MA, 2007), 134.

40. Schneeschuh-Verein München, "XV. Jahres-Bericht pro 1907/08" (Munich, 1908), 3–5.

41. Ibid., 7–13.

42. Ibid., 15–17.

43. *Der Winter* 1 (1906–7): 1.

44. *Der Winter* 2 (1907–8): 1. *Deutscher Wintersport* retained some reportage on sports such as ice skating and hockey, but its coverage was weighted heavily toward skiing by the end of the decade.

45. Hoek and Richardson, *Der Ski.*

46. "Allgemeine Einladung zur Versammlung Deutscher, Oesterreichischer und Schweizerischer Skiläufervereinigungen nach München zum 4. und 5. November 1905," in Gerd Falkner, *100 Jahre Deutscher Skiverband,* vol. 3 (Planegg, 2005), 122–29.

47. E. Thoma and Rudolf Nater, "Zum Austritt des S.S.V. aus dem M.E.S.V," *Der Winter* 2 (1907–8): 126.

48. Rudolf Gomperz, "Zur Auflösung des Mitteleuropäischen Ski-Verbandes," *Ski-Chronik* 5 (1913): 135.

49. For example, the ski division of the DÖAV's Bavarian section, Alpenverein-sektion Bayerland, began to offer insurance in 1912 that for as little as 2.10 marks per season (October 15–May 15) would provide skiers with a 3,000-mark invalidity payout and 3 marks in daily compensation in cases of catastrophic injury sustained while skiing. "An unsere Mitglieder!" January 18, 1912, *DAV,* SEK 6 SG/12/0. In the same year, a French insurance company published articles in the French Alpine journal offering coverage for skiing injuries. See "Les risques du ski," *La montagne* 8 (1912): 325.

50. "Satzungen des Deutschen Skiverbands," enacted November 4, 1905, in Falkner, *100 Jahre Deutscher Skiverband,* 3:150–63.

51. The German sport historian Christiane Eisenberg has shown that German sporting organizations before World War I tended toward the politicization, nation-alization, and bureaucratization of sport, whereas among the British, sporting organizations remained unquestionably in the private sphere. In general, Eisenberg's characterization of German sport also holds true for other continental sporting cultures. See Eisenberg, *"English Sports" und deutsche Bürger.*

52. G. Dumontel, "Skiing in Italy," *Year-Book of the Ski Club of Great Britain* 2 (1911): 49–50.

53. Allen, *Culture and Sport of Skiing,* 155.

54. Yves Ballu, "Les premières traces de skis dans les Alpes françaises," in Musée Dauphinois, *La grande histoire du ski,* 35–38.

55. "The Organization of Ski-Running in France," *Ski Club of Great Britain and National Ski Union Year-Book* (1913): 317–20.

CHAPTER THREE. A FAMILY FEUD

1. A. Dessauer, "Montecchi und Capuletti," in *Der mißhandelte Schnee: Eiskalte Geschichten,* ed. Toni Schönecker, E. Henel, et al. (Munich, 1921), 28–49.

2. Emil Zsigmondy and Wilhelm Paulcke, *Die Gefahren der Alpen,* 4th ed. (Innsbruck, 1908).

3. Michael Ponstingl, "Mathias Zdarskys 'Posen des Wissens': Zu einer fotografischen Kodierung des Skifahrens," in *Skilauf—Volkssport—Medienzirkus:*

Skisport als Kulturphänomen, ed. Markwart Herzog (Stuttgart, 2005), 125; Österreichischer Skiverband, *100 Jahre Österreichischer Skiverband* (Innsbruck, 2005), 21–23.

4. Mathias Zdarsky, *Alpine (Lilienfelder) Skifahr-Technik: Eine Anleitung zum Selbstunterricht* (Berlin, 1908), 3.

5. Anton Obholzer, *Geschichte des Schilaufs, mit besonderer Berücksichtigung Mitteleuropas* (Vienna, 1935), 34.

6. Erwin Mehl, "Mathias Zdarsky, Der Mann und das Werk," in *Zdarsky: Festschrift zum 80. Geburtstage des Begründers der alpinen Skifahrweise,* ed. Erwin Mehl (Vienna, 1936), 21.

7. W. R. Rickmers, "Der Newton der Skigesetze," in Mehl, *Zdarsky,* 154–56.

8. Heinrich Frank, "Die Entwicklung von Alpinistik und Wintersport in Österreich," in Ernst Bruckmüller and Hannes Strohmeyer, eds., *Turnen und Sport in der Geschichte Österreichs* (Vienna, 1998), 124; Heinz Polednik, *Das Glück im Schnee: 100 Jahre Skilauf in Österreich* (Vienna, 1991), 36.

9. Quoted in Luis Trenker, *Berge im Schnee* (Berlin, 1932), 101.

10. Polednik, *Das Glück im Schnee,* 12.

11. J. Simon, "Einiges über Schneeschuhlaufen in unserer deutschen Heimat," *Deutsche Alpenzeitung* 6 (1906–7): 302.

12. Ponstingl, "Mathias Zdarskys 'Posen des Wissens,'" 124–25.

13. Georg Löwenbach, "Ueber Lilienfelder Skitechnik," *Mitteilungen der Deutschen und Österreichischen Alpenvereins* 27 (1901): 6–7.

14. In reality, because of the logistics of taking part in club activities, the vast majority of members were Austrians.

15. Thor Tangvald, "A Norwegian Criticism of British Ski-ing," *British Ski Year Book* (1929): 123–24.

16. Arnold Lunn, *Ski-ing* (London, 1913), 49. Lunn initially criticized Zdarsky's Alpine school but later acknowledged Zdarsky's contributions to the development of the sport, noting that it was Zdarsky who first recognized that "the happy-go-lucky methods of downhill skiing on the comparatively gentle downhill slopes of Norway, required to be revolutionized when applied to steep Alpine ground." The enduring intransigence of many Norwegian ski bureaucrats to the development of institutions and competitions serving Alpine skiing softened Lunn's stance on Zdarsky considerably. Arnold Lunn, "Gruß aus England," in Mehl, *Zdarsky,* 8.

17. Zdarsky, *Alpine (Lilienfelder) Skifahr-Technik,* 95.

18. Willi Fleischmann, *Lilienfelder oder Norweger Skilauftechnik? Zur Aufklärung in einem alten Sportstreit!* (Diessen vor München, 1910), 16.

19. Wilhelm Paulcke, quoted in Fleischmann, *Lilienfelder oder Norweger Skilauftechnik?,* 81.

20. Wilhelm Paulcke, *Der Skilauf: Seine Erlernung und Verwendung im Dienste des Verkehrs, sowie zu touristischen, alpinen und militärischen Zwecken* (Freiburg im Breisgau, 1905), 190.

21. Zdarsky, *Alpine (Lilienfelder) Skifahr-Technik,* 3–6.

22. This contrast was certainly overdrawn by Zdarsky and his supporters, as most of their Central European interlocutors, such as Wilhelm Paulcke, also wished

to ski in the Alps. Many Norwegian proponents of the Nordic school, however, rejected skiing in the Alps out of hand.

23. Hugo Vondörfer, "Der Alpen-Skiverein," in Mehl, *Zdarsky,* 110.

24. "Zum Beginne," *Der Schnee* 6 (1910–11): 1–2.

25. Österreichischer Skiverband, *100 Jahre Österreichischer Skiverband,* 25.

26. Mehl, "Mathias Zdarsky," 45, 53.

27. Quoted in Fleischmann, *Lilienfelder oder Norweger Skilauftechnik?,* 97–98.

28. Wilhelm Paulcke, *Berge als Schicksal* (Munich, 1936), 59.

29. Paulcke, *Der Skilauf,* 188.

30. Lunn, *Ski-ing,* 39 & 152.

31. Vivian Caulfeild, *How to Ski and How Not To* (London, 1913), 15–18.

32. W. R. Rickmers, "An alle Skiläufer!," *Deutscher Wintersport* 14 (1904–5): 256–57.

33. Henry Hoek and E. C. Richardson, *Der Ski und seine sportliche Benutzung* (Munich, 1907).

34. Lunn, *Ski-ing,* 14.

35. Carl J. Luther, *Ski-Wörterbuch in fünf Sprachen* (Munich, 1934), 5.

36. Georg Bilgeri, *Der Alpine Skilauf* (Munich, 1910), 2.

37. Obholzer, *Geschichte des Schilaufs,* 53–55; Hannes Schneider and Arnold Fanck, *The Wonders of Ski-ing: A Method of Correct Ski-ing and its Applications to Alpine Running* (London, 1933), 13.

38. Hassa Horn, "Gruß aus Norwegen," in Mehl, *Zdarsky,* 8–10.

39. The historian of sport Erwin Mehl contended that "the triumphal procession of the ski moved from the Alps outward through the entire world (and not from the Nordic lands)." Erwin Mehl, *Grundriss der Weltgeschichte des Schifahrens, I: Von der Steinzeit bis zum Beginn der schigeschichtlichen Neuzeit (1860)* (Schorndorf bei Stuttgart, 1964), 12.

40. Trenker, *Berge im Schnee,* 45.

41. Carl Luther, *Das weiße Reich* (Berlin, 1935), 48.

42. Sepp Bildstein, "Wettläufe, ihre Grundlage und Bedeutung," *Ski-Chronik* 5 (1913): 19–21.

43. Quoted in Paulcke, *Der Skilauf,* 182.

44. Quoted in "Wintersportausschuss München," *Der Winter* 2 (1907–8): 49.

45. Mathias Zdarsky, "Die sportliche Ausrüstung in Skivereinen," *Der Winter* 1 (1906–7): 65–67.

46. On the antinomial nature of modernity and modernism, with their unresolved oppositions and inherent conflicts, see Michael Saler, "Modernity and Enchantment: A Historiographic Review," *American Historical Review* 111, no. 3 (2006): 692–716.

CHAPTER FOUR. JOY IN MOVEMENT

1. Carl Luther, "Erlebnis des Schnees und des Bergwinters," *Deutsche Alpenzeitung* 27 (1932): 53–54.

2. Diary of Nellie H. Friedrichs (née Bruell), March 11, 1935. Diary in possession of Christopher R. Friedrichs, Vancouver, British Columbia, Canada.

3. Ibid., March 12 and 13, 1935.

4. Between 1900 and 1939 Alpine skiing gained tens of thousands of converts, with the largest national ski club, the Deutscher Skiverband, expanding from fewer than 2,500 members at its founding in 1905 to over 100,000 members by 1932. The Österreichischer Skiverband expanded from 700 members in 1905 to nearly 25,000 in 1932; the Schweizerischer Skiverband grew from barely 600 members in 1905 to nearly 25,000 in 1934; and even the late-arriving French Fédération Française de Ski, founded only in 1924, counted nearly 20,000 members by 1932 (an increase of nearly 57 percent over 1931). Gerd Falkner, *100 Jahre Deutscher Skiverband* (Planegg, 2005), 1:116; "Verzeichnis der dem S.S.V. angehörenden Clubs/Liste des Clubs affiliés à l'A.S.C.S.," *SSV Jahrbuch* 30 (1934): 194–200; "Activité des sociétés," *La revue du ski* 3 (1932): xvii.

5. On "heroic" interwar modernism in culture and politics, see David Harvey, *The Condition of Postmodernity: An Enquiry into the Origins of Cultural Change* (Cambridge, UK, 1990), 30–31.

6. Oertel worked as a judge in a variety of Bavarian courts beginning in the Wilhelmine period (1871–1918) and in his free time was an avid sportsman and mountaineer. He served as the chairman of the Bavarian section of the DÖAV from 1903 to 1906 and from 1908 to 1920. Walter Welsch, *Geschichte der Sektion Bayerland des Deutschen Alpenvereins e.V.: Die Zeit des Ersten Weltkriegs und der Weimarer Republik, 1914–1933* (Munich, 2010), 321.

7. Eugen Oertel, "Sport, Alpinismus und Schilauf," *Mitteilungen des Deutschen und Österreichischen Alpenvereins* 35 (1909): 6.

8. On the second Industrial Revolution and the Long Depression, see David Landes, *The Unbound Prometheus: Technological Change and Industrial Development in Western Europe from 1750 to the Present,* 2nd ed. (Cambridge, MA, 2003), 193–358.

9. Georg Simmel, "The Metropolis and Mental Life," in *The Blackwell City Reader,* 2nd ed., ed. Gary Bridge and Sophie Watson (Chichester, UK, 2010), 108.

10. Descriptions of Europe's metropolises in the first half of the twentieth century are noteworthy for their ambivalence: the modern city was frightening and oppressive but also dynamic and novel. See Simmel, "Metropolis," and Walter Benjamin, *The Arcades Project* (Cambridge, MA, 1999).

11. H. Stuart Hughes, *Consciousness and Society* (New York, 1958).

12. Carl Schorske, *Fin-de-Siècle Vienna: Politics and Culture* (New York, 1980).

13. Oertel, "Sport, Alpinismus und Schilauf," 6.

14. Ibid., 7.

15. J. W. Burrow, *The Crisis of Reason: European Thought, 1848–1914* (New Haven, CT, 2000), 147–96.

16. Oertel, "Sport, Alpinismus und Schilauf," 8.

17. The idea that the human mind is tempestuous and conflicted became prevalent in the fin de siècle, represented, for example, by Sigmund Freud's description of

the conflict among the id, ego, and superego, and the schizophrenia of Robert Louis Stevenson's Dr. Jekyll and Mr. Hyde. See Sigmund Freud, *New Introductory Lectures on Psycho-analysis* (New York, 1989); Robert Louis Stevenson, *The Strange Case of Dr Jekyll and Mr Hyde* (London, 1886). On the history of modern subjectivity, see Jerrold Siegel, *The Idea of the Self: Thought and Experience in Western Europe since the Seventeenth Century* (New York, 2005); Charles Taylor, *Sources of the Self: The Making of Modern Identity* (Cambridge, MA, 1989).

18. Oertel, "Sport, Alpinismus und Schilauf," 18.

19. Ibid.

20. Friedrich Wilhelm Nietzsche, *Die fröhliche Wissenschaft* (Leipzig, 1887), 194.

21. Oertel, "Sport, Alpinismus und Schilauf," 8–9.

22. Ibid., 9.

23. Ibid.

24. Marco Armiero, *A Rugged Nation: Mountains and the Making of Modern Italy* (Cambridge, UK, 2011), 43. Thomas Lekan, "A 'Noble Prospect': Tourism, *Heimat,* and Conservation on the Rhine, 1880–1914," *Journal of Modern History* 81, no. 4 (2009): 824–58; Kerwin Lee Klein, "A Vertical World: The Eastern Alps and Modern Mountaineering," *Journal of Historical Sociology* 24, no. 4 (2011): 519–48.

25. Recent works have studied the importance of movement and sensory perception to the creation of a sense of place. See Justin Spinney, "A Place of Sense: A Kinaesthetic Ethnography of Cyclists on Mont Ventoux," *Environment and Planning D: Society and Space* 24, no. 5 (2006): 709–32; Tim Edensor, ed., *Geographies of Rhythm: Nature, Place, Mobilities and Bodies* (Farnham, UK, and Burlington, VT, 2010).

26. "Les sports de neige, II: Le ski," *Revue Olympique* 26 (February 1908): 28.

27. Hillel Schwartz, "Torque: The New Kinaesthetic of the Twentieth Century," in *Incorporations,* ed. Jonathan Crary and Sanford Kwintner (New York, 1992), 86, 108.

28. Letter from Arnold Lunn to Kurz, June 7, 1917. Sir Arnold Lunn Papers, Georgetown University, Washington DC, box 1, folder 10.

29. On the relationship between desirable and fearful landscapes in sport, see John Bale, *Landscapes of Modern Sport* (London, 1994), 120–21.

30. Emil Zsigmondy and Wilhelm Paulcke, *Die Gefahren der Alpen,* 4th ed. (Innsbruck, 1908).

31. See, for example, Nietzsche's evocation of the will to power in Friedrich Nietzsche, *Thus Spake Zarathustra: A Book for All and None* (New York, 1896); the importance of instinct to Sigmund Freud's tripartite model of the mind in Freud, *New Introductory Lectures;* and the celebration of instinct and the spirit in fascist politics, described in Simonetta Falasca-Zamponi, *Fascist Spectacle: The Aesthetics of Power in Mussolini's Italy* (Berkeley, 2000), 26–41, and in Robert O. Paxton, *The Anatomy of Fascism* (New York, 2005), 32–42.

32. Martin Jay has argued that the self-referentiality and "art for art's sake" ethos of modernist artists, which led them to privilege form over content and context, was a deliberate attempt to emancipate the artist by distancing art from the weight of history and preconceptions about the object represented. Martin Jay, "From

Modernism to Post-modernism," in *The Oxford Illustrated History of Modern Europe,* ed. T. C. W. Blanning (Oxford: Oxford University Press, 1996), 255–78.

33. Emil Petersen, "La technique du ski," in *L'enchantement du ski,* ed. Alfred Couttet, Arnold Lunn, and Emil Petersen (Paris, 1930), 15.

34. Marshall Berman, *All That is Solid Melts into Air: The Experience of Modernity* (New York, 1988), 5.

35. "Les sports de neige, II," 24–25. In 1903, Georg Simmel argued that urban modernity overwhelmed individuals with stimuli, and in response, moderns turned inward and urban life became "intellectual" in nature. Simmel believed that individuals in rural societies, by contrast, remained more "social" and "emotional."

36. Henry Hoek and E. C. Richardson, *Der Ski und seine sportliche Benutzung* (Munich, 1907), 20–22.

37. On the composition, performance, and reception of *Le sacre du printemps,* see Modris Eksteins, *Rites of Spring: The Great War and the Birth of the Modern Age* (Boston, 1989), 9–54.

38. Oskar Ewald, "Wintersport," *Der Schnee* 8 (1912–13): 134.

39. Berman, *All That Is Solid,* 5.

40. Wolfgang Schivelbusch, *The Railway Journey: The Industrialization of Time and Space in the Nineteenth Century* (Berkeley, 1986), 9.

41. Pierre de Coubertin, *Olympic Memoirs* (Lausanne, 1979), 49.

42. This attempt to blend instinctive action with intellectual contemplation had long vexed artists and cultural critics, forming the basis for Richard Wagner's attempt to create a *Gesamtkunstwerk* (total work of art) in his operas. On the sporting festival as a *Gesamtkunstwerk,* see Markwart Herzog, "Popularität und Ästhetik des Skisports," in *Skilauf-Volkssport-Medienzirkus: Skisport als Kulturphänomen,* ed. Markwart Herzog (Stuttgart, 2005), 18–19. On modernism in Pierre de Coubertin's thought, see Douglas Brown, "Modern Sport, Modernism and the Cultural Manifesto: De Coubertin's *Revue Olympique,*" *International Journal of the History of Sport* 18, no. 2 (2001): 78–109.

43. Eugen Oertel, "Die Schönheit des Skilaufs," *Ski-Chronik* 1 (1908–9): 10.

44. Joachim Radkau, *Nature and Power: A Global History of the Environment* (Cambridge, UK, 2008), 26.

45. Carl Luther, *Das weiße Reich* (Berlin, 1935), 52.

46. Wilhelm Paulcke, *Berge als Schicksal* (Munich, 1936), 268. On the historical meanings of *Heimat,* see Celia Applegate, *A Nation of Provincials: The German Idea of Heimat* (Berkeley, 1990); Alon Confino, *The Nation as Local Metaphor: Württemberg, Imperial Germany, and National Memory, 1871–1918* (Chapel Hill, NC, 1997); Thomas Lekan, *Imagining the Nation in Nature* (Cambridge, MA, 2004).

47. On the various functions and definitions of nature, see William Cronon, "Introduction: In Search of Nature," in *Uncommon Ground: Rethinking the Human Place in Nature,* ed. William Cronon (New York, 1996), 23–56.

48. F. Siebert, "Naturgenuß und Metaphysik," *Deutsche Alpenzeitung* 9 (1909–10): 115.

CHAPTER FIVE. ECSTASY IN SPEED

1. Tait Keller, "The Mountains Roar: The Alps during the Great War," *Environmental History* 14, no. 2 (2009): 253–74. See also Marco Armiero, *A Rugged Nation: Mountains and the Making of Modern Italy* (Cambridge, UK, 2011), 87–108.

2. On skiing in World War I, see Hermann Czant, *Alpinismus, Massenwintersport und Weltkrieg* (Munich, 1929); Carl J. Luther, *Schneeschuhläufer im Krieg* (Munich, 1915); Arnold Lunn, *The Mountains of Youth* (London, 1925), 132.

3. Modris Eksteins, *Rites of Spring: The Great War and the Birth of the Modern Age* (Boston, 1989); Stephen Kern, *The Culture of Time and Space, 1880–1918* (Cambridge, MA, 2003), 109–30, 259–86.

4. Kern, *Culture of Time and Space*, 3.

5. Jeremy Millar and Michiel Schwartz, "Introduction: Speed is a Vehicle," in *Speed: Visions of an Accelerated Age*, ed. Jeremy Millar and Michiel Schwartz (London, 1998), 16.

6. Peter Borscheid, *Das Tempo-Virus: Eine Kulturgeschichte der Beschleunigung* (Frankfurt, 2004).

7. F. T. Marinetti, "The Founding and Manifesto of Futurism," in *Futurism: An Anthology*, ed. Lawrence Rainey, Christine Poggi, and Laura Wittman (New Haven, CT, 2009), 51.

8. Borscheid, *Das Tempo-Virus*, 8–12.

9. Jeffrey Schnapp, "Crash (Speed as Engine of Individuation)," *Modernism/Modernity* 6, no. 1 (1999): 5, 21.

10. See Joachim Radkau, *Der Zeitalter der Nervosität: Deutschland zwischen Bismarck und Hitler* (Munich, 1998).

11. Borscheid, *Das Tempo-Virus*, 298–99, 7.

12. Enda Duffy, *The Speed Handbook: Velocity, Pleasure, Modernism* (Durham, NC, 2009), 4.

13. Lunn, *Mountains of Youth*, 31.

14. Ernst Bloch, "The Alps without Photography," in *Literary Essays* (Stanford, CA, 1998), 434.

15. Schnapp, "Crash," 2.

16. Lunn, *Mountains of Youth*, 31.

17. André Teissier, "Essai conçis," *Ski: Sports d'hiver* 2 (1933–34/1934–35): 74–76.

18. Sigmund Freud, *Civilization and Its Discontents* (New York, 2005), 75–76.

19. Hannes Schneider and Arnold Fanck, *The Wonders of Ski-ing: A Method of Correct Ski-ing and its Applications to Alpine Running* (London, 1933), 81. This book was an instructional book produced by a famed Austrian skier (Schneider) and a celebrated German *Bergfilm* director (Fanck) to accompany their film of the same name. The film was an international hit, and the accompanying book was quickly translated into French and English.

20. Lunn, *Mountains of Youth*, 33–34. See also Duffy, *Speed Handbook*, 106.

21. "One must be always drunk. Everything lies in that; it is the only question worth considering. In order not to feel the horrible burden of time which breaks your shoulders and bows you down to earth, you must intoxicate yourself without truce, but with what? With wine, poetry, or art?—As you will; but intoxicate yourself." Charles Baudelaire, "Intoxicate Yourself!" (*Enivrez-vous!*) in *Little Poems in Prose* (Chicago, 1995), 87.

22. Diary of Nellie H. Friedrichs (née Bruell), March 11, 1934. Diary in possession of Christopher R. Friedrichs, Vancouver, British Columbia, Canada.

23. Henry Hoek, "Kleine Ratschläge für eine Skifreundin," *Sport im Winter* 1 (1932–33): 211.

24. Jeffrey Schnapp notes that speed affects the body and mind simultaneously and in concert: "There is no simple way to disentangle somatic from cognitive iterations of velocity: the accelerated circulation of bodies from the accelerated circulation of thoughts, perceptual stimuli, or data; physical hyperactivity from mental hyperactivity." Jeffrey Schnapp, "Fast (Slow) Modern," in *Speed Limits,* ed. Jeffrey Schnapp (Milan, 2009), 31.

25. Carl J. Luther and G. P. Lücke, *Der Skitourist* (Munich, 1913), 92.

26. Schnapp, "Crash," 3–4. See also Duffy, *Speed Handbook,* 199–261.

27. Quoted in Arnold Lunn, *Switzerland and the English* (London, 1944). The original quote dates from 1935.

28. Lunn, *Mountains of Youth,* 35–36.

29. Diary of Nellie Friedrichs, March 15, 1935, and March 5, 1934.

30. Wolfgang Schivelbusch, *The Railway Journey: The Industrialization of Time and Space in the Nineteenth Century* (Berkeley, 1986).

31. Duffy, *Speed Handbook,* 9.

32. See Walter Adamson, *Embattled Avant-gardes: Modernism's Resistance to Commodity Culture in Europe* (Berkeley, 2007).

33. Eksteins, *Rites of Spring,* 241–74.

34. On the politics of speed and the "blatant" sexism of speed politics, see Duffy, *Speed Handbook,* 7–8, 55–56.

35. Stefan von Dévan, *Standard-Abfahrten in Europa* (Munich, 1938), 9.

36. Friedrich Nietzsche, *Thus Spake Zarathustra: A Book for All and None* (New York, 1896), 6.

37. Pierre de Coubertin, "The Philosophic Foundation of Modern Olympism," in *Olympism: Selected Writings,* ed. Norbert Müller (Lausanne, 2000), 583.

38. Kern, *Culture of Time and Space,* xiii; Schivelbusch, *Railway Journey,* 10. Enda Duffy has argued that when individuals deem speed alienating, as in Taylorist production processes, they stress that it collapses time, but when they deem it pleasurable, as in automobile travel, they stress that it collapses space. Duffy, *Speed Handbook,* 18, 270.

39. Marinetti, "Founding and Manifesto of Futurism," 51.

40. In 1894, a British vicar, Joseph Sanger Davies, published an account of his experiences climbing the Fünffingerspitze and other Dolomite peaks in the late 1880s and early 1890s: *Dolomite Strongholds: The Last Untrodden Alpine Peaks* (London, 1894). The subtitle alludes to the bittersweet nature of this conquest.

41. On the Alps as a frontier with positive moral implications, see Armiero, *A Rugged Nation,* 134–54, esp. 137; Kerwin Lee Klein, "A Vertical World: The Eastern Alps and Modern Mountaineering," *Journal of Historical Sociology* 24, no. 4 (2011): 519–48; Bernhard Tschofen, "Tourismus als Alpenkultur? Zum Marktwert von Kultur(kritik) im Fremdenverkehr," in *Der Alpentourismus: Entwicklungspotenziale im Spannungsfeld von Kultur, Ökonomie und Ökologie,* ed. Kurt Luger and Franz Rest (Innsbruck, 2002), 92.

42. Kurt Seeger, "Wir Skireisende," in *Deutscher Skilauf: Ein Querschnitt,* ed. Carl Luther (Munich, 1930), 98.

43. Paul Dinckelacker, "Geleitwort," in *Skiparadiese der Alpen,* ed. Carl Luther (Munich, 1933), 7.

44. Although the interwar period saw skiing become a major aspect of consumer culture, the relationship between sport, advertisers, and the press was already highly developed in the fin de siècle. In Germany, companies like Mercedes-Benz advertised heavily in the sporting press and used sporting images to associate their products with modernity, excitement, and youthfulness. The noted marketability of modern sports differed widely from the more serious and traditional, gymnastics-infused *Turnen* movement with which they competed for adherents. Products such as Ovomaltine (a malted-milk drink, the forerunner of Ovaltine in English-speaking markets), Leica cameras, and Nivea skin creams were advertised widely in the skiing press, often depicting skiers in action. On the general connection between turn-of-the-century sports and the advertising industry, see Christiane Eisenberg, *"English Sports" und deutsche Bürger: Eine Gesellschaftsgeschichte, 1800–1939* (Munich, 1999), 226–30.

45. On photography and Alpinism, see Klein, "Vertical World," 528.

46. On spectacle in mass culture, see Vanessa Schwartz, *Spectacular Realities: Early Mass Culture in Fin-de-Siècle Paris* (Berkeley, 1998). On speed culture and mass culture, see Duffy, *Speed Handbook,* 60, 270; Borscheid, *Das Tempo-Virus,* 176–214.

47. See Christian Rapp, "'Der weiße Rausch': Der Skisport im deutschen Bergfilm um 1930," in *Skilauf-Volkssport-Medienzirkus: Skisport als Kulturphänomen,* ed. Markwart Herzog (Stuttgart, 2005), 111–22.

48. Vera Martinelli, *Zwischen Telemarkschwüngen und Sportkorsetts: Frauen und Skisport; Das Beispiel Schwarzwald* (Schorndorf, 2008), 157–58.

49. E. John B. Allen, *The Culture and Sport of Skiing: From Antiquity to World War II* (Amherst, MA, 2007), 243.

50. Hans Fischer, *Skihaserl: Ein Bilderbuch* (Munich, 1935), 13.

51. Frank Becker, "Die Sportlerin als Vorbild der 'neuen Frau': Versuche zur Umwertung der Geschlechterrollen in der Weimarer Republik," *Sozial- und Zeitgeschichte des Sports* 8, no. 3 (1994): 36.

52. Luis Trenker, *Berge im Schnee* (Berlin, 1932), 87.

53. Becker, "Die Sportlerin," 36–39.

54. Fischer, *Skihaserl,* 22.

55. Ibid., 17, 23.

56. Ibid., 18, 24.

57. Trenker, *Berge im Schnee,* 88.

58. For other interpretations of this photo, see Armiero, *Rugged Nation,* 111, 147; Simonetta Falasca-Zamponi, *Fascist Spectacle: The Aesthetics of Power in Mussolini's Italy* (Berkeley, 2000), 73.

59. Enda Duffy persuasively argues that speed eliminates a sense of "place" and renders an area into meaningless "space." Duffy, *Speed Handbook,* 267.

60. Both Italy's Fascists and Germany's Nazis found in mountain sports an ideal combination of body cultures, heroism, and patriotic love of the landscape. Adolf Hitler stood and cheered Germany's victorious skiers at the Winter Olympic Games in Garmisch-Partenkirchen in 1936, and various Nazi officials glorified Alpine skiing as a historically Germanic *Volkssport* that trained body and mind. The Nazi leisure and tourism association Strength through Joy expanded access to the sport by providing affordable group excursions. Alpine skiing was not universally celebrated by fascist regimes, however. The Nazis expressed significant misgivings about the sport's bourgeois associations and egoism, which ran counter to the development of the *Volksgemeinschaft.* When the Nazi invasion of the Soviet Union bogged down in the winter of 1941, Propaganda Minister Joseph Goebbels delivered a radio address imploring Germans to donate their skis and winter clothes to the war effort. In early 1942, the regime banned the use of skis as a means of private transport, and German ski manufacturers reoriented their production toward the war effort, completing the regime's co-optation of the sport for the utilitarian needs of the Nazi Party. Armiero, *Rugged Nation,* 49; Klein, "Vertical World," 539; Lorenz Peiffer, "'Ski für die Ostfront': Der Aufruf des Reichssportführers im Winter 1941/42 und die Konsequenzen für die Entwicklung des Skisports in Deutschland," *SportZeiten* 2, no. 1 (2002): 53–64; Gertrud Pfister, "Sportfexen, Heldenmythen und Opfertod: Alpinismus und Nationalsozialismus," in *Sport und Faschismen/Sport e fascismi: Geschichte und Region/Storia e regione,* ed. Claudio Ambrosi and Wolfgang Weber, 13, no. 1 (2004): 21–60.

61. Rachel Josefowitz Siegel, *My Songs of Now and Then: A Memoir* (Bloomington, IN, 2012), 35–36.

62. On the equivocal nature of modernisms and modernity, see Marshall Berman, *All That is Solid Melts into Air: The Experience of Modernity* (New York, 1988); Susan Stanford Friedman, "Definitional Excursions: The Meanings of *Modern/ Modernity/Modernism," Modernism/Modernity* 8, no. 3 (2001): 493–513; Michael Saler, "Modernity and Enchantment: A Historiographic Review," *American Historical Review* 111, no. 3 (2006): 692–716; Peter Wagner, *Modernity as Experience and Interpretation: A New Sociology of Modernity* (Cambridge, 2008).

63. Erwin Mehl, *Grundriss der Weltgeschichte des Schifahrens, I: Von der Steinzeit bis zum Beginn der schigeschichtlichen Neuzeit (1860)* (Schorndorf bei Stuttgart, 1964), 12.

64. See Marinetti, "Founding and Manifesto of Futurism."

65. See Peter Bailey, "Leisure: Merrie to Modern," in *The Victorian World,* ed. Martin Hewitt (London, 2012), 619–35, esp. 625.

66. Markwart Herzog, "Popularität und Ästhetik des Skisports," in *Skilauf—Volkssport—Medienzirkus,* 16.

67. Eisenberg, *"English Sports" und deutsche Bürger,* 292–94, 434–35.

CHAPTER SIX. MODERNITY IN SPORT

1. *Les jeux de la VIIIe Olympiade Paris 1924: Rapport officiel* (Paris, n.d.), 688–90.

2. Vanessa Schwartz, *Spectacular Realities: Early Mass Culture in Fin-de-Siècle Paris* (Berkeley, 1998), esp. 1–12; Christiane Eisenberg, *"English Sports" und deutsche Bürger: Eine Gesellschaftsgeschichte, 1800–1939* (Munich, 1999); Georges Vigarello, "Le temps du sport," in *L'avènement des loisirs, 1850–1960,* ed. Alain Corbin (Paris, 1995), 193–221.

3. Allen Guttmann, *From Ritual to Record: The Nature of Modern Sports* (New York, 1978).

4. Arnold Lunn, "The Jungfraujoch Railway," unpublished manuscript. Sir Arnold Lunn Papers (hereafter ALP), Georgetown University, Washington, DC, box 9, folder 11.

5. Walter Amstutz, "The Elite and the Saisonniers," unpublished manuscript (ca. 1970), 1, ALP, box 8, folder 1. The article was later published in German as "Die Elite und die Saisonniers" in *Der Schneehase* 29 (1969–71): 45–47.

6. Arnold Lunn, *The Story of Skiing* (London, 1952), 62.

7. Arnold Lunn, *Ski-ing* (London, 1913), 49.

8. "Le rythme et la vitesse," *Revue Olympique* 45 (September 1909): 135–37.

9. Hillel Schwartz, "Torque: The New Kinaesthetic of the Twentieth Century," in *Incorporations,* ed. Jonathan Crary and Sanford Kwintner (New York, 1992), 70–127.

10. Douglas Brown describes Pierre de Coubertin's oeuvre as reflective of a unified modernist aesthetic based on balanced eurythmy and comprising both participation and spectatorship. See Douglas Brown, "Modern Sport, Modernism and the Cultural Manifesto: De Coubertin's *Revue Olympique,*" *International Journal of the History of Sport* 18, no. 2 (June 2001): 78–109; Douglas Brown, "Theories of Beauty and Modern Sport: Pierre de Coubertin's Aesthetic Imperative for the Modern Olympic Movement, 1894–1914" (PhD diss., University of Western Ontario, 1997).

11. Eisenberg, *"English Sports" und deutsche Bürger,* 434–35.

12. Letter from Arnold Lunn to A.G. Berdez, May 14, 1926, 1. Archive of the International Olympic Committee (hereafter IOC), Lausanne, Switzerland, International Ski Federation Series, Corr. 1926–59.

13. *Les jeux de la VIIIe Olympiade Paris 1924,* 689.

14. Lunn, *The Story of Skiing,* 45.

15. Carl Luther, "Nordische Meinungen zum mitteleuropäischen Skilauf," *Der Winter* 23 (1929–30): 51.

16. Letter from Carl CMR Hamilton to Arnold Lunn, March 4, 1927, 1. IOC, International Ski Federation Series, Corr. 1926–1959.

17. "Le Colonel Ivar Holmquist," interview conducted by F. Hallberg, *Revue du ski* 1 (1930): 297–301.

18. Ski Club of Great Britain, *International Racing Rules: The Case for Revision* (Uxbridge, 1926), 4.

19. Ibid., 6.

20. Hans Fischer, "Turistik und Abfahrtslauf," *Deutsche Alpenzeitung* 26 (1931): 50.

21. Richard Holt, "An Englishman in the Alps: Arnold Lunn, Amateurism and the Invention of Alpine Ski Racing," *International Journal of the History of Sport* 9 (1992): 428.

22. Heinrich Frank, "Die Entwicklung von Alpinistik und Wintersport in Österreich," in *Turnen und Sport in der Geschichte Österreichs,* ed. Ernst Bruckmüller and Hannes Strohmeyer (Vienna, 1998), 127.

23. Quoted from the Swiss journal *Sport* (October 30, 1929), in Walter Amstutz, "Über die Freiheit im Rennsportlichen Skilauf," *Der Schneehase* 3 (1929): 170.

24. "A New International Ski Association?" *British Ski Year Book* (1929): 113–14.

25. Quoted in Arnold Lunn, *Mountain Jubilee* (London, 1943), 131.

26. N. R. Oestgaard, "The International Ski Federation," in *Skiing: The International Sport,* ed. Roland Palmedo (New York, 1937), 27–28.

27. Organisationskomitee für die IV. Olympischen Winterspiele 1936, *IV. Olympische Winterspiele 1936, Garmisch-Partenkirchen: Amtlicher Bericht* (Berlin, 1936), 139.

28. Jacques Dieterlen, "IV Jeux Olympiques D'hiver," *Revue du ski* 7 (1936): 66–70.

29. Peter Borscheid, *Das Tempo-Virus: Eine Kulturgeschichte der Beschleunigung* (Frankfurt, 2004), 214.

30. Walter Amstutz, "The Kilometer Lancé on Skis: Speed Skiing," *Der Schneehase: Jahrbuch des Schweizerischen Akademischen Ski-Clubs* 34 (1986–1990): 87.

31. Ibid., 87–90.

32. Luis Trenker, *Berge im Schnee* (Berlin, 1932), 37.

33. France Ski de Vitesse, "World Records," www.kl-france.com/modules/edito/content.php?id=5, accessed August 15, 2013.

34. Amstutz, "The Kilometer Lancé on Skis," 92.

35. Ibid., 96.

36. Guttmann, *From Ritual to Record,* 85.

37. Franz Benk," Die Geschichte des Skilaufs und seine wirtschaftliche Bedeutung" (dissertation, Leopold-Franzens-Universität Innsbruck, 1953), 35.

38. "Protokoll über die Sitzung des Abfahrt und Slalom Komitees des Internationalen Skiverbandes des Fachausschusses für Abfahrt und Slalom in den Tagen vom 10. bis 12.V.35," German Bundesarchiv, fonds 70 Or 1, G154, 1935. Copies housed at IOC, JO-1936W-COJO, SD 4: Correspondance COJO. On microtime, see Jimena Canales, *A Tenth of a Second: A History* (Chicago, 2009), 4.

39. Édouard Frendo, *Le ski par la technique française* (Chamonix, 1946), 13.

40. The first metal ski tips appeared in Austria in 1926, and a Frenchwoman, Marie Marvingt, created the first full metal skis in 1928. Manufacturers slowly adopted these innovations in the 1930s. Gilbert Merlin, "Le ski alpin: Cent ans d'évolution technique," in *La grande histoire du ski,* ed. Musée Dauphinois (Grenoble, 1994), 65.

41. Ingo Rhomberg and August Burtscher, *Künstliche Skikanten* (Munich, 1933).

42. Frendo, *Le ski par la technique française,* 11.

43. Philippe Baehni, "Pourquoi toujours les autrichiens?" *Der Schneehase* 24 (1956–57): 112–14.

44. Josef Dahinden, *Ski und du* (Berlin, 1935), 18, 29–30.

45. Anson Rabinbach, *The Human Motor: Energy, Fatigue, and the Origins of Modernity* (New York, 1990), 2. See also Frank Becker, "Der Sportler als 'moderner Menschentyp': Entwürfe für eine neue Körperlichkeit in der Weimarer Republik," in *Körper mit Geschichte: Der menschliche Körper als Ort der Selbst- und Weltdeutung,* ed. Clemens Wischermann and Stefan Haas (Stuttgart, 2000), 223–43.

46. Henning Eichberg, *Body Cultures: Essays on Sport, Space and Identity* (London, 1998), 68.

47. Frendo, *Le ski par la technique française,* 133, 136.

48. Josef Dahinden, *Ski-Mambo: Der einfache und natürliche Skilauf* (Immenstadt im Allgäu, 1958), 3–4.

49. Schwartz, "Torque," 79.

50. "Ne laissons pas le ski tomber au niveau d'un sport athléthique," *Revue du ski* 9 (1938): 63–64.

51. Lunn, *Story of Skiing,* 100. See also Oswald Spengler, *The Decline of the West* (New York, 1961).

52. Arnold Lunn, "Olympic Supplement," *British Ski Year Book* (1936): 419.

53. Quoted in John Hoberman, *Mortal Engines: The Science of Performance and the Dehumanization of Sport* (Caldwell, NJ, 2001), 19.

54. R. Campell, "Des dangers du sport pour la formation du caractère," *Ski* (Switzerland) (1932–33): 36–37.

55. Stefan von Dévan, *Standard-Abfahrten in Europa* (Munich, 1938), 10–11.

56. "Olympic Hopefuls Start Meditating," *Observer* (UK), October 8, 1967.

57. Heinz Dramsch, "Marmolata: Ohne Rekordteufel," *Der Winter* 34 (1940–41): 101–2.

58. Jeffrey Schnapp, "Crash (Speed as Engine of Individuation)," *Modernism/Modernity* 6, no. 1 (1999): 1–49.

59. Dramsch, "Marmolata," 101–2.

60. John Bale, *Sports Geography,* 2nd ed. (London, 2003), 131.

CHAPTER SEVEN. CONSUMING ALPINE SKIING

1. Tom Gunning, "An Aesthetic of Astonishment: Early Film and the (In)Credulous Spectator," in *Viewing Positions: Ways of Seeing Film,* ed. Linda Williams (Rutgers, NJ, 1995), 114–33.

2. Bernhard Tschofen, "Tourismus als Alpenkultur? Zum Marktwert von Kultur(kritik) im Fremdenverkehr," in *Der Alpentourismus: Entwicklungspotenziale im Spannungsfeld von Kultur, Ökonomie und Ökologie,* ed. Kurt Luger and Franz Rest (Innsbruck, 2002), 92.

3. *Xèmes Jeux Olympiques d'Hiver/10th Winter Olympic Games: Official Report,* Comité d'Organisation des Xèmes Jeux Olympiques d'Hiver (Grenoble, 1969), 165.

4. Quoted in Otto Schantz, "The Presidency of Avery Brundage (1952–1972)," in *The International Olympic Committee: One Hundred Years; The Idea—The Presidents—The Achievements,* ed. Raymond Gafner (Lausanne, 1995), 2:86.

5. Avery Brundage, letter to Marc Hodler, January 6, 1953. Avery Brundage Collection (hereafter ABC), University of Illinois, Urbana-Champaign, box 218, folder: Fédération International de Ski (FIS) 1936–38, 1949–56, 1959.

6. William Rospigliosi, "Beau of Cortina," *Sports Illustrated,* February 13, 1956, http://si.com/vault/article/magazine/MAG1131075/index.htm, accessed January 20, 2014.

7. Ibid.

8. Curtis Casewit, "A Talk with Toni Sailer," *Skiing* (USA), March 1959, 8.

9. The IOC Archive in Lausanne possesses a file over an inch thick of press clippings detailing Sailer's lifestyle and business dealings. Archive of the International Olympic Committee (hereafter IOC), Lausanne, Switzerland, International Ski Federation Series, Folder: Toni Sailer 1958.

10. Casewit, "A Talk with Toni Sailer," 9.

11. Richard Gruneau, "'Amateurism' as a Sociological Program: Some Reflections Inspired by Eric Dunning," *Sport in Society* 9 (2006): 559–82.

12. "Reflections on the 10th Olympic Winter Games," attachment to circular letter from Avery Brundage to all IOC members, April 26, 1969, 2. ABC, box 71, ref: AB/M/487.

13. Walter Lutz, "1000mal teurer als 1948," *Sport* (Zurich), February 2, 1968.

14. *Xèmes Jeux Olympiques,* 134.

15. Friedl List, "Peinliche Fragen," *Skimagazin* 2, no. 6 (1968): 3.

16. "The Problem of Amateurism and Professionalism in Skiing," attachment to a letter from Marc Hodler to Cortlandt T. Hill, December 12, 1952, 1–2. ABC, box 218, folder: Fédération International de Ski (FIS) 1936–38, 1949–56, 1959.

17. Letter from Avery Brundage to Marc Hodler, August 18, 1950. ABC, box 58, folder: IOC Members, Marc Hodler (Switzerland).

18. Circular letter from Avery Brundage to IOC members, April 23, 1966. ABC, box 71, ref. 313.

19. "French Village Rewards Skiers," *New York Herald Tribune,* April 2, 1964.

20. Serge Lang, "Skisport: Ein mächtiger Wirtschaftsfaktor," *Ski* (DSV) 20 (1967–68): 128.

21. Ibid., 128–31.

22. Letter from Avery Brundage to the executive board, March 18, 1970. ABC, box 71, ref. EB/545.

23. For surveillance of alleged amateurism violations, see, e.g., ABC, box 219, folder: Ski Violations: Advertisements, 1970.

24. "Press Review: Articles and Pictures, Extracts from Some European Newspapers Concerning Advertising of Skiers," September 1971. ABC, box 218, folder: Fédération International de Ski (FIS) 1971.

25. "The Problem of the Olympic Winter Games," memorandum circulated by Avery Brundage, October 18, 1969. ABC, box 218, folder: Sports Federations, 1970–1973.

26. Hunter S. Thompson, "The Temptations of Jean-Claude Killy," in *The Great Shark Hunt: Strange Tales from a Strange Time* (New York, 1979), 79, 82, 87.

27. Ibid., 87.

28. Gert Kreyssig, "Das kritisch betrachtete Skivergnügen," *Der Winter* 44 (1956–57): 399.

29. Uta Poiger, *Jazz, Rock, and Rebels: Cold War Politics and American Culture in a Divided Germany* (Berkeley, 2000), 113.

30. The act of skiing itself, with its strong connections to the competitive racing circuit in the postwar era, remained implicitly masculine, and thus not the main object of representation in advertisements that depicted women. Indeed, the German ski journal *Der Winter* published a short exposé in 1965, asking rhetorically, "Does competitive sport make one ugly?," in which the editors published head shots of attractive female racers in an attempt to dispel fears among young girls (and their parents) that taking part in competitive sport would render their bodies and facial features masculine or homely. "Macht Leistungssport häßlich?" *Der Winter* 52 (1964–65), 486.

31. Orvar Löfgren has described tourism as "a cultural laboratory" and a socially liminal realm in which identities can be subverted, reworked, or discarded entirely. Orvar Löfgren, *On Holiday: A History of Vacationing* (Berkeley, 1999), 7.

32. Karl Pusch, "Skilauf und Volkswirtschaft," in *Festschrift zu den FIS-Wettkämpfen 1933 in Innsbruck und Tirol,* special issue of *Tirol* (1933): 21–22.

33. Shelley Baranowski and Ellen Furlough, "Introduction," in *Being Elsewhere: Tourism, Consumer Culture, and Identity in Modern Europe and North America,* ed. Shelley Baranowski and Ellen Furlough (Ann Arbor, MI, 2001), 6.

34. *Xèmes Jeux Olympiques,* 162.

35. Samivel, "La montagne, d'utilité publique," *La montagne* 72 (1947): 43.

36. John Urry, *Consuming Places* (London, 1995), 28–29.

37. Löfgren, *On Holiday,* 8; Dean MacCannell, *The Tourist: A New Theory of the Leisure Class* (Berkeley, 1999), xvi.

38. In the winter of 1950–51, foreign tourists spent a total of 1,593,000 nights in Austria, and 75 percent of them in Tirol, Salzburg, and Vorarlberg. Franz Benk, "Die Geschichte des Skilaufs und seine wirtschaftliche Bedeutung" (dissertation, Leopold-Franzens-Universität Innsbruck, 1953), 50–52.

39. Stefan von Dévan, *Mit Auto und Ski in die Alpen,* 2nd ed. (Munich, 1956), 5.

40. Walter Pause, *Ski Heil: Die Hundert schönsten Skiabfahrten in den Alpen* (Munich, 1958). The choices were widely dispersed but reflected the higher level of tourist development in Switzerland and Austria in the late 1950s. By the end of the following decade, both France and Italy had markedly improved their tourist offerings. Of Pause's one hundred selected downhill runs, 12 were in France, 30.5 in Switzerland, 8.5 in Italy (one run traversed the Swiss-Italian border), 38 in Austria, and 11 in Germany.

41. *VII Giochi Olimpici Invernali/7th Olympic Winter Games,* Comitato Olimpico Nazionale Italiano (Rome, n.d.), 108–11.

42. Josef Ritz, *Mit Auto und Ski,* 9th ed. (Munich, 1967), 24, 112, 134, 154, 180.

43. Claudia Bell and John Lyall have argued that extreme pursuits demand more advanced equipment to ensure safety, thus making them more socially exclusive than other leisure activities. Claudia Bell and John Lyall, *The Accelerated Sublime: Landscape, Tourism, and Identity* (Westport, CT, 2002), 63–64.

44. "Kleinigkeiten gross geschrieben," *Ski* (DSV) 8 (1955–56): 56. All currency conversions are drawn from Lawrence H. Officer, "Exchange Rates Between the United States Dollar and Forty-one Currencies," Measuring Worth, www.measuringworth.com/exchangeglobal/, accessed June 28, 2014. All inflation calculations are from Samuel H. Williamson, "Seven Ways to Compute the Relative Value of a U.S. Dollar Amount, 1774 to present," Measuring Worth, www.measuringworth.com/uscompare/, accessed June 28, 2014.

45. Hermann Kornacher, "Muß es immer das Teuerste sein?" *Ski* (DSV) 20 (1967–68): 168; "Weißer Sport und rote Zahlen," *Der Winter* 54 (1966–67): 294.

46. "Weißer Sport," 294.

47. Hans Magnus Enzensberger described choosing a vacation destination as analogous to choosing a brand of perfume, with certain choices possessing particular cachet. Hans Magnus Enzensberger, "Eine Theorie des Tourismus," in *Einzelheiten I. Bewußtseins-Industrie* (Frankfurt, 1962), 166.

48. On types of consumption as markers of social rank, see Pierre Bourdieu, *Distinction: A Social Critique of the Judgment of Taste* (Cambridge, MA, 1984) and "Programme pour une sociologie du sport," in *Choses dites* (Paris, 1987), 203–16.

49. Urry, *Consuming Places,* 130–31.

50. "Skifahren: Ein teurer Sport?" *Der Winter* 56 (1968–69): 493.

51. See Victoria de Grazia, *Irresistible Empire: America's Advance through Twentieth-Century Europe* (Cambridge, MA, 2005). See also Alain Corbin, "L'avènement des loisirs," in *L'avènement des loisirs, 1850–1960,* ed. Alain Corbin (Paris, 1995), 11.

52. Jacques Mouflier, "Historique de l'évolution des stations françaises," *Neige et glace,* November 1960, 20.

53. Jacques Mouflier, "Cent stations françaises prêtes au rendez-vous," *Neige et glace,* November 1958, 28.

54. Press Release of the Austrian National Olympic Committee, June 17, 1963, 8. ABC, box 170, folder: IX Olympic Winter Games—Innsbruck, Austria, 1964—Press Releases.

55. The cultural historian Peter Borscheid notes that the state has acted an accelerant rather a brake on innovation and change since Napoleonic France. Peter Borscheid, *Das Tempo-Virus: Eine Kulturgeschichte der Beschleunigung* (Frankfurt, 2004), 143.

56. Christian Rubi, "Ski Instruction in Switzerland," in *Skiing: The International Sport,* ed. Roland Palmedo (New York, 1937), 115–16.

57. Fred Rubi, "Der Wintertourismus in der Schweiz: Entwicklung, Struktur und volkswirtschaftliche Bedeutung" (dissertation, University of Bern, 1953), 7–8.

58. Anton Obholzer, *Geschichte des Schilaufs, mit besonderer Berücksichtigung Mitteleuropas* (Vienna, 1935), 67; Philippe Bourdeau, "Introduction," in *Les sports*

d'hiver en mutation: Crise ou révolution géoculturelle?, ed. Philippe Bourdeau (Paris, 2007), 18.

59. Kornacher, "Muß es immer das Teuerste sein?," 169; "Weißer Sport," 294.

60. Günter Bischof, "Der Marshall-Plan und die Wiederbelebung des österreichischen Fremdenverkehrs nach dem Zweiten Weltkrieg," in *"80 Dollar": 50 Jahre ERP Fonds und Marshall-Plan in Österreich 1948–1998*, ed. Günther Bischof and Dieter Stiefel (Vienna, 1999), 141.

61. Ibid., 134.

62. Ibid., 160.

63. Jon Mathieu, "Zwei Staaten, ein Gebirge: Schweizerische und österreichische Alpenperzeption im Vergleich (18.-20. Jahrhundert)," *Österreichische Zeitschrift für Geschichtswissenschaften* 15, no. 2 (2004): 91–105.

64. Von Dévan, *Mit Auto und Ski in die Alpen*, 50.

65. Antoine Borrel, "Pour un politique française des sports d'hiver," *Revue du ski* 5 (1934): 267.

66. Jean-François Lyon-Caen, "Les premières stations des Alpes françaises," in *La grande histoire du ski*, ed. Musée Dauphinois (Grenoble, 1994), 90–92.

67. Jacques Mouriquand, *L'or blanc: Le système des sports d'hiver* (Paris, 1988), 40. Swiss officials estimated that by the early 1970s, the French government was pouring six hundred million francs (US$140 million in 1975, or US$606 million in 2013) annually into winter resorts, not counting public spending on infrastructure, such as highways and rail lines, that benefited winter resorts directly. Hans Bachmann, "Das Skidorf aus der Retorte?" *Ski* (DSV) 24, no. 5 (1971–72): 23.

68. Mary L. Barker, "Traditional Landscape and Mass Tourism in the Alps," *Geographical Review* 72, no. 4 (1992): 407–8.

69. Gert Kreyssig, "Das kritisch betrachtete Skivergnügen," *Der Winter* 44 (1956–57): 399–400.

70. Gérard Blitz, "Une formule révolutionnaire de vacances de neige," *Ski: Revue mensuelle*, April 1958, 458; Ellen Furlough, "Making Mass Vacations: Tourism and Consumer Culture in France, 1930s to 1970s," *Comparative Studies in Society and History* 40, no. 2 (1998): 247–86.

71. Jacques-Louis Delpal, "Ces stations champignons qui changent le visage de vos vacances," *Ski* (France), no. 12 (1969): 41.

72. Gert Kreyssig, "Technik im Schneeparadies," *Skimagazin* 9, no. 2 (1973): 29.

73. Bachmann, "Das Skidorf aus der Retorte?," 21–22.

74. Ritz, *Mit Auto und Ski*, 175.

75. Bourdeau, "Introduction," 18–19.

CHAPTER EIGHT. THE PURSUIT OF WHITE GOLD

1. Organisationskomitee der IX. Olympischen Winterspiele in Innsbruck 1964, *Offizieler Bericht der IX. Olympischen Winterspiele Innsbruck 1964* (Vienna, 1967), 76–77.

2. Ibid.

3. "IX. Olympische Winterspiele, Bulletin 12/13" (May 1964), n.p. International Olympic Committee Archive, Lausanne, Switzerland (hereafter IOC), JO-1964W-BULLE, SD 2.

4. Kurt Bernegger, *Olympia Innsbruck 1964* (Vienna, 1964), 50.

5. Hansueli Rhyner, "Pistenpräparation—Beschneiungstechnik—Schneemanagement," in *3. FIS Forum Mainau: Zur Nachhaltigkeit des Schneesports,* ed. Fédération Internationale de Ski (Oberhofen am Thunersee, Switzerland, 2008), 122.

6. Jacques-Louis Delpal, "Ces stations champignons qui changent le visage de vos vacances," *Ski* (France), no. 12 (1969): 39. On the many conflicting definitions of nature in modern societies, see William Cronon, "Introduction: In Search of Nature," in *Uncommon Ground,* ed. William Cronon (New York, 1996), 23–56. On the utilitarian discourse of valuing "natural resources" over "nature," see James C. Scott, *Seeing Like a State: How Certain Schemes to Improve the Human Condition Have Failed* (New Haven, CT, 1998), 13.

7. Alison Frank, "The Air Cure Town: Commodifying Mountain Air in Alpine Central Europe," *Central European History* 45, no. 2 (June 2012): 185–207. On infrastructure and Alpine tourism, see Susan Barton, *Healthy Living in the Alps: The Origins of Winter Tourism in Switzerland, 1860–1914* (Manchester, UK, 2008).

8. On cultural landscapes, see Denis E. Cosgrove, *Social Formation and Symbolic Landscape* (London, 1984). On technical innovations in tourism and sport in Europe and North America, see, e.g., Wolfgang König, *Bahnen und Berge: Verkehrstechnik, Tourismus und Naturschutz in den Schweizer Alpen 1870–1939* (Frankfurt, 2000); Gertrud Pfister, "Sport, Technology, and Society: From Snowshoes to Racing Skis," *Culture, Sport, Society* 4, no. 1 (Spring 2001): 73–98; Michael W. Childers, *Colorado Powder Keg: Ski Resorts and the Environmental Movement* (Lawrence, KS, 2012); Annie Gilbert Coleman, *Ski Style: Sport and Culture in the Rockies* (Lawrence, KS, 2004); Hal Rothman, *Devil's Bargains: Tourism in the Twentieth-Century American West* (Lawrence, KS, 1998).

9. Richard White, *The Organic Machine: The Remaking of the Columbia River* (New York, 1995), 15.

10. John Bale, *Sports Geography,* 2nd ed. (London, 2003), 131.

11. Quoted from Jean-François Lyon-Caen, "Les premières stations des Alpes françaises," in *La grande histoire du ski,* ed. Musée Dauphinois (Grenoble, 1994), 86–87.

12. Pierre Ratinaud, "Les remontées mécaniques et les pistes," in *La grande histoire du ski,* 97.

13. "Les téléphériques de France," *Ski: Sports d'hiver* 4 (1937–38/1938–39), 59.

14. For an analogous case in Germany, see Thomas Lekan, "A 'Noble Prospect': Tourism, *Heimat,* and Conservation on the Rhine, 1880–1914," *Journal of Modern History* 81, no. 4 (2009), 824–58. See also Richard White's discussion of the Emersonian vision of nature, which viewed technology as a way to emulate and harmonize with nature rather than conquer it. As late as the 1930s, dams on the Columbia River were considered to represent "the final piece necessary to reveal nature's latent harmony." White, *Organic Machine,* 35, 57–58.

15. Carl Luther, "Kein Turm von Babel," *Der Winter* 30 (1936–37), 79–80; "Sestrières vient de réaliser son troisième téléphérique," *Revue du ski* 9 (1938): 21–23.

16. "Sestrières," 21.

17. Luther, "Kein Turm von Babel," 80.

18. Ratinaud, "Les remontées mécaniques," 99.

19. "Les téléfériques et les stations de sports d'hiver," *Revue du ski* 5 (1934), 270.

20. Henry Hoek, "Der Ski-Lift," *Der Schneehase* 12 (1938): 82.

21. Letter from the Deutscher Alpenverein to the Landrat des Landkreises Tölz, February 9, 1939. Archive of the German Alpine Association, Munich, Germany, DAV BGS 1 SG/14/3: Alpiner-Ski-Club (ASC): 3. Verschiedenes 1931–44.

22. See Frank, "Air Cure Town."

23. As Hal Rothman notes of skiing in the American West, these profits generally flowed to corporations and managers, not mountain residents. Rothman, *Devil's Bargains*.

24. Kurt Luger and Franz Rest, "Der Alpentourismus: Konturen einer kulturell konstruierten Sehnsuchtslandschaft," in *Der Alpentourismus: Entwicklungspotenziale im Spannungsfeld von Kultur, Ökonomie und Ökologie*, ed. Kurt Luger and Franz Rest (Innsbruck, 2002), 21. In Austria, the number of lifts grew from 350 in 1955 to 1,085 in 1965, 3,210 in 1975, and 4,005 in 1985. In France, the number expanded from 50 in 1945 to 400 in 1960, 1,809 in 1970, 3,270 in 1980, and 3,724 in 1986. Felix Jülg, "Faszination Schnee: Der Wintertourismus im Gebirge; Historische Entwicklung," in *Der Winter als Erlebnis: Zurück zur Natur oder Fun, Action und Mega-Events? Neue Orientierungen im Schnee-Tourismus,* ed. Wolfgang Isenberg (Bensburg, 1999), 21; Jacques Mouriquand, *L'or blanc: Le système des sports d'hiver* (Paris, 1988), 225.

25. Arnold Lunn, *Mountain Jubilee* (London, 1943), 24.

26. Franz Benk, "Die Geschichte des Skilaufs und seine wirtschaftliche Bedeutung" (PhD diss., Leopold-Franzens-Universität Innsbruck, 1953) 75.

27. Fritz Schmitt, "Wird das Bergsteigen wirklich unmodern?" *Der Winter* 38 (1950–51): 122.

28. W. L. Steinberger, "Wir können Zeit gewinnen," *Der Winter* 37 (1949–50): 63–64.

29. Organisationskomitee für die IV. Olympischen Winterspiele 1936, *IV. Olympische Winterspiele 1936, Garmisch-Partenkirchen: Amtlicher Bericht* (Berlin, 1936), 257–58.

30. "IX. Olympische Winterspiele, Bulletin 4/5" (June 1962), 19; "IX. Olympische Winterspiele, Bulletin 2" (December 1961), 91. IOC, JO-1964W-BULLE, SD 1: Bulletins 1–7, 1961–63.

31. Fédération Internationale de Ski, *The International Ski Competition Rules,* book 4 (Bern, 1983), 64, 78.

32. John Bale, *Landscapes of Modern Sport* (London, 1994), 10.

33. Marcel Ichac, "Pour et contre le ski sportif," *La montagne* 60 (1934): 136.

34. Karl Erb, "Alpiner Skisport im Wandel eines Vierteljahrhunderts," *Der Schneehase* 29 (1969–71): 13–16.

35. "Avalanche: The 'White Death' Strikes the Alps, Engulfing Whole Villages in Snow," *Life* (February 5, 1951), 19–25; Christian Pfister, *Wetternachhersage: 500 Jahre Klimavariationen und Naturkatastrophen (1496–1995)* (Bern, 1999), 258–60.

36. "Lawinenverbauungen," *Der Winter* 54 (1966–67): 304.

37. Ibid., 306.

38. Martin Kettle, "Slippery Slopes," *Marxism Today* (January 7, 1990): 7.

39. Gert Kreyssig, "Verkorkster Winter," *Skimagazin* 7, no. 6 (1971): 5.

40. Nigel Ellis, "Snow Guide to Europe," *Ski Survey* (September 1982): 18–19.

41. Ibid.

42. Bruno Abegg, "Palmen auf den Almen? Auswirkungen einer Klimaänderung auf den Wintertourismus," in *Der Winter als Erlebnis: Zurück zur Natur oder Fun, Action und Mega-Events? Neue Orientierungen im Schnee-Tourismus,* ed. Wolfgang Isenberg (Bensburg, Germany, 1999), 43; Hans Elsasser and Paul Messerli, "The Vulnerability of the Snow Industry in the Swiss Alps," *Mountain Research and Development* 21, no. 4 (2001): 336–38.

43. Ulrike Pröbstl, *Kunstschnee und Umwelt: Entwicklung und Auswirkungen der technischen Beschneiung* (Bern, 2006), 18.

44. Isabelle d'Erceville, "L'effet canons," *Ski* (France), January 1989, 99.

45. Pröbstl, *Kunstschnee und Umwelt,* 23.

46. Wolfgang Wagmann, "Sanfte Bergfahrt?" *Ski* (Switzerland), November 1987, 32.

47. Claude Francillon, "La Grogne au pays du Lognan," *Ski* (France), February 1982, 42.

48. Philippe Gaussot, "L'équipement du Super-Chamonix," *Ski: Revue mensuelle,* January 1958, 418–20.

49. Ibid., 421.

50. Ibid., 423.

EPILOGUE

1. On these back-to-nature movements, see John Alexander Williams, *Turning to Nature in Germany: Hiking, Nudism, and Conservation, 1900–1940* (Stanford, CA, 2007).

2. Arnold Lunn, *Ski-ing* (London, 1913), 152.

3. See Theodor Adorno, "Kitsch," in *Essays on Music,* ed. Richard Leppert (Berkeley, 2002), 501–5; Max Horkheimer and Theodor Adorno, "The Culture Industry: Enlightenment as Mass Deception," in *Dialectic of Enlightenment: Philosophical Fragments* (Stanford, 2002), 94–136.

4. Clement Greenberg, "Avant-Garde and Kitsch," in *Art Theory and Criticism: An Anthology of Formalist, Avant-Garde, Contextualist and Post-modernist Thought,* ed. Sally Everett (Jefferson, NC, 1991), 32.

5. Quoted in Hans Magnus Enzensberger, "Eine Theorie des Tourismus," in *Einzelheiten I. Bewußtseins-Industrie* (Frankfurt, 1962), 150.

6. Greenberg, "Avant-Garde and Kitsch," 32.

7. Ibid., 33.

8. Henning Böhme, "Skizentren, Nationalparks, und unberührte Landschaft," *Mitteilungen des Deutschen Alpenvereins* (hereafter *MDAV*) 35 (1983): 24–25.

9. Andrej Ziemilski, "Der Skilauf in der Zivilisation des 20. Jahrhunderts," *Der Winter* 48 (1960–61): 31.

10. Josef Dahinden, *Ski-Mambo: Der einfache und natürliche Skilauf* (Immenstadt im Allgäu, 1958).

11. Greenberg, "Avant-Garde and Kitsch," 32.

12. Gustav Prerowsky, "Probleme um den touristischen Skilauf," *Der Winter* 47 (1959–60): 270.

13. Helmut Sohre, "Ein Lob dem Skilift," *Der Winter* 38 (1950–51): 301.

14. Deutscher Skiverband, *50 Jahre Deutscher Skiverband, 1905–1955* (Munich, 1955): lvii.

15. Franz Grassler, "Vermassung und Herdenbetrieb im modernen Skilauf," *MDAV* 3 (1951): 38.

16. "Mehr laufen, statt fahren!" *Der Winter* 36 (1942–43): 2.

17. "La course à l'abîme," *Ski: Revue mensuelle* (October 1952): 1–2.

18. "Müssen Skiläufer so sein?" *Der Winter* 37 (1949–50): 1125.

19. Friedl List, "Ist Romantik unmodern?" *Der Winter* 49 (1961–62): 530, 532.

20. On this paradoxical role of postwar youth, see Uta Poiger, *Jazz, Rock, and Rebels: Cold War Politics and American Culture in a Divided Germany* (Berkeley, 2000); Richard Ivan Jobs, *Riding the New Wave: Youth and the Rejuvenation of France after the Second World War* (Stanford, CA, 2007).

21. Arnold Lunn, *Mountain Jubilee* (London, 1943), 28.

22. Konrad Klärner, "Ist Tourenskilauf unmodern?" *MDAV* 1 (1949): 3.

23. Werner Toth-Sonns, "Werden Gipfelfreuden unmodern?" *Der Winter* 44 (1956–57): 284–85.

24. Georg Frey, "Romantik des Skilaufs," *Der Winter* 42 (1954–55): 218.

25. Modris Eksteins, *Rites of Spring: The Great War and the Birth of the Modern Age* (Boston, 1989), 304.

26. Wolf Burger, "Bergerlebnis, Spiel und Sport," *Der Winter* 50 (1962–63): 304.

27. Hermann Kornacher, "Wer stoppt den Ausverkauf unserer Berge?" *MDAV* 7 (1955): 19.

28. Hans Bachmann, "Das Skidorf aus der Retorte?" *Ski* (DSV) 24, no. 5 (1971–72): 27.

29. Ibid., 26.

30. Dean MacCannell, *The Tourist: A New Theory of the Leisure Class* (Berkeley, 1999), 196.

31. Wolfgang Schivelbusch, *The Railway Journey: The Industrialization of Time and Space in the Nineteenth Century* (Berkeley, 1986), 41.

32. Quoted in Jacques Mouriquand, *L'or blanc: Le système des sports d'hiver* (Paris, 1988), 51.

33. Reinhard Bachleitner, "Sport- und tourismussoziologische Aspekte des Skilaufs," in *Alpiner Wintersport: Eine sozial-, wirtschafts-, tourismus- und ökowissenschaftliche Studie zum Alpinen Skilauf, Snowboarden und anderen alpinen Trendsportarten,* ed. Reinhard Bachleitner (Innsbruck, 1998), 16.

34. On the historiographical understanding of nature, see William Cronon, "The Trouble with Wilderness: Or, Getting Back to the Wrong Nature," in *Uncommon Ground: Rethinking the Human Place in Nature,* ed. William Cronon (New York: W. W. Norton, 1996), 69–90; Richard White, *The Organic Machine: The Remaking of the Columbia River* (New York, 1995); David Blackbourn, *The Conquest of Nature: Water, Landscape, and the Making of Modern Germany* (New York, 2006).

35. Martin Kettle, "Slippery Slopes," *Marxism Today,* January 7, 1990, 7.

36. Michael Lehning, "Globaler Klimawandel und die Alpine Schneedecke," in *3. FIS Forum Mainau: Zur Nachhaltigkeit des Schneesports,* ed. Fédération Internationale de Ski (Oberhofen am Thunersee, Switzerland, 2008), 29–61. See also Bruno Abegg, "Palmen auf den Almen? Auswirkungen einer Klimaänderung auf den Wintertourismus," in *Der Winter als Erlebnis: Zurück zur Natur oder Fun, Action und Mega-Events? Neue Orientierungen im Schnee-Tourismus,* ed. Wolfgang Isenberg (Bensburg, Germany: Thomas Morus-Akademie, 1999), 39–51.

37. Philippe Bourdeau, "Introduction," in *Les sports d'hiver en mutation: Crise ou révolution géoculturelle?,* ed. Philippe Bourdeau (Paris, 2007), 23–24.

38. On the inextricability of nature and technology (and of nature and culture more generally), see White, *Organic Machine.* See also Blackbourn, *Conquest of Nature;* David E. Nye, *Technologies of Landscape: From Reaping to Recycling* (Amherst, MA, 1999); Joseph E. Taylor III, *Pilgrims of the Vertical: Yosemite Rock Climbers and Nature at Risk* (Cambridge, MA, 2010).

BIBLIOGRAPHY

ARCHIVAL SOURCES

Avery Brundage Collection, University of Illinois, Urbana-Champaign, Illinois
Deutscher Alpenverein, Munich, Germany
Deutscher Skiverband, Munich, Germany
International Olympic Committee, Lausanne, Switzerland
Sir Arnold Lunn Papers, Georgetown University, Washington, DC

UNPUBLISHED DIARIES

Nellie H. Friedrichs (née Bruell), in possession of Christopher R. Friedrichs, Vancouver, British Columbia

PERIODICALS

English

British Ski Year Book, 1920–71
Downhill Only, 1959–74
Scottish Ski Club Journal, 1930–38
Scottish Ski Club Magazine, 1909–13
Ski Club of Great Britain and National Ski Union Yearbook, 1912–14
Ski Notes and Queries: The Periodical Publication of the Ski Club of Great Britain,
 1926–71
Ski Survey, 1972–90
Sports Illustrated, 1956–68
Year-Book of the Ski Club of Great Britain, 1911

French

Annuaire du Club Alpin Français, 1890–1904
La montagne, 1904–90
Neige et glace, 1958–1968
Revue Olympique, 1901–14
Revue du ski, 1930–39
Ski (France), 1967–71
Ski (Switzerland), 1969–90
Ski: Amtliches Korrespondenzblatt des Schweiz. Ski-Verbandes/Feuille de correspondance officielle de l'Association Suisse des Clubs de Ski, 1904–41
Ski: Feuille de correspondance officielle de l'Association Suisse des Clubs de Ski, 1941–62
Le ski: Revue mensuelle illustrée, 1947–67
Ski: Sports d'hiver; Revue mensuelle illustrée, 1931–46
Ski flash, 1972–89
Ski illustrée, 1963–68

German

Alpenvereins Jahrbuch, 1970–82
Berg: Alpenvereinsjahrbuch, 1983–90
Deutsche Alpenzeitung, 1901–43
Deutscher Wintersport, 1901–14
Durch Pulver und Firn: Das Buch der deutschen Skiläufer, 1939–42
Jahrbuch des Deutschen Alpenvereins, 1943–69
Mitteilungen des Deutschen Alpenvereins, 1949–90
Mitteilungen des Deutschen und Österreichischen Alpenvereins, 1890–1939
Der Skilehrer und seine Schüler, 1967
Der Schnee: Wochenschrift des Alpen-Skivereins, 1905–14
Der Schneehase: Jahrbuch des Schweizerischen Akademischen Ski-Club, 1928–90
Ski (Offizielles Organ des Deutschen Skiverbandes), 1951–90
Ski: Amtliches Korrespondenzblatt des Schweiz. Ski-Verbandes/Feuille de correspondance officielle de l'Association Suisse des Clubs de Ski, 1907–41
Der Ski: Österreichischer Skiverband—Amtliche Zeitschrift, 1933–38
Ski Bob Eis: Illustrierte Zeitschrift für Wintersport, 1948–50
Skileben in Österreich, 1935–38
Ski-Chronik: Jahrbuch des Mitteleuropäischen Ski-Verbandes, 1908–13
Ski-Magazin, 1967–90
Ski-Sport, 1938–41
Sport im Winter, 1932–34
Spur im Schnee: Jahrbuch des Fachamts Skilauf im Deutschen Reichsbund für Leibesübungen, 1938
SSV Jahrbuch, 1909–76
Der Winter, 1906–43, 1949–70
Zeitschrift des Deutschen und Österreichischen Alpenvereins, 1890–1942

Baretje, René. *Tourisme et hydrome : Essai bibliographique.* Aix-en-Provence: Centre des Hautes Études Touristiques, Faculté de droit, 1976.

Brinkmann, Heiner. *Skisport : Bibliographie von Anbeginn bis 1974.* Cologne: Sport und Buch Strauss, 1995.

———. *Skisport Bibliografie, 1975–1985.* Cologne: Sport und Buch Strauss, 1989.

———. *Skisport Bibliografie, 1986–1990.* Cologne: Deutsche Sporthochschule Köln, Abteilung Wintersport, 1992.

———. *Skisport Bibliografie, 1991–1995.* Cologne: Sport und Buch Strauss, 1996.

———. *Skisport-Bibliografie, 1996–1999.* Cologne: Sport und Buch Strauss, 2000.

Goeldner, Charles R. *Bibliography of Skiing Studies.* Boulder: University of Colorado, Graduate School of Business Administration, Business Research Division, 1978.

Hoek, Henry. *Die Schi-Literatur (bis 1. Januar 1908).* Munich: Gustav Lammers, 1908.

Perret, Jacques. *Guide des livres sur la montagne et l'alpinisme.* Grenoble: Éditions de Belledonne, 1997.

Schwartz, Gary H. *Skiing Literature: A Bibliographical Catalogue.* Mill Valley, CA: Wood River Publishing, 1995.

Yaple, Henry. *Ski Bibliography: A Classified List of English Language Books, Dissertations, Films, Government Documents, Videos, Sound Recordings, Computer Software, Ebooks, and Serial Titles on Skiing, 1890–2002.* Woodbury, CT: International Skiing History Association, 2004.

SECONDARY SOURCES

Adamson, Walter L. *Embattled Avant-gardes: Modernism's Resistance to Commodity Culture in Europe.* Berkeley: University of California Press, 2007.

Adorno, Theodor. "Kitsch." In *Essays on Music,* ed. Richard Leppert, 501–5. Berkeley: University of California Press, 2002.

Allen, E. John B. *The Culture and Sport of Skiing: From Antiquity to World War II.* Amherst: University of Massachusetts Press, 2007.

Allen, William Sheridan. *The Nazi Seizure of Power: The Experience of a Single German Town, 1922–1945.* Rev. ed. New York: Franklin Watts, 1984.

Amorous, Charles. "L'implantation du ski alpin dans les Alpes françaises: La tradition étayage de la modernité," *Revue de géographie alpine* 88, no. 4 (2000): 9–20.

Amstädter, Rainer. *Der Alpinismus: Kultur, Organisation, Politik.* Vienna: WUV Universitätsverlag, 1996.

Anderson, Benedict. *Imagined Communities: Reflections on the Origin and Spread of Nationalism.* Rev. ed. London: Verso, 1991.

Applegate, Celia. "A Europe of Regions: Reflections on the Historiography of Subnational Places in Modern Times," *American Historical Review* 104, no. 4 (October 1999): 1157–82.

———. *A Nation of Provincials: The German Idea of Heimat.* Berkeley: University of California Press, 1990.

Armiero, Marco. *A Rugged Nation: Mountains and the Making of Modern Italy; Nineteenth and Twentieth Centuries.* Cambridge: White Horse Press, 2011.

Ashburner, Tim. *The History of Ski Jumping.* Wykey, Shrewsbury, UK: Quiller Press, 2003.

Bachleitner, Reinhard, ed. *Alpiner Wintersport: Eine sozial-, wirtschafts-, tourismus- und ökowissenschaftliche Studie zum Alpinen Skilauf, Snowboarden und anderen alpinen Trendsportarten.* Innsbruck: StudienVerlag, 1998.

Bailey, Peter. "Leisure: Merrie to Modern." In *The Victorian World,* ed. Martin Hewitt, 619–35. London: Routledge, 2012.

Bale, John. *Landscapes of Modern Sport.* London: Leicester University Press, 1994.

———. *Sports Geography,* 2nd ed. London: Routledge, 2003.

Baranowski, Shelley, and Ellen Furlough, eds. *Being Elsewhere: Tourism, Consumer Culture, and Identity in Modern Europe and North America.* Ann Arbor: University of Michigan Press, 2001.

Barker, Mary L. "Traditional Landscape and Mass Tourism in the Alps," *Geographical Review* 72, no. 4 (October 1992): 395–415.

Bartaletti, Fabrizio. "What Role Do the Alps Play within World Tourism?," International Commission for the Protection of the Alps (CIPRA), http://alpsknowhow.cipra.org/background_topics/alps_and_tourism/alps_and_tourism_chapter_introduction.html, accessed August 18, 2013.

Barton, Susan. *Healthy Living in the Alps: The Origins of Winter Tourism in Switzerland, 1860–1914.* Manchester: Manchester University Press, 2008.

Bätzing, Werner. *Die Alpen: Geschichte und Zukunft einer europäischen Kulturlandschaft.* Munich: Verlag C. H. Beck, 2003.

Baudelaire, Charles. *Little Poems in Prose.* Chicago: Teitan Press, 1995.

Beattie, Andrew. *The Alps: A Cultural History.* Oxford: Oxford University Press, 2006.

Becker, Frank. "Der Sportler als 'moderner Menschentyp': Entwürfe für eine neue Körperlichkeit in der Weimarer Republik." In *Körper mit Geschichte: Der menschliche Körper als Ort der Selbst- und Weltdeutung,* ed. Clemens Wischermann and Stefan Haas, 223–43. Stuttgart: Steiner, 2000.

———. "Die Sportlerin als Vorbild der 'neuen Frau': Versuche zur Umwertung der Geschlechterrollen in der Weimarer Republik," *Sozial- und Zeitgeschichte des Sports* 8, no. 3 (1994): 34–55.

Bell, Claudia, and John Lyall. *The Accelerated Sublime: Landscape, Tourism, and Identity.* Westport, CT: Praeger, 2002.

Benjamin, Walter. *The Arcades Project.* Cambridge, MA: Belknap Press, 1999.

Benk, Franz. "Die Geschichte des Skilaufs und seine wirtschaftliche Bedeutung." PhD diss., Leopold-Franzens-Universität Innsbruck, 1953.

Berman, Marshall. *All That Is Solid Melts Into Air: The Experience Of Modernity.* New York: Viking Penguin, 1988.

Bernegger, Kurt. *Olympia Innsbruck 1964.* Vienna: Österreichischer Bundesverlag, 1964.

Bilgeri, Georg. *Der Alpine Skilauf.* Munich: Verlag der Deutschen Alpenzeitung, 1910.

Bischof, Günter. "Der Marshall-Plan und die Wiederbelebung des österreichischen Fremdenverkehrs nach dem Zweiten Weltkrieg." In *"80 Dollar": 50 Jahre ERP Fonds und Marshall-Plan in Österreich 1948–1998,* ed. Günther Bischof and Dieter Stiefel, 133–82. Vienna: Ueberreuter, 1999.

Blackbourn, David. *The Conquest of Nature: Water, Landscape, and the Making of Modern Germany.* New York: W. W. Norton, 2006.

———. "Das Kaiserreich transnational. Eine Skizze." In *Das Kaiserreich transnational: Deutschland in der Welt, 1871–1914,* ed. Sebastian Conrad and Jürgen Osterhammel, 302–324. Göttingen: Vandenhoeck & Ruprecht, 2006.

Bloch, Ernst. "The Alps without Photography." In *Literary Essays,* 433–41. Stanford, CA: Stanford University Press, 1998.

Borscheid, Peter. *Das Tempo-Virus: Eine Kulturgeschichte der Beschleunigung.* Frankfurt: Campus Verlag, 2004.

Bourdeau, Philippe, ed. *Les sports d'hiver en mutation: Crise ou révolution géoculturelle?* Paris: Lavoisier, 2007.

Bourdieu, Pierre. *Distinction: A Social Critique of the Judgement of Taste.* Cambridge, MA: Harvard University Press, 1984.

———. "Programme pour une sociologie du sport." In *Choses dites,* 203–16. Paris: Éditions de Minuit, 1987.

Braudel, Fernand. *The Mediterranean and the Mediterranean World in the Age of Phillip II.* Vol. 1. Berkeley: University of California Press, 1995.

Brown, Douglas. "Modern Sport, Modernism and the Cultural Manifesto: De Coubertin's *Revue Olympique,*" *International Journal of the History of Sport* 18, no. 2 (June 2001): 78–109.

———. "Theories of Beauty and Modern Sport: Pierre de Coubertin's Aesthetic Imperative for the Modern Olympic Movement, 1894–1914." PhD diss., University of Western Ontario, 1997.

Burns, Robert K., Jr. "The Circum-alpine Culture Area: A Preliminary View," *Anthropological Quarterly* 36, no. 3 (July 1963): 130–55.

Burrow, J. W. *The Crisis of Reason: European Thought, 1848–1914.* New Haven, CT: Yale University Press, 2000.

Canales, Jimena. *A Tenth of a Second: A History.* Chicago: University of Chicago Press, 2009.

Caulfeild, Vivian. *How to Ski and How Not To.* London: James Nisbet, 1913.

Chevallier, Marc. "Paroles de modernité: Pour une relecture culturelle de la station de sports d'hiver," *Revue de géographie alpine* 84, no. 3 (1996): 29–39.

Childers, Michael W. *Colorado Powder Keg: Ski Resorts and the Environmental Movement.* Lawrence: University Press of Kansas, 2012.

Coen, Deborah R. "Liberal Reason and the Culture of the *Sommerfrische*," *Austrian History Yearbook* 38 (2007): 145–59.

Coleman, Annie Gilbert. *Ski Style: Sport and Culture in the Rockies*. Lawrence: University Press of Kansas, 2004.

———. "The Unbearable Whiteness of Skiing," *Pacific Historical Review* 65, no. 4 (November 1996): 583–614.

Comitato Olimpico Nazionale Italiano. *VII Giochi Olimpici Invernali/VII Olympic Winter Games*. Rome: Comitato Olimpico Nazionale Italiano, n.d.

Comité d'Organisation des Xèmes Jeux Olympiques d'Hiver. *Xèmes Jeux Olympiques D'Hiver/Xth Winter Olympic Games: Official Report*. Grenoble: Comité d'Organisation des Xèmes Jeux Olympiques d'Hiver, 1969.

Comité Olympique Français. *Les jeux de la VIIIe Olympiade Paris 1924: Rapport officiel*. Paris: Librairie de France, n.d.

Confino, Alon. *The Nation as Local Metaphor: Württemberg, Imperial Germany, and National Memory, 1871–1918*. Chapel Hill: University of North Carolina Press, 1997.

Corbin, Alain, ed. *L'avènement des loisirs, 1850–1960*. Paris: Flammarion, 1995.

Cosgrove, Denis E. *Social Formation and Symbolic Landscape*. London: Croom Helm, 1984.

Coubertin, Pierre de. *Olympic Memoirs*. Lausanne: International Olympic Committee, 1979.

———. *Olympism: Selected Writings*, ed. Norbert Müller. Lausanne: International Olympic Committee, 2000.

Couttet, Alfred, Arnold Lunn, and Emil Petersen, eds. *L'enchantement du ski*. Paris: Editions Alpina, 1930.

Cronon, William. "A Place for Stories: Nature, History, and Narrative," *Journal of American History* 78, no. 4 (March 1992): 1347–76.

———, ed. *Uncommon Ground: Rethinking the Human Place in Nature*. New York: W. W. Norton, 1996.

Czant, Hermann. *Alpinismus, Massenwintersport und Weltkrieg*. Munich: Bergverlag Rudolf Rother, 1929.

Dahinden, Josef. *Ski-Mambo: Der einfache und natürliche Skilauf*. Immenstadt im Allgäu: Verlag J. Eberl KG, 1958.

———. *Ski und du*. Berlin and Bern: Martin Hillger Verlag, 1935.

Davies, J. Sanger. *Dolomite Strongholds: The Last Untrodden Alpine Peaks*. London: George Bell and Sons, 1894.

De Gex, Jenny. *The Art of Skiing: Vintage Posters from the Golden Age of Winter Sport*. Bath, UK: Palazzo, 2006.

De Grazia, Victoria. *Irresistible Empire: America's Advance through 20th-Century Europe*. Cambridge, MA: Belknap Press, 2005.

Deutsche Olympische Gesellschaft. *Die X. Olympischen Winterspiele Grenoble 1968: Das offiziele Standardwerk des Nationalen Olympischen Komitees*. Dortmund: Olympischer Sportverlag, 1968.

Deutscher Skiverband. *100 Jahre Deutscher Skiverband, 1905–2005*. Planegg: Deutscher Skiverband, 2005.

————. *50 Jahre Deutscher Skiverband, 1905–1955*. Munich: Deutscher Skiverband, 1955.

Di Bosso, Renato. *Aerosilografo, aeropittore, aeroscultore futurista*. Verona: Tipografia Massagrande, c. 1941.

Dickinson, Edward. "Germanizing the Alps and Alpinizing the Germans," *German Studies Review* 33, no. 3 (October 2010): 579–602.

Doyle, Arthur Conan. "An Alpine Pass on 'Ski,'" *Strand*, July–December 1894, 657–61.

Duffy, Enda. *The Speed Handbook: Velocity, Pleasure, Modernism*. Durham, NC: Duke University Press, 2009.

Eckert, Klaus. *Alpenbahnen*. Munich: Steiger, 2000.

Edensor, Tim, ed. *Geographies of Rhythm: Nature, Place, Mobilities and Bodies*. Farnham, UK, and Burlington, VT: Ashgate, 2010.

Eichberg, Henning. *Body Cultures: Essays on Sport, Space and Identity*. Edited by John Bale and Chris Philo. London: Routledge, 1998.

Eisenberg, Christiane. *"English Sports" und deutsche Bürger: Eine Gesellschaftsgeschichte, 1800–1939*. Munich: Paderborn, 1999.

————. "Massensport in der Weimarer Republik: Ein statistischer Überblick," *Archiv für Sozialgeschichte* 33 (1993): 137–77.

Eksteins, Modris. *Rites of Spring: The Great War and the Birth of the Modern Age*. Boston: Houghton Mifflin, 1989.

Elias, Norbert and Eric Dunning. *Quest for Excitement: Sport and Leisure in the Civilizing Process*. Oxford: Basil Blackwell, 1986.

Elsasser, Hans and Paul Messerli. "The Vulnerability of the Snow Industry in the Swiss Alps," *Mountain Research and Development* 21, no. 4 (November 2001): 335–39.

Enzensberger, Hans Magnus. "Eine Theorie des Tourismus." In *Einzelheiten I. Bewußtseins-Industrie*, 147–68. Frankfurt: Suhrkamp Verlag, 1962.

Falasca-Zamponi, Simonetta. *Fascist Spectacle: The Aesthetics of Power in Mussolini's Italy*. Berkeley: University of California Press, 2000.

Falkner, Gerd. *100 Jahre Deutscher Skiverband*. 3 vols. Planegg: Deutscher Skiverband, 2005.

————. "Ull und Skadi: Skibrauchtum und Götterglaube." Pamphlet accompanying exhibition of the German Ski Museum. Planegg: Deutscher Skiverband, 2006.

————. "Wilhelm Paulcke (1873–1949): Initiator der Gründung des Deutschen und des Mitteleuropäischen Skiverbandes," *SportZeiten* 8, no. 1 (2008): 79–99.

Fédération Internationale de Ski. *3. FIS Forum Mainau: Zur Nachhaltigkeit des Schneesports*. Oberhofen am Thunersee: Fédération Internationale de Ski, 2008.

————. *The International Ski Competition Rules*, book 4. Bern: Fédération Internationale de Ski, 1983.

Festschrift zu den FIS-Wettkämpfen 1933 in Innsbruck und Tirol: Sondernummer des Zeitschrift "Tirol". Innsbruck: Buch- u. Kunstdruckerei Tyrolia, 1933.

Fischer, Hans. *Skihaserl: Ein Bilderbuch*. Munich: Bergverlag Rudolf Rother, 1935.

Fleischmann, Willi. *Lilienfelder oder Norweger Skilaufttechnik? Zur Aufklärung in einem alten Sportstreit!* Diessen vor München: Jos. C. Huber, 1910.

Fleming, Fergus. *Killing Dragons: The Conquest of the Alps.* New York: Atlantic Monthly Press, 2002.

Frank, Alison. "The Air Cure Town: Commodifying Mountain Air in Alpine Central Europe," *Central European History* 45, no. 2 (2012): 185–207.

Frank, Heinrich. "Die Entwicklung von Alpinistik und Wintersport in Österreich." In *Turnen und Sport in der Geschichte Österreichs,* ed. Ernst Bruckmüller and Hannes Strohmeyer, 105–32. Vienna: ÖBV Pädogogischer Verlag, 1998.

Frendo, Édouard. *Le ski par la technique française.* Chamonix: Landru Éditeur, 1946.

Freud, Sigmund. *Civilization and Its Discontents.* New York: W. W. Norton, 2005.

———. *New Introductory Lectures on Psycho-analysis.* New York: W. W. Norton 1989.

Friedman, Susan Stanford. "Definitional Excursions: The Meanings of *Modern/Modernity/Modernism,*" *Modernism/Modernity* 8, no. 3 (2001): 493–513.

———. "Periodizing Modernism: Postcolonial Modernities and the Space /Time Borders of Modernist Studies," *Modernism/Modernity* 13, no. 3 (2006): 425–43.

———. "Planetarity: Musing Modernist Studies," *Modernism/Modernity* 17, no. 3 (2010): 471–99.

Furlough, Ellen. "Making Mass Vacations: Tourism and Consumer Culture in France, 1930s to 1970s," *Comparative Studies in Society and History* 40, no. 2 (April 1998): 247–86.

Gignoux, Paul. *Ski sur les Alpes.* Paris: La Table Ronde, 1956.

Goksøyr, Matti, Gerd von der Lippe, and Kristen Mo, eds. *Winter Games, Warm Traditions: Selected Papers from the 2nd international ISHPES seminar, Lillehammer 1994.* Sankt Augustin: Academia Verlag, 1996.

Greenberg, Clement. "Avant-Garde and Kitsch." In *Art Theory and Criticism: An Anthology of Formalist, Avant-Garde, Contextualist and Post-Modernist Thought,* ed. Sally Everett, 26–40. Jefferson, NC: McFarland, 1991.

Griffin, Roger. *Modernism and Fascism: The Sense of a Beginning under Mussolini and Hitler.* Basingstoke: Palgrave Macmillan, 2007.

Gruneau, Richard. "'Amateurism' as a Sociological Program: Some Reflections Inspired by Eric Dunning," *Sport in Society* 9, no. 4 (Oct. 2006): 559–82.

Guichonnet, Paul, ed. *Histoire et civilisations des Alpes.* 2 vols. Toulouse: Privat, 1980.

Gunning, Tom. "An Aesthetic of Astonishment: Early Film and the (In)Credulous Spectator." In *Viewing Positions: Ways of Seeing Film,* ed. Linda Williams, 114–33. Rutgers, NJ: Rutgers University Press, 1995.

Günther, Dagmar. *Alpine Quergänge: Kulturgeschichte des bürgerlichen Alpinismus (1870–1930).* Frankfurt: Campus, 1998.

GutsMuths, Johann Christoph Friedrich. *Gymnastik für die Jugend.* Schnepfenthal: Buchhandlung der Erziehungsanstalt, 1804.

Guttmann, Allen. *From Ritual to Record: The Nature of Modern Sports.* New York: Columbia University Press, 1978.

Habermas, Jürgen. *The Structural Transformation of the Public Sphere: An Inquiry into a Category of Bourgeois Society.* Cambridge, MA: MIT Press, 1991.

Harvey, David. *The Condition of Postmodernity: An Enquiry into the Origins of Cultural Change.* Cambridge: Blackwell, 1990.

Haupt, Heinz-Gerhard, and Jürgen Kocka, eds. *Comparative and Transnational History: Central European Approaches and Perspectives.* New York: Berghahn, 2009.

Herzog, Markwart, ed. *Skilauf—Volkssport—Medienzirkus: Skisport als Kulturphänomen.* Stuttgart: W. Kohlhammer, 2005.

Hoberman, John. *Mortal Engines: The Science of Performance and the Dehumanization of Sport.* Caldwell, NJ: Blackburn Press, 2001.

Hoek, Henry, and E.C. Richardson. *Der Ski und seine sportliche Benutzung.* Munich: Verlag von Gustav Lammers, 1907.

Hoibian, Olivier. *Les alpinistes en France, 1870–1950: Une histoire culturelle.* Paris: L'Harmattan, 2000.

Holt, Lee Wallace. "Mountains, Mountaineering and Modernity: A Cultural History of German and Austrian Mountaineering, 1900–1945." PhD diss., University of Texas at Austin, 2008.

Holt, Richard. "An Englishman in the Alps: Arnold Lunn, Amateurism and the Invention of Alpine Ski Racing," *International Journal of the History of Sport* 9, no. 3 (1992): 421–32.

Horkheimer, Max, and Theodor Adorno. *Dialectic of Enlightenment: Philosophical Fragments.* Stanford, CA: Stanford University Press, 2002.

Hudson, Simon. *Snow Business: A Study of the International Ski Industry.* London: Cassell, 2000.

Hughes, H. Stuart. *Consciousness and Society.* New York: Knopf, 1958.

Huntford, Roland. *Two Planks and a Passion: The Dramatic History of Skiing.* London: Continuum, 2008.

Hussey, Elisabeth. "The Man Who Changed the Face of Alpine Racing," *Skiing Heritage Journal* 17, no. 4 (Dec. 2005): 7–12.

Hyde, Walter Woodburn. "The Alps in History," *Proceedings of the American Philosophical Society* 75, no. 6 (1935): 431–42.

Isenberg, Wolfgang. *Der Winter als Erlebnis: Zurück zur Natur oder Fun, Action und Mega-Events? Neue Orientierungen im Schnee-Tourismus.* Bensburg, Germany: Thomas Morus-Akademie, 1999.

Jay, Martin. "From Modernism to Post-modernism." In *The Oxford Illustrated History of Modern Europe,* ed. T.C.W. Blanning, 255–78. Oxford: Oxford University Press, 1996.

Jenkins, Jennifer. "Locating Germany," *German History* 29, no. 1 (March 2011): 108–26.

Jobs, Richard Ivan. *Riding the New Wave: Youth and the Rejuvenation of France after the Second World War.* Stanford, CA: Stanford University Press, 2007.

Keller, Tait. "Eternal Mountains — Eternal Germany: The Alpine Association and the Ideology of Alpinism, 1909–1939." PhD diss, Georgetown University, 2006.

———. "The Mountains Roar: The Alps during the Great War," *Environmental History* 14, no. 2 (April 2009): 253–74.

Kern, Stephen. *The Culture of Time and Space, 1880–1918: With a New Preface.* Cambridge, MA: Harvard University Press, 2003.

Keys, Barbara J. *Globalizing Sport: National Rivalry and International Community in the 1930s.* Cambridge, MA: Harvard University Press, 2006.

Klein, Kerwin Lee. "A Vertical World: The Eastern Alps and Modern Mountaineering," *Journal of Historical Sociology* 24, no. 4 (Dec. 2011): 519–48.

König, Wolfgang. *Bahnen und Berge: Verkehrstechnik, Tourismus und Naturschutz in den Schweizer Alpen 1870–1939.* Frankfurt: Campus Verlag, 2000.

Koshar, Rudy. *German Travel Cultures.* Oxford: Berg, 2000.

———, ed. *Histories of Leisure.* Oxford: Berg, 2002.

Landes, David. *The Unbound Prometheus: Technological Change and Industrial Development in Western Europe from 1750 to the Present.* 2nd ed. Cambridge: Cambridge University Press, 2003.

Landry, Marc. "Europe's Battery: The Making of the Alpine Energy Landscape, 1870–1955." PhD diss, Georgetown University, 2013.

Lauterwasser, Erwin, Rainer Mülbert, and Fritz Wagnerberger, eds. *Faszination Skilauf: Vor hundert Jahren fing es an.* Heidelberg: Edition Braus, 1995.

Lekan, Thomas. *Imagining the Nation in Nature.* Cambridge, MA: Harvard University Press, 2004.

———. "A 'Noble Prospect': Tourism, *Heimat,* and Conservation on the Rhine, 1880–1914," *Journal of Modern History* 81, no. 4 (December 2009): 824–58.

Löfgren, Orvar. *On Holiday: A History of Vacationing.* Berkeley: University of California Press, 1999.

Luger, Kurt and Franz Rest, eds. *Der Alpentourismus: Entwicklungspotenziale im Spannungsfeld von Kultur, Ökonomie und Ökologie.* Innsbruck: StudienVerlag, 2002.

Lunn, Arnold. *Come What May: An Autobiography.* Boston: Little, Brown and Company, 1941.

———. *A History of Ski-ing.* London: Oxford University Press, 1927.

———. *Mountain Jubilee.* London: Eyre & Spottiswoode, 1943.

———. *The Mountains of Youth.* London: Oxford University Press, 1925.

———. *Ski-ing.* London: Eveleigh Nash, 1913.

———. *The Story of Ski-ing.* London: Eyre & Spottiswoode, 1952.

———. *Switzerland and the English.* London: Eyre & Spottiswoode, 1944.

Luther, Carl J. *Schneeschuhläufer im Krieg.* Munich: J. Lindauersche Universitäts Buchhandlung, 1915.

———. *Ski-Wörterbuch in fünf Sprachen.* Munich: Bergverlag Rudolf Rother, 1934.

———. *Das weiße Reich.* Berlin: Verlag Ludwig Simon, 1935.

————, ed. *Deutscher Skilauf: Ein Querschnitt.* Munich: Bergverlag Rudolf Rother, 1930.

————, ed. *Skiparadiese der Alpen.* Munich: Verlag F. Bruckmann, 1933.

Luther, Carl J., and G. P. Lücke. *Der Skitourist.* Munich: J. Lindauersche Buchhandlung, 1913.

MacCannell, Dean. *The Tourist: A New Theory of the Leisure Class.* Berkeley: University of California Press, 1999.

Macfarlane, Robert. *Mountains of the Mind.* New York: Pantheon, 2003.

Magnus, Louis, and Renaud de la Fregeolière. *Les sports d'hiver.* Paris: Pierre Lafitte & Cie, 1911.

Maier, Charles. "Consigning the Twentieth Century to History: Alternative Narratives for the Modern Era," *American Historical Review* 105, no. 3 (2000): 807–31.

Mann, Thomas. *The Magic Mountain.* New York: Knopf, 1939.

Marinetti, Filippo Tommaso. "The Founding and Manifesto of Futurism." In *Futurism: An Anthology,* ed. Lawrence Rainey, Christine Poggi, and Laura Wittman, 49–53. New Haven, CT: Yale University Press, 2009.

Marjanen, Jani. "Undermining Methodological Nationalism: Histoire Croisée of Concepts as Transnational History." In *Transnational Political Spaces: Agents—Structures—Encounters,* ed. Mathias Albert, Gesa Bluhm, Jan Helmig, Andreas Leutzsch, and Jochen Walter, 239–63. Frankfurt: Campus, 2009.

Martinelli, Vera. *Zwischen Telemarkschwüngen und Sportkorsetts: Frauen und Skisport; Das Beispiel Schwarzwald.* Schorndorf: Hofmann, 2008.

Mathieu, Jon. *History of the Alps, 1500–1900: Environment, Development, and Society.* Morgantown: West Virginia University Press, 2009.

————. "Zwei Staaten, ein Gebirge: Schweizerische und österreichische Alpenperzeption im Vergleich (18.-20. Jahrhundert)," *Österreichische Zeitschrift für Geschichtswissenschaften* 15, no. 2 (2004): 91–105.

McDowell, Matthew L. "Sports History: Outside of the Mainstream? A Response to Ward's 'Last Man Picked,'" *International Journal of the History of Sport* 30, no. 1 (2013): 14–22.

McNeill, J. R. *The Mountains of the Mediterranean World.* New York: Cambridge University Press, 1992.

————. "Observations on the Nature and Culture of Environmental History," *History and Theory* 42, no. 4 (December 2003): 5–43.

Mehl, Erwin. *Grundriss der Weltgeschichte des Schifahrens, I: Von der Steinzeit bis zum Beginn der schigeschichtlichen Neuzeit (1860).* Schorndorf bei Stuttgart: Verlag Karl Hofmann, 1964.

————, ed. *Zdarsky: Festschrift zum 80. Geburtstage des Begründers der alpinen Skifahrweise.* Vienna: Deutscher Verlag für Jugend und Volk, 1936.

Millar, Jeremy, and Michiel Schwarz, eds. *Speed: Visions of an Accelerated Age.* London: Photographer's Gallery, 1998.

Mouriquand, Jacques. *L'or blanc: Le système des sports d'hiver.* Paris: Lieu Commun, 1988.

Müller, Michael G., and Cornelius Torp. "Conceptualising Transnational Spaces in History," *European Review of History/Revue européenne d'histoire* 16, no. 5 (Oct. 2009): 609–17.

Mumelter, Hubert. *Skifibel*. Munich: Nymphenburger Verlagshandlung, 1951.

———. *Der Skiteufel*. Vienna: Paul Neff Verlag, 1950.

Musée Dauphinois. *La grande histoire du ski*. Grenoble: Musée Dauphinois, 1994.

Nansen, Fridtjof. *The First Crossing of Greenland*. London: Longmans, Green, 1890.

Nassauer, Max. *Gebirge und Gesundheit: Hygienische Winke besonders für die Frauen*. Munich: Verlag von Gustav Lammers, 1908.

Nicholson, Marjorie Hope. *Mountain Gloom and Mountain Glory: The Development of the Aesthetics of the Infinite*. New York: W. W. Norton, 1959.

Nietzsche, Friedrich Wilhelm. *Der fröhliche Wissenschaft*. Leipzig: E. W. Fritzsch, 1887.

———. *Thus Spake Zarathustra: A Book for All and None*. New York: Macmillan, 1896.

Nye, David E., ed. *Technologies of Landscape: From Reaping to Recycling*. Amherst: University of Massachusetts Press, 1999.

Obholzer, Anton. *Geschichte des Schilaufs, mit besonderer Berücksichtigung Mitteleuropas*. Vienna: Deutscher Verlag für Jugend und Volk, 1935.

Officer, Lawrence H. "Exchange Rates Between the United States Dollar and Forty-one Currencies," Measuring Worth, 2014, www.measuringworth.com/exchange-global/, accessed June 28, 2014.

Organisation for Economic Co-operation and Development. *Climate Change in the European Alps: Adapting Winter Tourism and Natural Hazards Management*. Paris: Organisation for Economic Co-operation and Development, 2007.

Organisationskomitee der IX. Olympischen Winterspiele in Innsbruck 1964. *Offizieler Bericht der IX. Olympischen Winterspiele Innsbruck 1964*. Vienna: Österreichischer Bundesverlag für Unterricht, Wissenschaft, und Kunst, 1967.

Organisationskomitee für die IV. Olympischen Winterspiele 1936. *IV. Olympische Winterspiele 1936, Garmisch-Partenkirchen: Amtlicher Bericht*. Berlin: Reichssportverlag, 1936.

Österreichischer Skiverband. *100 Jahre Österreichischer Skiverband*. Innsbruck: Österreichischer Skiverband, 2005.

Palmedo, Roland, ed. *Skiing: The International Sport*. New York: Derrydale Press, 1937.

Paulcke, Wilhelm. *Berge als Schicksal*. Munich: Verlag F. Bruckmann, 1936.

———. *Der Skilauf: Seine Erlernung und Verwendung im Dienste des Verkehrs, sowie zu touristischen, alpinen und militärischen Zwecken*. Freiburg im Breisgau: Fr. Wagner'sche Universitäts-Buchhandlung, 1905.

Pause, Walter. *Ski Heil: Die Hundert schönsten Skiabfahrten in den Alpen*. Munich: BLV Verlagsgesellschaft, 1958.

Paxton, Robert O. *The Anatomy of Fascism*. New York: Vintage, 2005.

Peiffer, Lorenz. "'Ski für die Ostfront': Der Aufruf des Reichssportführers im Winter 1941/42 und die Konsequenzen für die Entwicklung des Skisports in Deutschland," *SportZeiten* 2, no. 1 (2002): 53–64.

Penny, H. Glenn. "German Polycentrism and the Writing of History," *German History* 30, no. 2 (2012): 265–82.

Pfister, Christian. *Wetternachhersage: 500 Jahre Klimavariationen und Naturkatastrophen (1496–1995).* Bern: Paul Haupt, 1999.

Pfister, Gertrud. "Gracefully and Elegantly Downhill . . . Women and the Sport of Skiing in Germany (1890–1914)." In *Winter Games, Warm Traditions: Selected papers from the 2nd international ISHPES seminar, Lillehammer 1994,* ed. Matti Goksøyr, Gerd von der Lippe, and Kristen Mo, 227–37. Sankt Augustin: Academia Verlag, 1996.

——. "Sport, Technology, and Society: From Snowshoes to Racing Skis," *Culture, Sport, Society* 4, no. 1 (Spring 2001): 73–98.

——. "Sportfexen, Heldenmythen und Opfertod: Alpinismus und Nationalsozialismus," in *Sport und Faschismen/Sport e fascismi: Geschichte und Region/ Storia e regione* 13, no. 1 (2004), ed. Claudio Ambrosi and Wolfgang Weber, 21–60.

Philpott, William. *Vacationland: Tourism and Environment in the Colorado High Country.* Seattle: University of Washington Press, 2013.

Poiger, Uta. *Jazz, Rock, and Rebels: Cold War Politics and American Culture in a Divided Germany.* Berkeley: University of California Press, 2000.

Polednik, Heinz. *Das Glück im Schnee: 100 Jahre Skilauf in Österreich.* Vienna: Amalthea, 1991.

Pröbstl, Ulrike. *Kunstschnee und Umwelt: Entwicklung und Auswirkungen der technischen Beschneiung.* Bern: Haupt, 2006.

Rabinbach, Anson. *The Human Motor: Energy, Fatigue, and the Origins of Modernity.* New York: Basic Books, 1990.

Radkau, Joachim. *Nature and Power: A Global History of the Environment.* Cambridge: Cambridge University Press, 2008.

——. *Der Zeitalter der Nervosität: Deutschland zwischen Bismarck und Hitler.* Munich: Carl Hanser Verlag, 1998.

Rhomberg, Ingo, and August Burtscher. *Künstliche Skikanten.* Munich: Bergverlag Rudolf Rother, 1933.

Ring, Jim. *How the English Made the Alps.* London: John Murray, 2000.

Ritz, Josef. *Mit Auto und Ski.* 9th ed. Munich: ADAC Verlag, 1967.

Rothman, Hal. *Devil's Bargains: Tourism in the Twentieth-century American West.* Lawrence: University Press of Kansas, 1998.

Rubi, Fred. "Der Wintertourismus in der Schweiz: Entwicklung, Struktur und volkswirtschaftliche Bedeutung." PhD diss., University of Bern, 1953.

Saler, Michael. "Modernity and Enchantment: A Historiographic Review," *American Historical Review* 111, no. 3 (June 2006): 692–716.

Schantz, Otto. "The Presidency of Avery Brundage (1952–1972)." In *The International Olympic Committee: One Hundred Years: The Idea—The Presidents—The Achievements,* vol. 2, ed. Raymond Gafner, 77–200. Lausanne: International Olympic Committee, 1995.

Schivelbusch, Wolfgang. *The Railway Journey: The Industrialization of Time and Space in the Nineteenth Century.* Berkeley: University of California Press, 1986.

Schnapp, Jeffrey T. "Crash (Speed as Engine of Individuation)," *Modernism/Modernity* 6, no. 1 (1999): 1–49.

———, ed. *Speed Limits*. Milan: Skira, 2009.

Schneeschuh-Verein München. "XV. Jahres-Bericht pro 1907/08." Munich, Schneeschuh-Verein München, 1908.

Schneider, Hannes, and Arnold Fanck. *The Wonders of Ski-ing: A Method of Correct Ski-ing and its Applications to Alpine Running*. Translated by George Gallowhur. London: George Allen & Unwin Ltd, 1933.

Schönecker, Toni, E. Henel, et al. *Der mißhandelte Schnee: Eiskalte Geschichten*. Munich: Bergverlag, 1921.

Schorske, Carl. *Fin-de-Siècle Vienna: Politics and Culture*. New York: Knopf, 1980.

Schwartz, Hillel. "Torque: The New Kinaesthetic of the Twentieth Century." In *Incorporations*, ed. Jonathan Crary and Sanford Kwintner, 70–127. New York: Urzone, 1992.

Schwartz, Vanessa. *Spectacular Realities: Early Mass Culture in* Fin-de-Siècle *Paris*. Berkeley: University of California Press, 1998.

Scott, James C. *Seeing Like a State: How Certain Schemes to Improve the Human Condition Have Failed*. New Haven, CT: Yale University Press, 1998.

Senger, Max. *Wie die Schweizer Alpen erobert wurden*. Zurich: Büchergilde Gutenberg, 1945.

Shand, Alexander Innes. *Old-Time Travel: Personal Reminiscences of the Continent Forty Years ago Compared with Experiences of the Present Day*. New York: James Pott, 1904.

Siegel, Jerrold. *The Idea of the Self: Thought and Experience in Western Europe since the Seventeenth Century*. New York: Cambridge University Press, 2005.

Siegel, Rachel Josefowitz. *My Songs of Now and Then: A Memoir*. Bloomington, IN: iUniverse LLC, 2012.

Simmel, Georg. "The Metropolis and Modern Life." In *The Blackwell City Reader*, 2nd ed., ed. Gary Bridge and Sophie Watson, 103–10. Chichester, UK: Wiley Blackwell, 2010.

"The Sir Arnold Lunn Papers: Collection Description," Georgetown University Special Collections, www.library.georgetown.edu/dept/speccoll/cl143.htm, accessed January 13, 2014.

Ski Club of Great Britain. *International Racing Rules: The Case for Revision*. Uxbridge, UK: King and Hutchings, 1926.

Smyth, Edward. "Sir Arnold Lunn (1888–1974)," *Alpine Journal* 94 (1989–90): 213–16.

Spengler, Oswald. *The Decline of the West*. New York: A. A. Knopf, 1961.

Spinney, Justin. "A Place of Sense: A Kinaesthetic Ethnography of Cyclists on Mont Ventoux," *Environment and Planning D: Society and Space* 24, no. 5 (2006): 709–32.

Stevenson, Robert Louis. *The Strange Case of Dr Jekyll and Mr Hyde*. London: Longmans, Green, 1886.

Szymanski, Stefan. "A Theory of the Evolution of Modern Sport." *Journal of the History of Sport* 35, no. 1 (Spring 2008): 1–32.

Taylor, Charles. *Sources of the Self: The Making of Modern Identity.* Cambridge, MA: Harvard University Press, 1989.

Taylor, Joseph E., III. *Pilgrims of the Vertical: Yosemite Rock Climbers and Nature at Risk.* Cambridge, MA: Harvard University Press, 2010.

Thompson, Christopher. *The Tour de France: A Cultural History.* Berkeley: University of California Press, 2006.

Thompson, Hunter S. "The Temptations of Jean-Claude Killy." In *The Great Shark Hunt,* 77–96. New York: Summit, 1979.

Trenker, Luis. *Berge im Schnee.* Berlin: Neufeld & Henius Verlag, 1932.

Trenker, Luis, and Walter Schmidkunz. *Berge und Heimat: Das Buch von den Bergen und ihren Menschen.* Berlin: Neufeld & Henius Verlag, 1933.

Turner, Frederick Jackson. *The Frontier in American History.* New York: Henry Holt, 1921.

Umbach, Maiken, and Bernd-Rüdiger Hüppauf, eds. *Vernacular Modernism: Heimat, Globalization, and the Built Environment.* Stanford, CA: Stanford University Press, 2005.

Urry, John. *Consuming Places.* London: Routledge, 1995.

———. *The Tourist Gaze: Leisure and Travel in Contemporary Societies.* London: Sage Publications, 1990.

Verwaltungen der k.k. österreich. Staatsbahnen und der österreich. Südbahn. "Wintersport in Österreich." Vienna: k.k. Hof- und Staatsdruckerei, 1914.

Von Dévan, Stefan. *Mit Auto und Ski in die Alpen.* 2nd ed. Munich: Allgemeiner Deutscher Automobil-Club, 1956.

———. *Standard-Abfahrten in Europa.* Munich: Bergverlag Rudolf Rother, 1938.

Wagner, Peter. *Modernity as Experience and Interpretation: A New Sociology of Modernity.* Cambridge: Polity Press, 2008.

———. *A Sociology of Modernity: Liberty and Discipline.* London: Routledge, 1994.

Weber, Max. *The Protestant Ethic and the Spirit of Capitalism.* Hoboken, NJ: Routledge, 2001.

Welsch, Walter. *Geschichte der Sektion Bayerland des Deutschen Alpenvereins e.V.: Die Zeit des Ersten Weltkriegs und der Weimarer Republik, 1914–1933.* Munich: Holzer Druck und Medien, 2010.

Werner, Michael, and Bénédicte Zimmermann. "Beyond Comparison: *Histoire croisée* and the Challenge of Reflexivity," *History and Theory* 45, no. 1 (February 2006): 30–50.

———. *De la comparaison à l'histoire croisée.* Paris: Le Seuil, 2004.

———. "Vergleich, Transfer, Verflechtung: Der Ansatz der Histoire croisée und die Herausforderung des Transnationalen," *Geschichte und Gesellschaft* 28, no. 4 (2002): 607–36.

White, Richard. *The Organic Machine: The Remaking of the Columbia River.* New York: Hill and Wang, 1995.

Williams, John Alexander. *Turning to Nature in Germany: Hiking, Nudism, and Conservation, 1900–1940*. Stanford, CA: Stanford University Press, 2007.

Williamson, Samuel H. "Seven Ways to Compute the Relative Value of a U.S. Dollar Amount, 1774 to present," Measuring Worth, 2014, www.measuringworth.com/uscompare/, accessed June 28, 2014.

Wolff, Larry. *Inventing Eastern Europe: The Map of Civilization on the Mind of the Enlightenment*. Stanford, CA: Stanford University Press, 1994.

Zdarsky, Mathias. *Alpine (Lilienfelder) Skifahr-Technik: Eine Anleitung zum Selbstunterricht*. Berlin: Konrad W. Mecklenburg, 1908.

———. *Beiträge zur Lawinenkunde*. Vienna: A-B-Z-Druck- und Verlagsanstalt, 1929.

———. *Die Lilienfelder Skilauf-Technik: Eine Anleitung für Jedermann, den Ski in kurzer Zeit vollkommen zu beherrschen*. Hamburg: Verlagsanstalt und Druckerei, 1897.

Zsigmondy, Emil, and Wilhelm Paulcke. *Die Gefahren der Alpen*. 4th ed. Innsbruck: A. Edlinger's Verlag, 1908.

Zweig, Arnold. "Dialektik der Alpen: Fortschritt und Hemmnis." In *Berliner Ausgabe* 3, no. 4, 7–269. Berlin: Aufbau-Verlag, 1997.

INDEX

St. Anton am Arlberg, 102
St. Moritz, 35, 42–43, 60, 92, 117, 120–21,
    144–45, 167, 177
Straumann, Richard, 120–21
Stravinsky, Igor, 86
Styria, 41
Suez Canal, 87
Sulden, 77, 97
Sweden, 31, 55, 110, 115
Switzerland, 1, 3, 7, 21–22, 24, 26–29,
    34–35, 41–43, 47, 52, 56, 66, 84, 90, 107,
    116, 119–20, 138–39, 147–51, 156–58, 163,
    172, 177

Taylorism, 84–85, 93, 125, 199n38
technology, 3, 5, 7, 13, 35, 38, 43, 61, 67, 72,
    83, 86, 93–95, 98–100, 110, 118, 120,
    122–23, 127, 153, 155–63, 165–69, 171–73,
    176, 181, 184n24
Telemark, 34, 63
téléphériques. See ski lifts
television, 14, 132–34, 140, 144, 153
Thomas Cook Company, 28
Thompson, Hunter S., 140
Tirol, 25, 35, 75–76, 90, 149
tobogganing, 35–36, 48
tourism: industry of, 28–29, 35, 41, 43, 72,
    132–33, 137–41, 143–52, 155–59, 162–63,
    165, 167–68, 171, 173, 177, 180; summer,
    3, 28, 30, 35, 41–42, 82–83, 152, 157, 180;
    winter, 1, 3, 6, 14, 30, 34, 39, 41–42,
    44, 47, 90, 92, 103, 125, 127, 138–39,
    144–46, 148–51, 157, 167–68, 171,
    173, 78–79
tourists, 24, 28–29, 34, 43, 90, 139, 144
Trenker, Luis, 26–27, 69, 103–4
Trondheim, 32

Tromsø, 32
Turin, 55
Turnen, 32, 60, 188n39, 200n44

Übermensch, 98
urbanization, 80, 88

Val d'Isère, 138–39
Valle d'Aosta, 158, 159 *fig. 25*
Verne, Jules, 38
Viard, Charles, 156
Vichy France, 124, 150
Vienna, 48–49, 54, 61, 86, 148
Volkssport, 65, 67, 70, 145, 200n61
von Dévan, Stefan, 98, 126
Vosges, 34, 62

Walde, Alfons, 75–76, 76 *fig. 8*
Weber, Max, 48, 80
Der weiße Rausch, 102–3, 102 *fig. 13*, 117,
    120, 132
Wirtschaftswunder, 143, 145
World War I, 23, 27, 40, 45, 47, 52, 68–70,
    72, 76, 79, 90, 92–93, 103, 114, 149
World War II, 15–16, 83, 89, 98, 108–9, 121,
    123, 125, 140, 144, 148–51, 153, 155, 157,
    162–63, 167
Wundt, Theodor, 61

youth culture, 175–76

Zakopane, 117
Zdarsky, Mathias, 38, 47, 52, 60–70, 62 *fig.
    6*, 72, 112, 115, 172 193n16, 193n22
Zermatt, 1, 3, 5, 35
Ziemilski, Andrzej, 5–9, 14, 171, 174, 180
Zweig, Arnold, 27